# THE GLORY OF THE SULTANS

Slipcase. The Rang Mahal with its marble fountain in the Red Fort, Delhi.

Cover. Detail of the *jali* and inlay decoration on marble, mausoleum of Itimād al-Dawla, Āgra, India, 1628.

Back cover. Incrusted mirror-glass decoration, Shish Mahal, Lahore.

Translated from the French **David Radzinowicz**

Design and Typesetting **Thierry Renard**

Copyediting **Chrisoula Petridis**

Proofreading **Marc Feustel**

Color Separation **IGS, Angoulême**

Printed in **Singapore by Tien Wah Press**

Simultaneously published in French as *L'Inde des sultans*
© Flammarion, Paris, 2009

English-language edition
© Flammarion, Paris, 2009

All rights reserved.
No part of this publication may be reproduced in any form or by any means, electronic, photocopy, information retrieval system, or otherwise, without written permission from Flammarion S.A.
87, quai Panhard et Levassor
75647 Paris Cedex 13

editions.flammarion.com

09 10 11   3 2 1

ISBN-13: 978-2-08-030110-9
Dépôt légal: 09/2009

YVES PORTER - GÉRARD DEGEORGE

THE GLORY OF THE SULTANS

ISLAMIC ARCHITECTURE IN INDIA

Flammarion

CONTENTS

07 Foreword
09 Introduction
12 Glossary

14 FROM THE ARAB-MUSLIM INCURSIONS TO THE FOUNDATION OF THE MUGHAL EMPIRE

22 India's Earliest Contacts with Islam
    22 The Arab invasions
    26 Ghaznavids and Ghūrids

32 The Sultanate of Delhi (c. 1191–1414)
    34 The architecture of the Mu'izzi
    44 The Khaljī of Delhi
    49 The Tughluqs

65 The Sultanate of Delhi from the Sayyid Dynasty to the Mughals (1414–1555)
    66 The Sayyid (1414–51) and the Lodî (1451–1526) dynasties
    77 The rule of the first Mughals
    83 The Sûri parenthesis, before the return of the Mughals (1540–55)
    93 Partial assessment on the eve of the Mughal artistic explosion

96 THE INDEPENDENT SULTANATES

105 Bengal (1336–1576)
    105 The path to Islamic cultural assertion in Bengal
    113 The monuments of the Gaur or the architectural maturity of the Sultanate

122 Kashmir (1346–1589)

125 The Sultanates of the Deccan
    125 The Bahmanid Sultanate (1347–1527) and its Barīd Shāhīs successors (1504–1600)
    134 The 'Ādil Shāhīs and Bijāpur; or the full-blown originality of a capital
    143 The Qutb Shāhīs (1543–1687)
    145 Golconda: the rigors of a martial capital
    149 Hyderābād: a mature capital
    151 The legacy of the architecture of the Deccan Sultanates

152 The Sultanate of Gujarāt (1391–1583)
- 153 From province to sultanate
- 153 The reign of Ahmed I (1411–42): the assertion of Gujarati identity
- 155 The successors of Ahmed I
- 157 The reign of Mahmūd Beghada (1458–1511)
- 170 The late architecture of a declining sultanate
- 170 The architecture of Gujarāt: a highly individual synthesis in the Indian world

172 The Sharqī of Jaunpur (1394–1479)
- 180 The legacy of the Sharqī of Jaunpur

181 The Sultanate of Mālwa (1401–1531)
- 181 The Ghauri in power (1401–36)
- 188 The Khaljī sovereigns (1436–1531)
- 194 The later monuments
- 195 The legacy of the sultanate of of Mālwa

196 THE GREAT MUGHALS AND THEIR HEIRS

204 The Great Mughals, from Akbar to Aurangzeb
- 205 Akbar (1556–1615)
- 212 Fatehpur Sīkri

226 Jahāngīr (r. 1605–27)
- 232 Royal nomadism: Jahāngīr, from Māndu to Kashmir
- 233 The Gardens of Jahāngīr
- 235 Tomb architecture during the Reign of Jahāngīr

240 Shāh Jahān (1628–1657)
- 250 Religious architecture of the time of Shāh Jahān
- 267 Shāhjahānābād, or the consecration of Delhi

274 Aurangzeb (1658–1707) and his successors
- 274 Aurangzeb: absolute power and harbingers of decline
- 278 The heirs to the Great Mughals (1707–57)
- 282 The nabobs of Oudh
- 288 Bahādur Shāh Zafar (r. 1837–58), the last Mughal

290 Conclusion
From Identity to Universality

292 Appendixes

FOREWORD

In spite of its geographical extent and chronological longevity, few texts have tackled the subject of Muslim architecture in the Indo-Pakistani subcontinent as a whole. It is striking how this region—which, after Indonesia, contains the greatest number of Muslims in the world—has been neglected by general works on Islamic architecture.

To make good this neglect is what lies behind this attempt to draw a panorama of the architecture of this vast and glorious region—although an in-depth study would necessarily stretch to several volumes. The present text can then only provide an outline in which, although India enjoys the lion's share, Pakistan also has an important part to play. Only a rapid overview of Bangladesh has proved practicable.

Rather than embark on an exhaustive survey then, we have chosen to adopt a dual perspective: a chronological account exploring the major phases of the Islamic architecture of the subcontinent is illustrated by Gerard Degeorge's splendid photographs, adding a personal touch to our narrative development. Completing the visuals, several plans and cross-sections place the monuments in their spatial context or illustrate the proportions of an architectural complex. Following the survey, the inquisitive reader will find a glossary of architectural terms, as well as a bibliography enabling him to further enrich his or her knowledge.

The languages of India are rich in phonemes; these vernacular languages were supplemented first by Arabic and Persian, and later by English, a history that renders a coherent system of transcription almost impossible. Thus, the vernacular "kh" is an aspirated "k," whereas the same character of Arab-Persian origin corresponds, in their source languages, to the Spanish *jota*.

I would like here to express my profound gratitude to Richard Castinel for his assistance when writing this volume.

INTRODUCTION

The first contacts between Islam and the Indian subcontinent date to the eighth century and laid the foundations for the dominance of Muslim dynasties over the majority of this territory that was to last some six hundred years. The patronage of successive reigns produced many brilliant artistic achievements, but its glories are particularly evident in architecture, as illustrated by such universally acknowledged masterpieces as the Qutb Minār in Delhi and the Tāj Mahal of Āgra.

Historically, these waves of Muslim invasion were staggered over a lengthy period. Over time, the effects fed into some of the architectural currents that had developed in the newcomers' geographical sphere of origin, proving crucial in asserting Islamic religious identity over the regions they had lately conquered. The earliest Muslim occupants, in Sindh and Kerala, left hardly any archaeological vestiges of importance, and no significant monument testifies to their settlement. The foundation of the sultanate of Delhi in the last years of the twelfth century, on the other hand, marked the beginning of an era in which monumental architecture was viewed as a tool to make visually manifest the power of the new overlords. The landscape was dotted with mosques and mausoleums that legitimized the grandeur of the victors, while palaces and administrative buildings embodied the government.

Specific features can be discerned in Islamic architecture in India. Initially, an investigation of building typology demonstrates how, besides the mosque—literally "place of prostration," it, above and beyond the conceptual variations the differences in its construction conveyed, imposed itself as the Islamic monument par excellence—other edifices sprung up. These included the minaret, whose frequency varied depending on the area concerned and whose dimensions were extremely variable.

After the mosque, Islamic identity in India was chiefly characterized by the mausoleum, perhaps because it is a monument that expresses a clean break with the Hindu world, which practiced and practices cremation. Thus, throughout the period of Muslim dominion, and across all the regions in the subcontinent where it exerted its power, a vast number of such edifices were erected. In comparison with other Islamic territories, such as those in North Africa, where such monuments remain rare and of modest dimensions, in India the mausoleum developed into a dramatic statement of the Muslim identity of believers. The importance conferred on it can be deduced from the dimensions chosen: in addition to the great Tāj Mahal, there exists a plethora of mausoleums of vast size in the subcontinent. If the best-known shelter the tombs of the Great Mughals, and sometimes their wives, others contain the remains of saints and are still a focus for ceremonies and veneration. This Indian peculiarity is especially evident in the mausoleums of the "saints" of the Chishti order of Sufism in Ajmer, Delhi, and Lahore, which regularly play host to gatherings of *qawwāls* during which chants are sung in praise of these saints. On the other hand, buildings common in certain Islamic geographical regions, such as the madrassa, remain underrepresented in the subcontinent. Notwithstanding, Muslim dominance in India never resulted in numerical superiority over other confessions in the conquered regions. Thus the power of the sultan of Delhi initially relied on an army and then on a government made up of adepts of local religions as well as recent converts.

The architecture of this heterogeneous society was forged from an amalgam of imported forms—such as the dome on squinches and the dropped arch—local motifs, and regional materials. This resulted in unique examples of hybrid monuments marrying forms and materials enriched by stylistic and concrete contributions from the new territories over which the power of the sultanate extended as successive regions increasingly distant from the central power were absorbed (i.e., Bengal, the Deccan, and Kashmir). However, the expansion of the zone under dominion weakened the political structures of the sultanate, to the point that, by the end of the fourteenth century, Timur the Conqueror (Tamburlaine) could take advantage of the decline of the state to sweep into Delhi and put an end to its supremacy by 1398. He occupied the country only for a short while, however, before returning to Samarkand, leaving his governors to hold sway over the devastated tracts of land in his absence.

From the late fourteenth century to the sixteenth century, independent sultanates endeavored to consolidate their identity through architecture: from Gujarāt to Bengal and Kashmir to the Deccan, variations in climate and geography—as well as the diversity of vernacular languages, age-old traditions, and building materials—urged each local potentate to give full expression to his individuality. Thus, on flood plains such as Sindh and Bengal, brick dominated, whereas central India privileged stone. In this context the wonderfully rich creativity and variety of the legacy of the Indian sultanates is readily understandable.

From 1526, Bābur, a distant descendant of Timur, began to lay the foundations of the Mughal Empire in India that went on to subdue the sultanates, attaining its geographical and political high-water mark under Aurangzeb. At the death of the latter in the early eighteenth century, the empire shattered. Provinces shook themselves free from the central power, thereby favoring the resurgence of the Rājput dynasties that up to that point had been kept at bay. The sack of Delhi by Nādir Shāh in 1738–39 accelerated the decline of a Mughal power further weakened by ceaseless attacks from brigands. By the end of the eighteenth century, the British, through the East India Company, had vast chunks of the subcontinent under their control, while in Delhi the descendants of the Great Mughals were reduced to playing second fiddle. For a few months in 1857, the revolt of the sepoys—locals drafted into the British army that a mass of vexatious measures had induced to rebel—gave a further twist to the inexorable loss of influence. After heavy losses, the British army eventually crushed the uprising, going on to put the whole of India under the direct rule of Her Majesty's Empire (except for princely states in which nabobs and maharajas enjoyed tepid autonomy). British India subsequently took part in the two world wars for which it provided "colonial" quotas, before the Empire gave out in 1947, when India proclaimed its independence, resulting in the partition of Pakistan—two territories divided by 1,055 miles (1,700 kilometers), both demanding the setting up of an Islamic state. At the end of a conflict opposing the two parts of the country, East Pakistan became independent in 1971 and took the name Bangladesh.

Islam has clearly had an enormous effect on the history of the subcontinent and, to contemporary eyes, the evidence of its splendid architecture testifies to the grandeur and variety of a Muslim presence that, over such an immense territory, was confronted with the vivacity of preexistent cultures whose artistic techniques and traditions were blended with contributions from the invaders. Even after the period of the sultans under British dominion, Muslim influence resurfaced in the "Indo-Saracenic" style of architecture—continental Europeans might dub it "Orientalist"—that blends Victorian construction principles with elements lifted wholesale from the Indo-Islamic architectural vocabulary, such as *chhatris* (small decorative pavilions), "Persian arch" profiles, onion domes, and pinnacles in the form of miniature minarets. These were all elements that invaded Mughal mausoleums and Rājput palaces as much as British administrative buildings, such as the Town Hall in Mysore or the Victoria Hall in Madras (currently the National Art Gallery).

The subcontinent's recent history has witnessed a revival in communal "identity politics." Pakistan, for example, is busy unearthing every last scrap of its Muslim past, while the situation in India—whose 1947 constitution enshrines its secular nature—is necessarily more contrasted. Partition and border tensions between these feuding brothers, however, have sometimes resulted in Muslim buildings failing to be granted the historic status they deserve. Thus, as late as 1992, the Babri Masjid in Ayodhya, a mosque whose construction is attributed to Bābur, was demolished after allegations that it was built on the birthplace of Rama. Elsewhere, other instances of the Hindu recuperation of Islamic sites can be observed, such as the conversion of the pavilion of Nilkhant in Māndu into a temple to Shiva and the erection of a polychrome statue of Durgā in the middle of the prayer hall in the Friday Mosque at Daulatābād. However, though it spawned the jewels of one of the most remarkable civilizations in world history, the extraordinary cultural synthesis that took place over the centuries of Muslim presence could only impose itself through a combination of monarchal rule and the combined effort of all Indians in a technical and artistic cohabitation rich in interchange.

The intention of the present volume is to describe this collaboration with particular insistence on the neglected and complex period of the sultanates that preceded the arrival of the Mughals.

GLOSSARY

The terms in this glossary come from Arabic, Persian, and Hindustani (an Indian language derived from Sanskrit) words.

Baoli (Hindustani): stepped or tiered water-tank; known as a *wāv* in Gujarāt.
Baradari (Hindustani): (literally "twelve doors") a pleasure pavilion, often characterized by a radially symmetrical plan.
Chabutara (Hindustani): dais or platform in a garden.
Chahār-bāgh (Persian): (literally "four gardens") quadripartite garden.
Chajja (Hindustani): projecting eaves or awning.
Chau-chala (Hindustani): pyramidal four-pitched dome.
Chhatri (Hindustani): (from "parasol") pavilion or kiosk that may stand on its own (funerary *chhatri*) or adorn the summit of an edifice.
Dargāh: Sufi sanctuary.
Darwāza (Persian): monumental door.
Guldasta (Persian): (literally "bouquet of flowers") pinnacle or pseudo-minaret.
Gunbad (Persian): cupola; by synecdoche, the mausoleum it domes.
Hansa (Hindustani): ("sacred goose") a decorative motif borrowed from the Hindu repertory, appearing especially on pier or column bases.
Hauz (Arabic): tank, pool, or reservoir.
Iwan (Persian): a great archway vaulting a space enclosed to three sides and open on the fourth. As an entrance, often confused with *pishtāq* (literally, "before the archway"), the vaulted, arched entryway to a building.
Jali (Hindustani): screen with *claustrae* in stone openwork.
Jharokha (Hindustani): balcony. *Darshan jharokha:* a balcony at which the sovereign would appear.
Kufic (Arabic): Arabic script, originating in the city of Kufa, characterized by its angular appearance and an absence of diacritic points.
Madrassa (Arabic): a university in which the traditional Islamic sciences are taught.
Mahal (Arabic): palace.
Masjid (Arabic): mosque. *Jama' Masjid:* main congregational mosque or Friday mosque.
Mihrab (Arabic): niche or recess indicating the direction of Mecca towards which Moslems face when praying.
Minār (Arabic): minaret; by extension, any "tower," that may not have the function of calling the faithful to prayers. "Pseudo-minaret": an architectural element that mimics the form of a minaret but without its use.
Minbar (Arabic): pulpit generally situated to the right of the mihrab.
Muqarnas (Arabic): cells corbelled in rows; "stalactite" squinches.
Naqqāra-khāna (Persian): a pavilion serving as a "bandstand" placed at the entrance to a palace.
Qibla (Arabic): the direction to which prayers must be addressed (towards Mecca).
Riwāq (Arabic): porticos surrounding a mosque courtyard.
Sahn (Arabic): courtyard (of a mosque).
Shir-o-Khorshid (Persian): ("lion and sun") a decorative motif showing the sun rising behind a lion; also served as the coat of arms of the Iranian throne.
Suraj-mukh (Hindustani): ("sun face") a decorative motif taken from the Hindu repertoire, found especially at the summit of an arch.
Thuluth (Arabic): Arabic script employed for large inscriptions on monuments, distinguished by the height of its ascenders.
Zenāna (Persian): part of a mosque or a residence reserved for women.

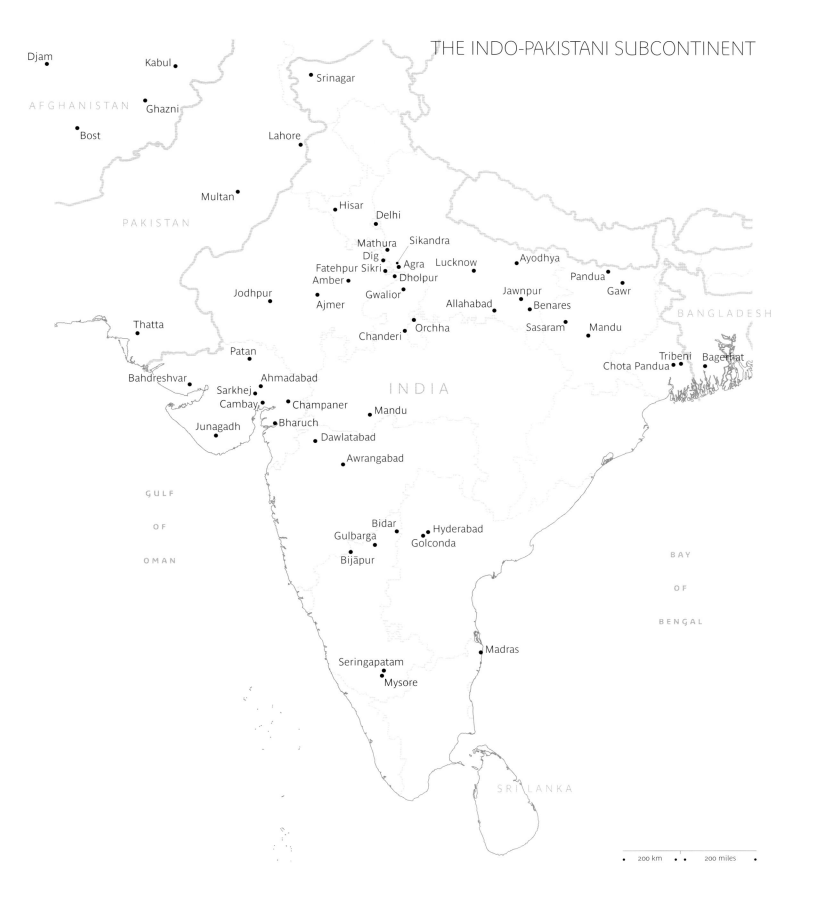

FROM THE ARAB-MUSLIM INCURSIONS TO THE FOUNDATION OF THE MUGHAL EMPIRE
(eighth–sixteenth centuries)

Facing page. The Qutb Minār, begun in 1199, Delhi, India; the two upper levels, in white marble, are a fourteenth-century restoration.

Pages 15–16. The Mān Mandir palace in Gwalior, India, late fifteenth century.

Pages 17–18. Details of the Arabic inscriptions carved on the Qutb Minār, late twelfth–early thirteenth century.

Pages 18–19. Detail of the decoration on the central arch of the Bara Gumbaz mosque, in the Lodī Gardens, Delhi, India, dated 1494.

India's Earliest Contacts with Islam

The presence of Muslim communities in the Indian subcontinent dates back far earlier than the advent of the sultanate of Delhi in 1206. Sometimes this presence amounted to peaceful settlement, as in Kerala and Sri Lanka, where Arab merchants had been cultivating commercial outposts since antiquity; sometimes events proved more turbulent. The historical episodes during which these confrontations occurred —from the Arab conquest of Sindh in 711 to the arrival of the Ghūrids in the late twelfth century—however, remain little known, as do the characteristics of the architecture that flowered at the time. In point of fact, the earliest Islamic monuments on the subcontinent were due to trade flows between Arabs and local populations that clearly preceded the Hegira, and which subsequently continued. It remains nonetheless the case that the mercantile concerns presiding over these initial contacts in southern Indian coastal cities resulted for the most part in the construction of the kind of utilitarian buildings that are not conducive to the conservation of architectural vestiges of any great quality. It is now certain that the Indus plain to the north was the theater of the earliest urbanization in the Indian sphere (at Harappā and Mohenjo-daro, for example). Yet, the wealth of the region, which also constituted a strategic corridor between India and the Arab-Persian arena, attracted invaders and plunderers over the centuries. For that very reason—especially if one also takes into consideration the devastation wreaked by natural phenomena (earthquakes, mudslides in the delta, tidal waves, etc.)—it is little short of miraculous that any vestiges have survived. Nonetheless they can give contemporary observers only a shadowy notion of the refinement and expertise of the civilizations that gave birth to them.

The Arab invasions

Probably at some time in the fifth century, the Sindh region experienced the emergence and eventual consolidation of the power of the Rai dynasty, whose founder is supposed to have been the rajah Diwaij. Around 485 in Alor, he established the capital of a kingdom that extended to Kashmir in the northeast and to Makrān to the west, the limits of its influence being marked by the port of Daybul in the south and the mountains of Kurdān and Kikānan in the east respectively. There then followed a succession of five sovereigns before a Brahman named Chāch, in the service of the king's chamberlain, seized power, assassinating the last of the rajahs, Rai Sāhsi II. After a reign lasting forty years, Chāch's brother Chandra ruled over the kingdom for a further seventeen. His two sons then divided up the territory, one keeping a capital at Alor, while the second chose Brahmanābād; in 670, one of the brothers died and the kingdom was reunified under the scepter of the survivor, Dahār. It was in his reign that the first armed Arab forays occurred.[1]

By as early as 661, the meteoric expansion of Islam had been consolidated by the Umayyad caliphate at Damascus. The near totality of what is today Iran was at that time under its control, and in 692 the province fell under the rule of Hajjāj ibn Yūsuf al-Thaqafī. The latter made the most of a singular incident to push home his advantage in regions distant from the seat of caliphate power: a ship laden with gifts intended for the caliph and the governor Hajjāj, and transporting the widows of Arab merchants from Ceylon, was boarded by pirates in the seas off Daybul. Hajjāj promptly issued a protest to King Dahār in an effort to obtain compensation for the loss sustained, as well as for the return of the wealthy widows. Dahār turned a deaf ear, so Hajjāj ordered in the troops. As the first two expeditions proved fruitless, the caliph authorized Hajjāj to raise a larger contingent containing some six thousand horsemen and as many camel drivers, equipped with siege machines, the whole commanded by a nephew of the governor, Muhammad ibn al-Qāsim al-Thaqafī. In the autumn of 711, the invader crossed the Makrān and arrived at the port of Daybul, while a fleet dispatched by Hajjāj blocked the seaward escape route. After fierce resistance, the city fell into the hands of the besiegers the same year the Arabs reached Gibraltar in the west.

Sindh as a province of the Umayyad caliphate
Once Daybul was finally in his grasp, Muhammad ibn al-Qāsim al-Thaqafī, in reprisal for the defeat inflicted on his troops prior to its capture, ordered the execution of all inhabitants over the age of seventeen who refused to convert to Islam; the rest of the population was enslaved. To repopulate the city, he brought in four thousand Muslims from the Makrān, establishing them in a new district complete with a mosque. This mosque is probably the oldest on the entire subcontinent. Between 1958 and 1965, excavations carried out at Bambhore—the presumed site of ancient Daybul—brought to light a mosque.[2] Its plan replicates that of the ancient mosque of Kufa in Iraq, though on a smaller scale, since it measures about 120 feet (37 meters) down the side.[3] The walls were erected in coursed blocks of chalkstone [limestone], while wooden piles resting on stone plinths (some of which have been unearthed) bore the roof frame. The prayer hall is fitted with thirty-three columns that form three aisles parallel to the *qibla* wall; the central courtyard was arranged between the porticoes (*riwāq*) over two bays. An inscription (disputed by some scholars) indicates a date of 727—that is, only forty years after the construction of the mosque at Kufa. If its authenticity were proven beyond doubt, it would constitute the oldest Muslim

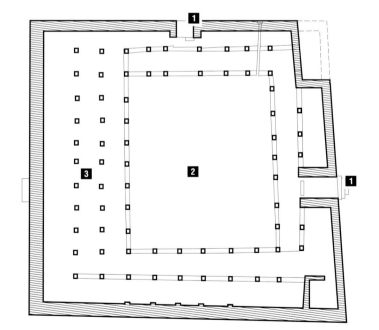

Plan of the great mosque in Bambhore, Pakistan (after Kāmil Khān Mumtāz): **(1)** entrances; **(2)** courtyard; **(3)** prayer hall.

vestige in the entire Indo-Pakistani area. The building presents no trace of a mihrab, but in the first half of the eighth century the presence of these recesses indicating the direction of Mecca was not yet widespread. The site also reveals a citadel overlooking the city, girt by a rampart studded with towers and pierced by three gates. To the north outside the walls sprung up a suburb where craftsmen and tradesmen worked. Lastly, thanks to its sizable stone foundations, a large building that probably had some administrative purpose has been located in the citadel opposite the mosque.

Once he had a firm grip on Daybul, Muhammad ibn al-Qāsim al-Thaqafī went on to attack other cities in Sindh. In the process he was pleasantly surprised to discover that a large proportion of the local population—Buddhists, Mazdeans, and underprivileged Hindus feeling downtrodden by the Brahmans—were ready to join forces under his authority. He thus quickly seized Nerūn (current Hyderābād) and then Sehwān. Reinforcements dispatched by Hajjāj allowed the general to pursue Dahār's army as it crossed the Indus. During a pitched battle, Dahār was killed and his widow and son forced to retrench to the fort of Rāwar where they put up a desperate resistance. As the inevitable end approached, the queen and her women set themselves on fire. Finally the conqueror took the stronghold, making off with Dahār's treasure and massacring the surviving men of the besieged army, but sparing the merchants, craftsmen, and farmers. A tax—the *jizya*—that Caliph 'Umar had instituted to be levied on infidels was then imposed on all the landowners who refused conversion.

The conquest of Sindh blazed a path for Muhammad ibn al-Qāsim al-Thaqafī, who then went on to besiege Multān. There again, once the city was in his hands after a resistance lasting seven days, he observed that many Hindus, dissatisfied with their lot under the preceding regime, promptly swore allegiance to him. In response, he decreed that Hindu temples, as well as synagogues and churches, should be respected. On the point of carrying the offensive to the kingdom of Kannauj in the mid Ganges valley, he received news of the sudden death of his uncle, Hajjāj, and turned on his heel. The epic accounts of his homeward journey and tragic demise are the stuff of legend. Disgraced, Hajjāj's family seems to have been eliminated by a new caliph, Sulaymān, who reigned but from 715 to 717. The Arab army of Sindh, however, although shorn of its chief, remained under arms.

Then the caliph named several governors—including 'Umar, one of Muhammad ibn Qāsim's sons, appointed by Hishām (r. 724–43), to whom fell the thorny problem of how to reassert Umayyad authority in the provinces where local princes were champing at the bit. With this aim in mind, he founded a first bastion, called al-Mahfūza, "the Protected," in Sindh, and mustered all the forces still faithful to the caliphate. In 737, he set up the town of Mansura, "the Victorious," which affirmed its status as *the* dominant stronghold of the Arab presence in Sindh and as the base from which expeditions to preserve the territorial integrity of the province would set out. By then Muslim soldiers were marrying local women and putting down roots. The armed forces were organized into garrison cities (*amsār*) and in camps (*junūd*), particularly in Multān and Mansura. In 750, however, the Umayyad dynasty was swept aside by the revolt of the Abbasids: the new caliphs dispatched governors to Sindh, although they were unable to prevent the inexorable split of Multān and Mansura into two smaller, autonomous principalities in the late eighth century.

Mansura and Multān under the Abbasids
In the early twentieth century, excavation campaigns by archaeologist Henry Cousens, who rediscovered the site of Mansura at Brahmanābād, were revealing a large building he regarded as the Friday mosque, together with three smaller mosques.[4] The great mosque was built in a mix of stone and brick with some parts being dressed in marble.[5] In the ninth century, Arab historians of the Abbasid era describe Mansura as an abundantly populated and commercially flourishing city measuring a mile long and located on an island embraced by two arms of the Indus. Mansura leather, and particularly its shoes, was much vaunted in Baghdad, including in the caliph's family. Later in the tenth century, the geographer al-Maqdisī set down his observations on the Friday mosque, which he places at the center of the city, with the booths of a bazaar running around the nearby arcades.[6]

Our knowledge of the Arab monuments of Multān, the ancient capital of Punjab, comes solely from later historical sources, Ibn Rustah, Mas'ūdī, and Istakhri, ninth-century Arab authors, who provide details of the city monuments in their descriptions. The scarcity of surviving buildings from the period should not obscure the fact that the caliphate's province of Sindh was at that time a significant centre for the arts in the Islamic world. A point of convergence between the Indian and Muslim worlds, it was a melting pot where the sciences of the former were transmitted to the latter—particularly mathematics (the use of zero, for example) and astronomy. During the caliphate of al-Mansūr (r. 753–74) the Arabs of Sindh brought Indian manuscripts back to Baghdad, including the *Brahmā-Siddhānta* and the *Khāndkhādyaka*, two astronomical treatises written in Sanskrit. It was also from Sindh that India extended its influence westwards as regards music, literature, and mysticism —and that the game of chess reached Iran in the Sassanid period.

In the course of excavations in the region, various ceramic workshops and thousands of shards of local pottery have been exhumed, as well as examples of stoneware and porcelain from China—ancient witnesses to its place in international trade. It is regrettable, however, that so few pieces of quality have survived until to the present day, while the absence of any scientific synthesis of the material recently unearthed forestalls informed conclusions about the typology of the objects executed and the techniques employed.

While some consider the Arab conquest of Sindh a failure,[7] such a judgment cannot be accepted en bloc. Arab-Muslim power was admittedly concentrated at Sindh and in the Multān region, and it must be recognized that this outlying province of the empire of the caliphate gravitated more readily into the orbit of its western neighbors—the Makrān and Kabul—than into the sphere of influence of the plains of the Ganges. The Indian world thus remained essentially resistant to Muslim influence, but the corollary is infinitely more debatable. Moreover, the Ghaznavids initially staged sorties and raids that were to carry them far from their bases in what is now Afghanistan. Subsequently, in the late twelfth century, the Ghūrids furthered the interest of Muslim princes in the interior of the subcontinent, initiating a decisive movement of interpenetration of what at the time could be decidedly antagonistic worlds.

Ghaznavids and Ghūrids

As the tenth century wore on, the gradual weakening of the power centers of the Abbasid caliphate resulted in much muscle-flexing on the part of local dynasties. Thus, the line of the Sāmānids (864–1005) came to dominate a region in eastern Iran extending to Transoxiana in the north and Kabul in the east. These Iranian princes, however, took into their service soldiers of Turkic origin, captured as youths and raised in the Islamic religion. Though of servile extraction, some were to rise through the ranks, the most fortunate attaining the rank of general or provincial governor. As it turned out, on the death of the Sāmānid prince 'Abd al-Malik in 961, one of his generals, a governor in the remote province of Ghaznī in present-day Afghanistan, voiced genuine aspirations to autonomy; his son-in-law Sebüktigin, meanwhile, declared independence, though this freedom only became a reality during the reign of his son, Mahmūd. Since the capital of the new principality was established at Ghaznī, it was this city that gave its name to a dynasty that initially grew at the expense of its onetime masters, the Sāmānids, the star of the latter waning as the glory of Ghaznavid rule burned brighter.

The Ghaznavids (977–1186)

The dynasty's expansionist aims came to the fore in the reign of Sebüktigin (977–97), although at the time his position was still being disputed by the Sāmānids. Sebüktigin translated his policies by annexing part of Sīstān and by repeated incursions into the Indian kingdoms. Punjab was then under the control of the Hindu kingdom of the Shāhi family, whose territories included Kabul. Sebüktigin quickly succeeded in grabbing Kabul before launching expeditions over on the eastern banks of the Indus. This lineage reached its zenith under Mahmūd, who succeeded his father after his death in 997. Under his dominion (998–1030), the emirs of Khorāsān in eastern Iran were crushed and he was recognized as an independent sovereign (sultan) by the Abbasid caliph, al-Qādir Billāh. He then marched out to conquer the Shāhi kingdom, whose king, Jayapāla, he soundly beat in 1001. The latter's brother, Ānandapāla, put up a staunch defense of Punjab, yet was driven out the following year and harried into the mountains. Mahmūd returned to Ghaznī laden with valuable spoils, vowing to send his troops on campaigns into Indian territory every year: no less than seventeen raids followed, securing immense riches for the Ghaznavid court.

The minarets of Ghaznī, Afghanistan: in the foreground, minaret of Mas'ūd III, early twelfth century; in the back ground, minaret of Bahrām Shāh, mid-twelfth century.

Mahmūd also extended his domain to Multān. There Abu al-Fath Dā'ud Lodī, a descendant of the first Arab invaders and the city's governor, had offered refuge to the Qarmatians (a dissident Ismaili branch of Shiism considered heretical by the Sunni majority). The Qarmatians had already sparked riots in Syria and Iraq and in 930 even attacked Mecca, where they made off with the black stone of the Ka'bah that they kept for twenty-two years, returning it only in exchange for a hefty ransom. Settling for a time in Bahrain, they then took refuge in Sindh, where Multān afforded them asylum. Brandishing the banner of orthodoxy, Mahmūd saw a heaven-sent occasion to attack the city, which Dā'ud Lodī ceded after a week-long siege. Spared as a Muslim, the sovereign was condemned to pay an astronomical annual tribute to Mahmūd and to swear never again to offer support to the Qarmatians. Mahmūd was by now the lord of possessions covering a vast tract of land from Punjab to the borders of Transoxiana. A series of revolts broke out in Punjab that Mahmūd crushed one after the other, snatching much booty that was dispatched to Ghaznī where it was put on show. The wonder this aroused among the populace naturally proved a considerable spur to undertake fresh sorties.

Mahmūd, however, did not care to give a firm foundation to the territorial conquests he had made in India, considering the subcontinent more as a storehouse from which he could draw immense wealth. He was thus satisfied with incursions and plundering the Indo-Gangetic plain, using the spoils to turn Ghaznī into a thriving capital. Only Punjab and its capital, Lahore, became Ghaznavid possessions in the full sense. The gold brought back from the various campaigns was also for the greater part exported to Ghaznī, melted down and minted. Nothing, however, has survived of Mahmūd's loot. The prisoners, included a host of craftsmen whose styles and expertise exerted substantial influence on Ghaznavid artistic production. It was also at the court of Ghaznī that the great scholar Bīrūnī composed what is undoubtedly the first objective study of a foreign culture—on India. Once Mahmūd died, the Seljuk surge in Khorāsān forced the Ghaznavids to retrench to Punjab, to the point that by the mid-eleventh century their empire had been reduced to this Indian province alone. It was in this period that Lahore developed into a prosperous urban center in which the cultural force fields of the Indian, Iranian, and Central Asian worlds converged.

Alas, the splendor of the Ghaznavid capital of Punjab can only be imagined since the city was razed in 1217 by the armies of Genghis Khan, before being sacked again in 1398 by Timur. The vestiges of the monuments of Ghaznī—including minarets bearing the names of Mas'ūd III (r. 1099–1115) and Bahrām Shāh (r. 1118–52) and foreshadowing the Qutb Minār in Delhi—and the ruins of Lashkarī Bāzār, also in Afghanistan, represent the types of architectural models that might have been applied in the Ghaznavid Punjab.

The Ghūrids (1100–1215)
The privilege of presiding over the decline of the Ghaznavids fell to a dynasty called the Ghūrids, who took their name from Ghūr (modern Ghowr), a mountainous region in central Afghanistan. To begin with, the Ghūrids were vassals of the Ghaznavids, but in the early eleventh century they joined forces with the Seljuks, who were in the ascendant. The Ghaznavid Bahrām Shāh certainly must have made a bid to restore his authority over Ghūr, but his only reward was a violent backlash that culminated in the sack of Ghaznī by the Ghūrids in 1150–51 and the concomitant loss of Ghaznavid territory in eastern Afghanistan. For this feat of arms that relegated the

Terra-cotta decoration in a private mosque belonging to the Ghūrid sultans, Kabul, Afghanistan, late twelfth century.

Ghaznavids to their Indian possessions, Alā 'Al-Dīn of Ghūr earned the nickname, Jahān-suz ("The World Burner"). The high point of this lineage was attained during the reign of Ghiyāth al-Dīn Muhammad (1163–1203). Starting out from his capital, Fīrūzkūh, the potentate directed military actions against his neighbors to the west and shared the throne with his brother Mu'izz al-Dīn, who had established his capital at Ghaznī, using it as a base for several incursions into Indian lands.

In 1186, Mu'izz al-Dīn crushed the last Ghaznavid, Khosrow Malik (1160–1186), annexing Punjab and continuing his march east, in the process facing down several Indian rajahs: Prithvirāj III, the Chauhān sovereign of Ajmer and Delhi was defeated in 1192, while Jayachandra, king of Benares and Kannauj, capitulated in 1194. After 1191, Mu'izz al-Dīn entrusted the administration of these newly conquered provinces to one of his generals, Qutb al-Dīn Aybak. On the death of his lord in 1206, the general took on the title of *malik* (prince), and governed these regions in the name of the Ghūrid sultan of Fīrūzkūh—an explanation of why the early sovereigns of Delhi, whose line took the appellation Mu'izzi (after Mu'izz al-Dīn), were also known as "Slave Dynasty." The destiny of the Ghūrids, however, was soon rocked by the expansion of the Khwārezm-Shāhs, before being crushed entirely by the sledgehammer of the Mongols.

The suzerainty of the rulers of Ghūr over the first princes of Delhi may well imply that the monuments erected at the time of the fledgling sultanate of Delhi had some relationship with the art of the Ghūrids, but, the relative neglect of Ghūrid remains—still very much the case today—makes such a hypothesis far from easy to support. It was only in 1957 that the site of the Ghūrid capital of Fīrūzkūh was rediscovered, just as the minaret in Jām, Afghanistan, was being surveyed for the first time.[8] Entirely made of brick and decorated with turquoise glazed ceramics, this monument was erected in the reign of Ghiyāth al-Dīn Muhammad bin Sām (1163–1202), whose titulary it bears. Its tapering form somewhat resembles other major minarets such as the Qutb Mīnar of Delhi, begun in 1199, the minarets of Ghaznī (already mentioned), and the Kalān minaret of Bukhara (1127).

The site of the ancient city of Bost in Afghanistan was where Ghūrid princes built magnificent palaces atop Ghaznavid ruins.[9] The subsumed constructions provide a limited idea of what the no longer extant Ghaznavid and Ghūrid palaces of Lahore may have looked like. Certain architectural characteristics of Ghūrid monuments reoccur in buildings erected by the sultans of Delhi, although they were inevitably subjected to adaptations in response to the specific context of their construction (this is particularly the case with the "Persian" arch and the dome on squinches).

Pre-sultanate Bhadreshvar and other sites
In keeping with a Muslim presence motivated by foreign policy expedients that extended to the economy and culture, settlements were found in various sectors of the subcontinent. They amounted in fact to more or less isolated outposts that preceded the foundation of the sultanate of Delhi or were independent of its establishment. This is clearly the case with the village of Bhadreshvar, located on the gulf of Kachchh in Gujarāt, which boasts a mausoleum bearing the date 1159, making it the oldest dated monument of its kind within the present-day borders of India.[10] The exact date of Muslim settlement in the Kachchh remains unknown. Mahmūd of Ghaznī certainly carried out a raid there in 1025–26 on his way back from plundering Somnāth[11]; but during the period when the mausoleum was being erected, it seems that power still lay in the hands of a Jain governor. A major trading hub at the time, Bhadreshvar was a bone of contention in several wars opposing the Islamic kings of Sindh and the Jain prince Jagadeva, a vassal of the Chaulukyas. The victorious Jagadeva had initiated a rebuilding program that covered several monuments in the city, including, paradoxically enough, a mosque begun in 1166, probably intended for the local Ismaili community composed of the Arab merchants who presided over the significant commercial links with the Red Sea ports. Similar examples of communities of Ismaili merchants and sailors can be found in other coastal cities, such as Somnāth.[12] The mausoleum at Bhadreshvar is known as the mausoleum of Ibrāhīm or Dargāh La'l Shahbāz. Arguably this monument had links to the Shiite, and, in all probability, originally to the Ismaili community.

The funerary function was, of course, an innovation in Indian lands, but both the architectural techniques and decoration were mainly influenced by local idioms. A system of monolithic columns supports a series of concentric entablatures rising to form a kind of "dome" that owes nothing to the techniques employed in Islamic lands. The carved motifs in the moldings at the level of the cornice, as well as the corbels, meanwhile, also derive from a local repertory. The unimpeachably Muslim character of the monument is evident, however, in the presence of a mihrab and a dated inscription in Arabic.

On the same site can be found the remnants of two mosques; the first relatively large and is known locally as the Solahkhambi Masjid ("mosque with sixteen columns"), whereas the second, smaller in size, is known as the Chhoti Masjid. Neither

Bhadreshvar, India.
Above left: Chhoti Masjid mosque, twelfth century; right: entrance to the mausoleum known as the Dargāh La'l Shahbāz, dated 1159; center: dome of the mausoleum (photos Richard Castinel); bottom: plan of the site (after M. Shokoohy):
(1) reservoir. **(2)** temple. **(3)** tomb of Ibrahim. **(4)** Solakhambi Masjid. **(5)** mosque.

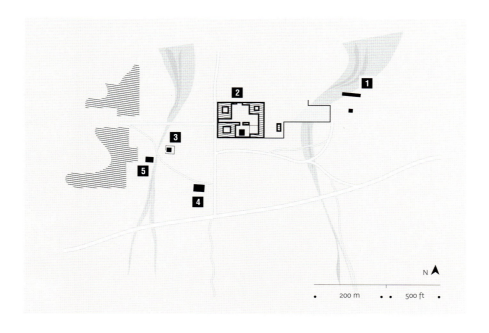

is dated, but the tombstones encircling the larger of the two date from 1177 to 1227, indicating the period of the mosque's activity. If the year 1177 were authenticated—the more likely date as it is corroborated by a Jain historical chronicle—the building would be the oldest surviving mosque in India. To judge from their architectural style, the construction of the two buildings seems to have been simultaneous.

Two other monuments in Bhadreshvar also bear the imprint of this Islamic twelfth- and thirteenth-century community. One is a *chhatri*, or funerary "pavilion," and the other a tiered tank, or *baoli*, called Dūdhā Wāv. Evidence to support the Muslim origin of the *baoli* is rather weak as it is based on the absence of figurative carvings whose presence is more usual in a Hindu or Jain context for this type of building.

A mosque located at Junāgadh on the Saurāshtra peninsula in Gujarāt features an inscription dating to 1286–87,[13] a date posterior to the foundation of the sultanate of Delhi, but prior to the conquest of Gujarāt by this new power in 1298–99. The building thus attests to the presence of isolated Muslim communities before the establishment of the great Indian sultanates. Other examples testify to this type of occupation in various localities, such as Nāgaur in Rājasthān, again well before the sultanate of Delhi emerged as Islam's overarching power in India.[14]

The general situation on the eve of the Delhi sultanate
The Islamic stamp on Indian lands thus remained relatively modest during the period from the Hegira to the foundation of the sultanate of Delhi. Yet it was the growth in contact between the Indian and Muslim worlds throughout these years that paved the way for the impressive cultural fusion that took place over subsequent centuries.

Certain settlements were peaceful, based on shared economic interests—to the extent that, as we have seen, a Jain sovereign permitted the construction of a mosque at Bhadreshvar, since it was the Muslim community that drove the commercial prosperity of the city. Other contacts, motivated by the expansionist policies that accompanied the growing power of the Muslim empires, proved, however, more violent. Still, in general the invaders could rely on the adhesion of entire swathes of the indigenous society for which Islam appeared as a way out of their subservient condition. Moreover, apart from the odd outburst of intolerance punctuated by massacres, the Muslims also learned how to absorb and even promote the local elites, for whom systematic conversion was not deemed imperative. Over time, first Sindh, then Punjab, together with many other more or less durable footholds of the Muslim princes, became forcing grounds for social intercourse between once antagonistic worlds—a crucible in which knowledge, foodstuffs, and attitudes, for instance, could be readily exchanged.

Although the evidence is scanty, the first buildings forged on the template of the Islamic approach to architecture to appear in the Indian sphere generally deployed local techniques of construction and indigenous decorative idioms. In prestigious centers such as Lahore this blossomed into a style embodied by buildings, now long vanished, that available evidence suggests were consummate masterpieces. It was these building that prepared the ground for the summits of the art that arose from the fusion of the diverse genius of the peoples involved. Through its own achievements, the sultanate of Delhi imposed itself as the heir apparent to the combined influences from these trade links and territorial conquests.

The Sultanate of Delhi (c. 1191–1414)

At the time Qutb al-Dīn Aybak acceded to power, he could never have imagined that he was inaugurating, in the footsteps of his former Ghūrid master, a succession of dynasties whose glory was to resound from one end of the old world to the other. Aybak's lineage (the Mu'izzi) is often designated as the "slave kings," although only three sovereigns were of servile origin, Aybak, Iltutmish, and Balban, and even they had been manumitted before ascending to the throne. Moreover, all three descended from different scions. The true progenitor of the sultanate of Delhi was actually Iltutmish (r. 1211–36), one of Qutb al-Dīn Aybak's sons-in-law, and it was during his reign that Sindh, in the hands of a Ghūrid governor up to that point, was incorporated into the sultanate. Iltutmish's reputation was further enhanced by his preservation of the integrity of the territory against incursions from the Khwārezm-Shāhs, whereas his successors were unable to slow those of the Mongols and failed to prevent the invaders from laying waste to Lahore and Punjab in 1241. At the outset, Iltutmish received his investiture from the Abbasid caliph, al-Mustansir, and the fidelity of the Mu'izzi to the Abbasids was so unwavering that, even after the assassination of its last caliph, al-Musta'sim, in 1258, they continued striking currency in his name so as to assert their unaffected position at the heart of the legitimate Sunni majority. Among the long line of Iltutmish's successors, the reign of his daughter Raziya Sultān (1236–40) merits especial mention, since the emergence of a female ruler was exceptional in a political world dominated by men. The rule of Balban (1266–87) was also characterized by the extraordinary political status of this figure and by the period of relative stability he brought, even though Balban, like Iltutmish, had to constantly defend his lands against Mongol raids.

The Mu'izzi were succeeded by the Khaljī sovereigns (1290–1320). They belonged to Turkic—or Turkized—tribes from eastern Afghanistan, whose clan had played a preponderant role during the Ghūrid push into India; it was incidentally a Khaljī, Ikhtiyār al-Dīn Muhammad, who introduced Islam to Bengal in about 1195. The high point of this line was embodied by 'Alā' al-Dīn Muhammad, who ruled from 1296 to 1316. Although he had to confront a growing threat from the Chagatai Mongols, it was he who kick-started the territorial expansion of the sultanate of Delhi towards the Deccan. For this reason, the seizure of Devagiri in 1296, formerly the capital of the Yādava kingdom and renamed Daulatābād, won him colossal spoils and opened the door to fresh conquests to the south. The dynasty, however, was to collapse following the usurpation of Khosrow Khān, a converted Hindu who made the most of the confidence he had acquired as a favorite of the last sovereign, Mubārak Shāh (r. 1316–20).

Pillar originally from a pre-Islamic temple, Quwwat al-Islām mosque, Delhi, India.

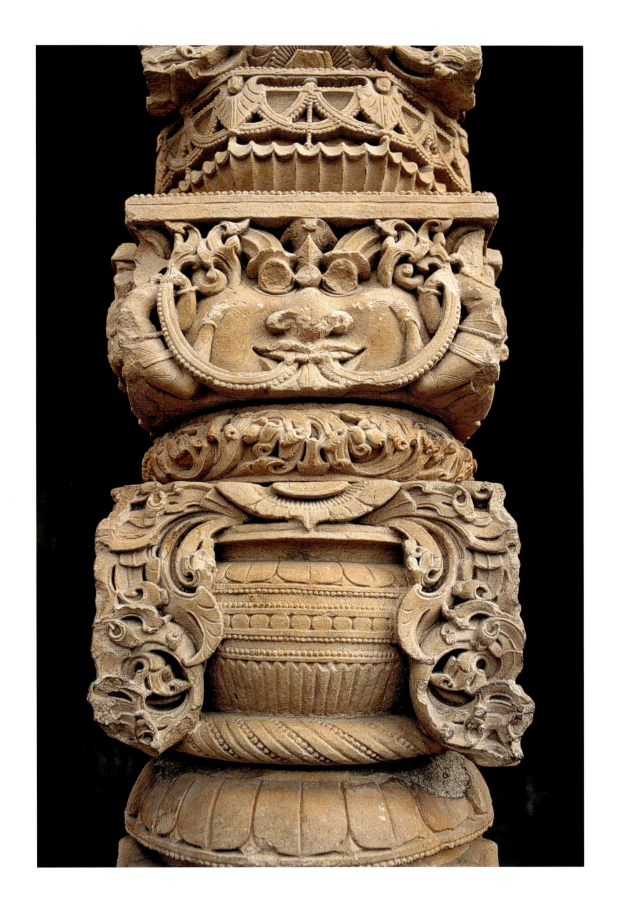

That same year, the Ghāzi general, Malik Tughluq, with the assistance of his son, quelled the disorder sparked by a coup and founded the dynasty of the Tughluqs that was to hold on to power from 1320 to 1414. His twofold objective was to restore economic and administrative stability within the borders of the sultanate and to continue propagating Islam throughout the Deccan. It was, moreover, with this aim in mind that Muhammad Shāh Tughluq (r. 1325–51) temporarily transferred his capital from Delhi to Daulatābād in 1327 and raised taxes in an effort to straighten out the finances of the empire. This, however, only attracted hostility on the part of his flock and a reputation as an unpopular and controversial figure that history has entrenched. One of his successors, Fīrūz Shāh III (r. 1351–88), however, made his mark, overseeing a prosperous period marked by intense architectural activity.

The line's grip subsequently relaxed; this weakness was a boon for Timur, who invaded the sultanate in 1398–99, laying waste to the capital and dealing a death blow to the power base of the Tughluqs. Following these disastrous invasions, the sultanate fissured into a plethora of independent principalities. The fragmentation was such that by 1414 the lineage of the Sayyids, vassals of the Timurids, asserted its authority over an insignificant parcel of land in the Delhi region.

The architecture of the Mu'izzi (c. 1191–1290)

Although it might be logical to assume that the early monuments of the sultanate of Delhi would be indebted to the architecture of the Ghūrid invader, it appears that the builders devised from the start a synthesis of specific forms related to the functions of constructions unknown in the indigenous culture (mosques, mausoleums)—and the new demands they brought with them—with local materials and decorative idioms. An initial era of conquest was characterized by constructions that made use of spolia from preexistent temples; this was, however, followed by a second, politically less unstable, period characterized by architecture in a style specific to the sultanate.

The period of conquest (c. 1191–1211)

On the site of what would become Delhi there rose an ancient Hindu city known as Qila Rai Pithora. This was the creation of the Chauhān, Prithvirāj III, who in fact simply proceeded by enlarging the fortress of Lāl Kot. In 1192 Qutb al-Dīn Aybak laid the foundations of his eastern capital on the ruins of this first settlement. Few and far between, vestiges of the ramparts of this "old" Delhi subsist today and are visible from the summit of the nearby minaret (the Qutb Mīnār).[15] The walls were pierced by no less than thirteen gates, of which some are partially preserved, but the heart of the Muslim city was organized around the Friday Mosque, called Quwwat al-Islām ("power of Islam"). Nowadays, the imposing and majestic silhouette of the Qutb Mīnār casts a protective shadow over the last trace of this founding establishment, in the shape of a succession of interlocked courtyards.

Screen in the prayer hall, Quwwat al-Islām Mosque, with a carved decoration of Arabic inscriptions and plant motifs, early thirteenth century.

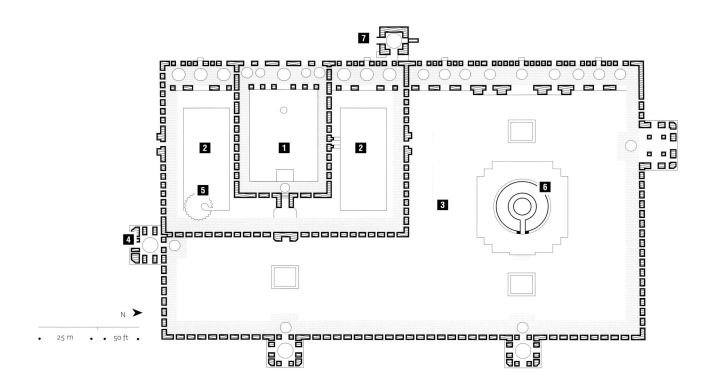

Plan of the Quwwat al-Islām Mosque: **(1)** original mosque; **(2)** additions by Iltutmish (from 1211); **(3)** additions by 'Alā al-Dīn Khaljī (from 1296); **(4)** gate known as 'Alā'i Darwāza (1311); **(5)** Qutb Minār; **(6)** unfinished minaret; **(7)** tomb of Iltutmish (after H. Stierlin).

The Quwwat al-Islām Mosque

Founded in 1193, the mosque at that time was a rectangle measuring 197 by 138 feet (60 by 42 meters). Spolia from twenty-seven Hindu and Jain temples stand around a stone colonnade completed by porticoes over three bays surrounding the central courtyard, the whole resting on a coursed earthwork; there is also a staircase rising from an earlier earthwork. To attain the approximate height of a traditionally columnated mosque, the recycled elements were superposed in pairs.

Although the figurative motifs of its opulent carved decoration have been obliterated by hammering, they often remain identifiable. At this stage of the construction, the columns supported horizontal lintels and a roof covered in flagstones, some overhanging, with in places sculptural effects reminiscent of little domes. On the side of the *qibla* (in the direction of Mecca, to the west here), the prayer hall was originally designed to have a depth of five bays, its volume modeled beneath a row of five "domes" formed of overhanging entablatures, the largest being the one in the middle facing the mihrab. In the same axis, but in the courtyard space, towers the "Iron Pillar," a metal column originally used as a plinth for a statue plundered from a temple of Vishnu in the region of Mathura. At the entrance to the mosque an inscription recalls the name of the builder, Qutb al-Dīn Aybak. At the completion of building work in 1198, the composite monument remained an amalgam of various stylistic borrowings with little unifying principle.

It was in all probability this defect that led a little later to the erection of a stone screen parading a majestic array of five pointed arches. This splendid elevation is applied to the courtyard façade of the prayer hall, which—due to its "Persian" appearance—forms from afar an astonishing contrast with the first colonnades that, in a tradition characteristic of Indian architecture, merely serve to support the stone lintels and flagstone roof. However, closer examination of the construction process has demonstrated that the blocks of red sandstone do not quite follow the curve of an arch ring in the way of voussoirs, but are laid in cantilevered tiers. The visible faces are moreover decorated with delicate trails of plants and lively calligraphic friezes in Arabic. Such fusion hints at the stylistic and technical synthesis that native craftsmen were forging for themselves in response to the demands of their new overlords. This is the (rather overdone) description Ibn Battuta provides of the monument:

> The Cathedral Mosque occupies a vast area; its walls, roof and paving are all constructed of white stone, admirably squared and firmly cemented with lead. There is no wood in it at all. It has thirteen domes of stone, its *minbar* also is of stone, and it has four courts. In the centre of the mosque is the awe-inspiring column [*sic*] of which [it is said] nobody knows of what metal it is constructed. One of their learned men told me it is called Haft Jush, which means 'seven metals'... At the eastern gate of the mosque there are two enormous idols of brass prostrate on the ground and held by stones, and everyone entering or leaving the mosque treads on them. The site was formerly occupied by a budkhana, that is an idol temple, and was converted into a mosque on the conquest of the city.[16]

The Qutb Minār
The construction of the Qutb Minār minaret began in 1199 under Qutb al-Dīn Aybak. At that point in time it stood outside the mosque, more exactly at its southeastern corner; today its 238 feet (72.5 meters) tower over its vestiges. While for the mosque it fulfilled the function of a true minaret, its awe-inspiring height also exemplifies the desire to proclaim the grandeur of Islam, in the manner of the (local) Indian "towers of victory" (*jayastambha*) in a pre-Islamic context. The minaret barrel is punctuated by four balconies—only the first three are original—and topped by a lantern. Qutb al-Dīn Aybak would probably have seen only the lower level completed, with the construction of the other levels occurring under Iltutmish. The lower level presents alternately round and wedge-shaped moldings. A balcony with corbelling heralds the break to a second zone of gadrooned section, while a second balcony ensures the transition to a third level of star-shaped section. The two upper levels, built in white marble, betray later restorations. Mention of several building campaigns is to be found in the inscriptions on the monument itself, as well as in historical accounts. The minaret stairway comprises some 379 steps today.

We have already underscored the relationship between Qutb Minār and the minaret at Jām in Afghanistan; less in the form of loans and copying, it amounts instead—due to the radical differences in materials and construction techniques employed—to the adaptation of architectural forms. Jām is built chiefly in brick decorated with turquoise ceramics, while the Qutb Minār was erected in coursed red

Facing page. The Qutb Minār and the 'Alā'i Darwāza; foreground, mausoleum of Imām Muhammad 'Alī, called Imām Zamīn, early sixteenth century.

Above. The cornice on the first balcony of the Qutb Minār, with a corbelled carved decoration.

sandstone with white marble trim at the summit, while the decorations are carved entirely in the stone. The opposition between a brick construction typical of the Iranian or Afghanistan plateau and the stone architecture prevalent in India marks the emergence of one of the crucial features of architectural expression distinguishing these two geographical entities.

The Arhai-din-ka-Jhonpra Mosque of Ajmer
The Hindu kingdom incorporating Delhi also included the town of Ajmer in Rājasthān. This shared historical destiny arguably accounts for the many similarities between Quwwat al-Islām and the congregational mosque in Ajmer, constructed between 1200 and 1206. The monument, whose name designates a mosque built "in half a day," stands on a platform of almost perfectly square shape approximately 256 feet (78 meters) along the side. As in Delhi, considerable spolia from Hindu temples have been redeployed, but greater effort has been made to integrate them and the general proportions are more elegant. Tiers three barrels high allow each column

to reach the ceiling height of some twenty-three feet (seven meters). Porticoes four bays across and set with uniform "domes" adorn three sides of a vast courtyard. The volume of the prayer hall extends over six full bays, reiterating the alignment of the domes ornamenting the porticoes. Originally, there was no minaret, but, as in Delhi, and subsequently between 1220 and 1229 during the reign of Iltutmish, a screen was erected whose central archway is flanked by two "mock minarets."

Too constricted to contain stairs, the purpose of these towers was purely decorative. They are reminiscent of the disposition of certain Seljuk monuments in Anatolia.

Iltutmish and his successors (1211–90)

By the time Iltutmish took power, succeeding his father-in-law Qutb al-Dīn Aybak, the period of conquest had been completed, and the return to stability led to a prosperity that the many monuments built at that time would reflect.

Facing page and below. The screen in the prayer hall of the Arhai-din-ka-Jhonpra Mosque, Ajmer, India, early thirteenth century.

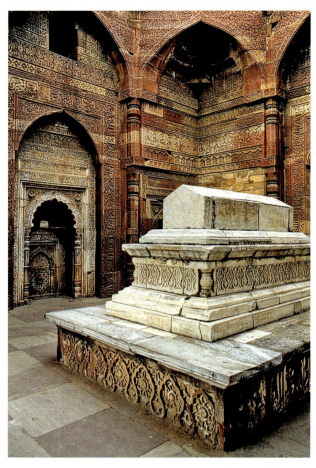

Mosque and mausoleums

At the outset, the sovereign turned his attention to the mosque of Quwwat al-Islām, which he first enlarged in about 1220–29 with the construction of a new compound incorporating its predecessor, as well as with the erection of the Qutb Minār within a vast rectangle 394 feet (120 meters) wide by 230 feet (70 meters) deep. Moreover, the *qibla* wall was extended by three cupolas on both sides of the old enclosure, which was kept intact.

Outside this complex, Iltutmish had his tomb, thirty-foot (nine-meter) square in plan, erected. The mausoleum is built of stone; once topped by a dome on squinches, its decoration is remarkable and delicately carved. Arguably, the tomb also shows the first occasion on which decoration exploiting the contrast between white marble and sandstone appears in the architecture of the sultanate. This characteristic marks an important stage in the emergence of an architectural language specific to the Islamic Indian domain.

When in 1231 Iltutmish had the misfortune to lose the son he hoped would succeed him, Nāsir al-Dīn Muhammad, he determined to honor his memory. In consequence, he ordered the construction of a sumptuous mausoleum, some three miles (five kilometers) from the city at the time. The proportions of what is today dubbed the Sultān Ghāri, or "vault of the sultan," are decidedly more imposing than the tomb of Iltutmish. At the center of an compound measuring almost 280 square feet (26 square meters), flanked by corner towers and opened by a monumental gate with a staircase allowing access to a terrace, stands an isolated octagonal platform covering the crypt, while the space for a prayer hall opens out at the rear of the courtyard. The mass of materials recycled from Hindu temples contribute to a profoundly original construction, although parallels—none of them particularly convincing in the end—have been made with Seljuk mausoleums. Moreover, the contrast between the splendor of this building and the extremely modest tomb known as the Raziya Sultān—supposed to contain the remainders of the intrepid queen, Iltutmish's daughter, who succeeded him in 1236 and reigned for four years—is striking. This tomb barely emerges from an open-air courtyard today submerged under the dense urban fabric of Old Delhi at the back of an alley close to the Turkman Gate.

Above and facing page. Mausoleum of Iltutmish (died 1236); the cenotaph and the mihrab, where white marble alternates with the red sandstone on the walls.

Pools and tanks

The tribute Indian architectural heritage should pay to Shams al-Dīn Iltutmish means that the excavation, in about 1230, of the great pool bearing his name, the Hauz-e Shamsi, should be mentioned. Its purpose was to catch the runoff from many gullies; at that time, it constituted the biggest water reserve in Delhi and was hugely admired by the Moroccan traveler Ibn Battuta in around 1330:

> Outside Delhi is the large reservoir named after the Sultan Shams al-Din Lalmish [Iltutmish] from which the inhabitants of the city draw their drinking water. It lies close to the *musalla* [place of prayer]. Its contents are collected from rainwater and it is about two miles in length by half that in breadth. Its western side, in the direction of the *musalla* is constructed with stones, and disposed like a series of terraces one above the other, and beneath each terrace are steps leading down to the water. Beside each terrace is a stone pavilion [dome] containing seats for those who have come out to visit the place and to enjoy its attractions. In the centre of the tank there is

a great pavilion [dome] built of dressed stones, two stories high. When the reservoir is filled with water it can be reached only in boats. Inside there is a mosque, and at most times it is occupied by poor brethren devoted to the service of God and placing their trust in him. When the water dries up at the sides of this reservoir, they sow sugar canes, gherkins, cucumbers, and green and yellow melons.[17]

This description poses a number of questions, in particular as regards the building containing a mosque; if a domed pavilion does indeed stand on an "island" linked to the bank of the pool by a bridge, it appears to be posterior to the thirteenth century. The banks of the pool have been further embellished over the dynasties, while the Jahāz Mahal, or "boat palace," was built under the Lodī in the fifteenth century.

Finally, the installation of a curious stepped pit-well that collects water from a sulfurous spring, the Ghandak-ki-Baoli, is likewise attributed to the era of Iltutmish. A flight of steps on one side allows access to the basin whose water is celebrated for improving skin conditions. On the axis of this staircase—but on the other side of the pool—a gallery supported by five pillars opens up to form a hall where one can take the air.

Balban and Kayqobād
No remarkable monument marks the reign of Nāsir al-Dīn (1246–66). The sovereign, whose reputation was for extreme devotion, had abandoned the business of state to his vizier, Balban. Starting out as Iltutmish's slave, Balban became Nāsir al-Dīn's father-in-law, enabling him to succeed when the latter passed away without heir. The buildings of the rule of Balban (1266–87) are little known and few have survived. The chronicles say Balban built palaces, but even their location remains doubtful. The mausoleum bearing his name in the town of Mehrauli is unfortunately in extremely poor condition. Square in plan and pierced with four arches to generate a tetrapylon, it is built in stone and its dome has long gone. It amounts however to a noteworthy landmark in the history of Indian architecture, since it is presumably the first monument to feature a true arch-ring with stone *cunei*.

The brief reign of Mu'izz al-Dīn Kayqobād (or Kaikobad, 1287–90) is worthy of note for the construction of a palace complex on the banks of the Yamuna surrounded by gardens called Kiloghari. Only scant traces remain of this building, which is mainly known from ancient records,[18] but represents the earliest attempt to urbanize Delhi along the riverbank, a planning option that foreshadows the one that Fīrūz Shāh Tughluq—among others—was to subsequently adopt.

The Khaljī of Delhi (1290–1320)

The first two sovereigns of the line of Khaljī left hardly any evidence of their reign. Their successor, 'Alā' al-Dīn Khaljī (1296–1316), on the contrary, bequeathed a substantial amount, initially as the conqueror of the Deccan and then as a megalomaniac builder. His military victories and attendant conquests earned him the nickname "the second Alexander," but more relevantly they provided him with immense quantities of booty that allowed him to give free rein to his architectural mania. What is more, he could indulge it with impunity, since the Mongolian threat seemed at that point to have been contained.

The Mu'izzi era was one of sometimes questionable stylistic juxtapositions in the course of which elements were combined, giving rise to the most individual characteristics of all the Islamic architecture in the subcontinent. In this regard, the buildings erected under the authority of the Khaljī mark the final phase of these experiments, materialized by genuine arches and cupolas in the full sense of the term, as well as in specific decorative elements, such as, for example, lotus-bud friezes around arches.

Hydraulic systems and town planning

The reign of 'Alā' al-Dīn Khaljī was one of plenty and it fostered a considerable surge in both the population and economy of Delhi. At this time, however, the city stood some distance from the course of the Yamuna, imposing rigorous strictures on the use of water. To ameliorate this situation, Iltutmish's pool, long clogged up with alluvia, was dredged and resupplied with water. The sovereign then went on to commemorate his reign with a new foundation, erecting to the north of the ancient site of Delhi the citadel of Siri. Apart from the ramparts, few scattered vestiges remain of this fortress, while the exact location of the palace named in the sources as the Hezār Sotūn ("palace with the thousand columns") remains unclear. To the west of the citadel, the monarch also had a new pool with even more imposing dimensions dug, the Hauz-i 'Alā'i, now called the Hauz-Khas. This installation, the principal source of water for Siri, was later re-excavated, in particular under Fīrūz Shāh Tughluq. The prestige of the tank earned a glowing tribute from Ibn Battuta:

Tribute from the poet Amīr Khosrow to Sultan 'Alā' al-Dīn Khaljī. Page from a dismembered *Khamsa* ("Quintet") by Amīr Khosrow, India, gouache on paper, mid-fifteenth century. Courtesy of the Art Institute of Chicago, 1962–640.

> Between Delhi and the "Abode of the Caliphate" [Siri] is the private [imperial] reservoir [*hauz-khas*] which is larger than the other [that of Sultan Iltutmish]. Along its sides there are about forty pavilions and around it live the musicians. Their place is called *Tharb-abad* ["the dwelling of joy"] and they have there a most extensive bazaar, a cathedral mosque and many other mosques besides. I was told that the singing girls living there, of whom there are a great many, take part in a body in the *tarawih* prayers in these mosques during the month of Ramadan, and the *imans* lead them in these prayers.[19]

Major extensions at Quwwat al-Islām

The sovereign's almost excessive architectural ambitions are also apparent in the works he inaugurated on the venerable Friday Mosque. Incredibly, 'Alā' al-Dīn Khaljī decided to go one better than the Qutb by erecting a minaret double its height. The challenge was never met, however, as the construction advanced no farther than the first, lower level, now rising 80 feet (24.5 meters). After seeing the edifice during his travels, Ibn Battuta waxed lyrical. He noted in particular: "The width of its passage is such that three elephants could go up it. The third that is built equals in height the whole of the short minaret in the north [this assertion is demonstrably false]."[20]

The sovereign was, moreover, to enlarge the Quwwat al-Islām mosque with a third enclosure. As well as incorporating the new minaret, the perimeter of this new compound doubled the surface area of the two preceding structures, without marring them in any way. The planned elevation was for four monumental gates, of which only one, located on the southern side, remains in a pristine state of preservation. Known as the 'Alā'i Darwāza (a pun meaning both "sublime gate"—as in "Sublime Porte"—and "gate of 'Alā' al-Dīn"), it takes the form of a tetrapylon gateway of square plan surmounted by a dome on squinches that is perhaps the earliest of the kind to survive in India. Three projecting external facades are inlaid with white marble that stands out against the red sandstone; the decorative schema included several inscriptions, some notably in Arabic, giving a date of 1311. A barely horseshoe-shaped arch springing from corner imposts adorns the entrance, its edge decorated with a characteristic lotus-bud frieze. The windows are shut off by *jali*, or screens, that rapidly became a calling card for Muslim architects in India. The refined and ingenious ornamental rhythm alternates plain surfaces punctuated

Below and facing page. The 'Alā'i Darwāza, Delhi, clad in red sandstone and white marble to bring out the delicate carved ornamentation, 1311.

Above. The unfinished minaret of 'Alā' al-Dīn Khaljī, Quwwat al-Islām, Delhi.

Facing page. The mosque of the *dargāh* of Nizamuddin, or Jamā'at-Khāna, Delhi, early fourteenth century.

with niches and moldings with complete openings attenuated by the curves of the arches and the openwork *jalis*, together composing a harmony of consummate delicacy. This subtlety of execution by no means dilutes the coherence of the overall decorative scheme; indeed, it emphasizes the structure's balanced proportions, making the 'Alā'i Darwāza one of the finest masterpieces erected during the Delhi sultanate.

Finally, in the southwestern corner of the new mosque compound were erected a series of buildings now in ruins, which are presumed to comprise the tomb and funerary madrassa of 'Alā' al-Dīn Khaljī. If this identification were borne out, the complex would be probably the first of its kind in India. Furthermore, while the combination in a funerary context of mausoleum and madrassa was relatively frequent in the Seljuk or Mamluk Orient, it was more exceptional in the subcontinent.

The mosque of Jamā'at-Khāna, Nizamuddin
In about 1286, ten years before the accession to power of 'Alā' al-Dīn Khaljī, a young Sufi named Nizām al-Dīn Chishti and known as the Awliyā of Chisht, Afghanistan, settled in the Ghiyāspur district of Delhi.[21] It was during the reign of this sultan that his son Khizr Khān is thought to have erected a mosque known as the Jamā'at-Khāna or "congregational mosque," which survives in the heart of a complex (*dargāh*) that also shelters the remains of the saint. The red sandstone front is decorated with three arches that open on to the court, each leading to a domed hall; the somewhat ponderous central cupola is the most impressive. Notwithstanding the thesis of certain authors, who suggest a far later date for the construction of the mosque, the influence of the 'Alā'-i Darwāza clearly transpires in a wealth of details, such as the lotus-bud friezes bordering the arches, the Koranic inscriptions, and certain

floral motifs. The same Khizr Khān resurfaces as the hero of a verse narrative composed by the great Indo-Persian poet Amīr Khosrow, the panegyrist of Sultan 'Alā' al-Dīn as well as a disciple of Nizām al-Dīn Chishti. Shortly after the construction of the mosque, in around 1320, the latter also had the *baoli* constructed that to this day supplies the district and which in that period constituted the primary store for drinking water. There is a curious legend concerning this construction: the Tughluq sovereign is supposed to have had his fortress at Tughluqābād erected just as the *baoli* was being dug and to have prohibited anyone from working on other constructions. The workmen at the *baoli* initially tried to get round this constraint by working at night, but when the sultan learned of their trick, he forbade the sale of oil for the lamps. The saint, however, ordered that the lamps be filled with water from the tank and they miraculously ignited. When Nizām al-Dīn Chishti died in 1325 during the reign of Ghiyāth al-Dīn Tughluq, he was interred in front of the Jamā'at-Khāna mosque. Several times rebuilt, his mausoleum still attracts pilgrims and is the object of passionate devotion.

The Tughluqs (1320–1414)

The founder of a new dynasty, Ghiyāth al-Dīn Tughluq, saluted the event by building a whole new city: Tughluqābād (1320–25). Whereas architecture under the Khaljīs had on occasion been exuberant, Ghiyāth al-Dīn Tughluq's achievements are better remembered for their reserve and sobriety. Prior to ascending to the throne, Ghiyāth al-Dīn Tughluq had once been governor of Punjab and a remarkable monument testifies to this period: the mausoleum of Rukn-e 'Alam in Multān. It is a construction that crowns Multān's particular status; while, administratively speaking, the city was little more than the seat of a governorship, artistic activity there was worthy of the capital it had once been. The grandeur of the constructions with which it is embellished earns it the excursus we will devote to its original historical position that is evident up to and during the administration of the Tughluqs.

In this connection, the mausoleum built for Ghiyāth al-Dīn Tughluq himself in Delhi redeployed some elements from the Rukn-e 'Alam.

From a present-day perspective, Muhammad Tughluq seems a key figure in the upheaval that affected the regime. He instituted the eventually disastrous attempt to transfer the capital to Daulatābād, before undertaking the construction of a whole new city in Delhi: Jahānpanāh, the "Refuge of the World." In contrast, the reign of Fīrūz Shāh seems to have been more serene, with renowned buildings springing up and a remarkable urbanization policy, in particular in respect of plans for irrigation. The intensity of these building activities inclines one to believe that the period must have been one of prosperity, a kind of calm before the storm, which, by the late fourteenth century, was about to break over the region in the form of the invasions of Timur the Lame, a violent prelude to the brutal end of the supremacy of the Delhi sultanate.

Ghiyāth al-Dīn Tughluq (r. 1320–25)

Qutb al-Dīn Mubārak Shāh (r. 1316–20), the last sovereign of the Khaljī line, was assassinated by his favorite, a converted Hindu by the name of Khosrow Khān. The regicide promptly seized the crown, sparking a legitimist reaction by General Ghāzi Malik, the then governor of Punjab. Since no male descendant of the Khaljī dynasty survived, at the conclusion of a victorious march against the usurper, whom he had decapitated, it was the general himself who was proclaimed king in 1321 under the name of Ghiyāth al-Dīn Tughluq (or Tughluq Shāh).

The fortress at Tughluqābād

The new monarch arrived with a military past boasting firsthand knowledge of the disasters occasioned by Mongol incursions into Punjab. He was thus immediately sensitive to the vulnerability of the original settlement of Delhi as much as to that of Siri, neither particularly compatible in his eyes with the role of "royal seat" that these urban centers were expected to play.

At this point, he decided to undertake the construction of a veritable fortified city that was to bear his name: Tughluqābād. To this end, he chose a site about five miles (eight kilometers) from the Qutb Minār and the Yamuna River. It amounted to a rock outcrop which provided a stronghold not only complete with the materials

Mausoleum of Ghiyāth al-Dīn Tughluq, Tughluqābād, Delhi, c. 1325.

necessary to build it nearby, but also a firm underpinning on which the foundations of such a complex might rise. The locally quarried gray stone was arranged to build an enclosing wall of irregular form delimiting two quite distinct zones. On the one hand, there stands an almost rectangular royal citadel separated from the fortified city proper by its own compound and, on the other, a covered bazaar, today in ruins, together with a palatial ensemble. The city itself lay next to the royal citadel, but is today a low-lying stretch of vestiges that provide scant indications of the street layout or the plans of the various dwellings.

Between the rock on which the city stood and the hills opposite, a natural pool that formed during monsoon season provided a reservoir for the site that filled with runoff water. The king had it closed off to the east with a dam, while at the western edge of the pool, the fortress is linked to the tomb of Tughluq Shāh by a bridge-cum-dam. The building of this imposing construction was a subject on which the chronicles wax lyrical, describing it in often overblown language, as in the following example:

> I was informed that at the time of the fourth year of the reign of Ghiyāth al-Dīn, he completed a fortress located a *parasange* [approximately three miles] from Siri. From the foundations to the turrets, the fortress was built out of sturdy stone and its underpinnings were hewn out of the rock. Then a reservoir lake was dug at the foot of this fortress, so that its clear waters constantly would splash it with waves and it was said there was a seventh sea at the foot of the Caucasus mountain. This fortress was named Tughluqābād because it was built by this blessed monarch.[22]

The preoccupation with security that presided over this austere and imposing defensive complex implies that its basic purpose was to survive a siege, so water supplies were guaranteed by cisterns cut into the rock. It seems, however, that the whole immense construction was hardly occupied at all. In effect, the reign of Ghiyāth al-Dīn Tughluq was brutally cut short in 1325, when he was returning to Lakhnautī from a military campaign. Together with his son and heir, Prince Mahmūd, he was crushed to death when a wooden pavilion that another of his children, the future Muhammad Shāh, had erected in his honor collapsed. It is generally supposed that Muhammad Shāh, in his desire for power, had given destiny a helping hand.

The mausoleum of Ghiyāth al-Dīn Tughluq

This is the building located on a fortified island on Lake Tughluqābād, which is accessible over the bridge-cum-dam just mentioned. Square in plan, it is remarkable for its strongly battered (that is, inclined) external walls, as well as the calculated two-color appearance of its courses of alternate red sandstone and white marble— also used to frame the windows—in the manner of the wooden lintels and tie beams of Punjab. While the salient features of the monument are directly inspired by the mausoleums of Multān, the materials used are common in central India. Three gates with Persian arches rimmed by lotus buds open majestically onto the spacious funerary hall. The arches tend to widen out, passing from a simple pointed arch to the "Persian" (four-centered) variety.[23]

Finally there stands a distinctive dome on an octagonal drum clad in white marble. In both its silhouette and materials, and its finial floret—although it has not yet taken on the onion profile—one can see the beginnings of the future Mughal dome style.

Above. Mausoleum of Yusuf Gardizi, Multān, Pakistan, founded in 1152; the ceramic dressings date from much later.

Facing page. Mausoleum of Bahā' al-Dīn Zakarīyā, Multān, Pakistan, after 1262.

An original creative unity: the mausoleums of Multān

Now located in Pakistan, the city and region of Multān boasts several monuments remarkable for their age and for testifying to an architectural panache with specific characteristics that both reflect and extrapolate an intellectual and religious life endemic to the sphere of influence of the ancient capital.

One example is the 1152 building bearing the name of Yusuf Gardizi containing the remains of a saint presumed to have died four centuries previous, around 752. The cladding of the quasi-cubic structure was added to the building at a time significantly posterior to its construction. In addition, three further mausoleums stand to the glory of personages, who passed away during the thirteenth century, venerated for their holiness: Shāh Bahā'-i Haqq (or Bahā' al-Dīn Zakarīyā, 1262), Shādnā Shahīd (1270), and Shāh Shams al-Dīn Tabrizi (1276). These grand statements are rounded out by the huge mausoleum of Rukn-e 'Alam, completing a prime illustration of an architectural tradition profoundly representative of Punjab, but which, because it remained a place of devotion until the present day, has undergone some significant modifications that may well have had a deleterious effect on the unity of its decoration.

Mausoleum of Bahā' al-Dīn Zakariyā (after 1262)
Bahā' al-Dīn Zakariyā, who introduced the Suhrawardīyah brotherhood to the subcontinent, was one of the most distinguished disciples of the great Sufi, Suhrawardī of Aleppo. Born in Sindh in 1171, he traveled to the major religious centers to deepen his knowledge of Islam before settling at Multān, where he founded a *khāneqāh*, or "house of dervishes." In the course of his spiritual life, he was to initiate many adepts, including Rukn-e 'Alam himself. The base of the mausoleum of Bahā' al-Dīn is square and serves as the plinth for a second, octagonal level from which springs a cupola. The corners of the building are highlighted by small buttresses in the shape of minarets or pinnacles. The battered walls of the first level, and still more those of the second, contribute greatly to the impression of elevation that gives the edifice such a dynamic aesthetic. The fact that the brick used as a building material is left visible imposes an overall tonality touched off by colorful notes in enamel tiles of a predominantly turquoise hue.

Mausoleum of Rukn-e 'Alam (after 1335)
Known by the name Rukn al-Dīn, or Rukn-e 'Alam, this sheikh was a saint belonging to the Sufi Suhrawardīyah brotherhood. Grandson of and spiritual successor to Sheikh Bahā' al-Dīn Zakarīyā, he was born in Multān in 1251 and resided primarily in that city, although he made several journeys to Delhi, exerting a considerable influence on successive sultans, from 'Alā' al-Dīn Khaljī to Muhammad Tughluq. On his death in 1335, he was initially interred beside his father before being transferred to the mausoleum that now bears his name.

This remarkable monument cannot be dated with certitude; one local tradition retold by many chroniclers ascribes its construction to Ghiyāth al-Dīn Tughluq at the time when he was a governor of the region, the implication being that the future sovereign had intended the building for himself. The presumption of such a noble birth is undermined by several inconsistencies, however: first, General Ghāzi Malik would have been occupied by his ceaseless battles against the Mongols (or "Tatars"), and one can hardly picture him delighting in architectural design before even ascending to the throne of Delhi; and secondly, the sizable proportions of the building presuppose a protracted and costly campaign, scarcely compatible with the resources of an embattled governor—one who, moreover, two witnesses of the time (Amīr Khosrow and Ibn Battuta) mention as having built a mosque at Multān, without though breathing word of a mausoleum. It is instead more probable that the expenses of the construction were in fact borne by the powerful Suhrawardīyah brotherhood itself.[24]

Standing within an enormous compound, the mausoleum of Rukn-e 'Alam rises more than ninety-eight feet (thirty meters) in height, the culmination of the towering city and a spectacular landmark. Arranged around an octagonal plan and ninety feet (27.5 meters) in diameter, it is flanked by eight corner towers and its elevation covers three levels. In spite of its perpendicular walls, the flanged towers— wider at the base than above—are powerfully dynamic. The exterior walls are entirely in brick reinforced with timber lintels; the relative austerity is enlivened by a decoration of blue and white glazed ceramic tiles. To the south, the main entrance in the form of a rectangle joins the first level octagon, generating a complex vestibule structure. The funerary hall, also octagonal, features a mihrab facing west.

Muhammad Shāh Tughluq (1325–1351)

Muhammad Shāh Tughluq had an ambivalent and controversial impact on his time. While some ancient and modern authors see him as an unpredictable, capricious individual whose inconsistent actions drained the coffers of the state, others consider him a blend of wily politician and acute strategist. As we hinted above, he did in all probability hasten the demise of his father and his brother, before, at the beginning of his reign, applying his stamp to the sultanate in a radical manner by ordaining the capital to be transferred. In 1327 or 1328 it was thus moved to Daulatābād in the Deccan and at a stroke a significant proportion of the Delhi population of all and every social class was forced to accept its exile to the new site. This enforced transhumance proved, however, short-lived, and when Ibn Battuta visited Delhi a few years later, it had recovered its status as the capital of the sultan, who was, moreover, then making efforts to erect a new enceinte there.

Facing page. Mausoleum of Rukn-e 'Alam, Multān, after 1335.

Below. The fort of Daulatābād, India, and the Chand Minār; in the foreground, the ramparts of the lower town.

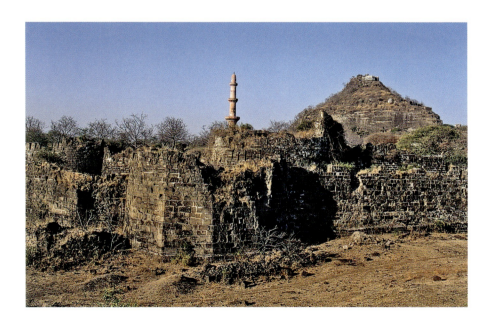

From Tughluqābād to Jahānpanāh
The relationship of Muhammad Shāh Tughluq with his capital is still partly veiled in mystery; the reasons for the construction of Tughluqābād and its subsequent abandonment four years later by Muhammad Shāh remain no less obscure. Calculated to rebuff a siege at a time when the Mongol threat was almost constant, the immense enclosure included a royal citadel and cost a phenomenal amount of money, but it seems that the city rising behind the ramparts was never actually inhabited. Our astonishment only increases on noting that the sultan added a palace-citadel to the city at the other end of the Tughluqābād dam, to which he gave the name of Ādilābād. Be that as it may, neither project seems to have supplanted the cities of Delhi and Siri, which continued to expand.

In 1334, Ibn Battuta described Delhi as an agglomeration of four contiguous cities: "old" Delhi, built in the late twelfth century by the Chauhān kings; followed by Siri, founded by 'Alā' al-Dīn Khaljī; preceding Tughluqābād, the creation of Ghiyāth al-Dīn Tughluq; and finishing up finally with Jahānpanāh, built by Muhammad Shāh.[25] This fourth enceinte was supposed to connect the first Delhi foundation to Siri by way of a fortification. The great pool of the Hauz-Khas borders the northwestern wall, with a gate providing access to its waters. On the eastern flank of the enclosing wall, close to the Khirkī Mosque, an impressive-looking and ingenious bridge-dam with seven arches—the Satpula—traverses a drain to form a reservoir; these works were an integral part of Muhammad Tughluq's compound and offered the possibility of diverting the water flow for the purposes of irrigation.

The Begumpurī Masjid
In the center of the new city stands the Great Mosque of Jahānpanāh, now known as the Begumpurī Masjid. It is organized around a virtually square plan—295 by 308 feet (90 by 94 meters)—and is clearly Persian in inspiration. It was probably the first mosque in Islamic India that adopted an "Iranian"-type plan, with four *iwans* (large entrance arches that project into the courtyard). Notwithstanding, the

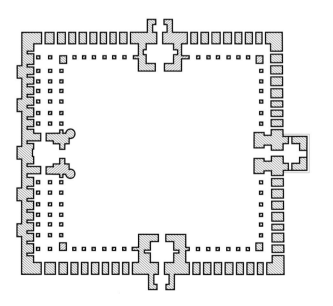

Left. Plan of the Begumpuri Masjid, Delhi (after C. Tadgell).

Facing page. Entrance to the mosque of the Kotla Fīrūz Shāh, Delhi, second half of the fourteenth century.

relationship with Iranian architectural models is tempered by the use of strictly indigenous materials: the masonry course is coated in mortar, with small turquoise ceramic tiles alleviating in places the sense of austerity conveyed by the structure of the edifice. Each side of the court is graced with porticoes supported on stone columns, while in the center rises a great *iwan*. Opposite the prayer hall, the portico facing the main entrance is flanked by massive, truncated cone-shaped "pseudo-minarets" characteristic of Tughluq architecture.

Timur himself might well have gazed on this mosque. Perhaps it was here that he learned the principles later applied to its famous counterpart in Samarkand, the Bibi Khanum; in this connection, one should note not only the engaged minarets to either side of the prayer hall *iwan* and the monumental entryway, but also the appearance of carved stone columns and panels, all elements rare in the Iranian and Central Asian worlds. The construction does, however, offer visitors an opportunity to observe the sorts of crosscurrents that must have influenced teams of artists and craftsmen all over this part of the Islamic world.

On a site near the mosque there emerge the ruins of a palatial complex today identified as the Bijai Mandal, whose foundation is dated by certain authors to the time of Muhammad Tughluq, while others point to a later era, such as the period (late fifteenth century–early sixteenth century).

Fīrūz Shāh Tughluq (r. 1351–88)

The advent to power of Fīrūz Shāh heralds the onset of a new epoch. The sovereign, probably motivated by the steadily growing population of the various zones of Delhi, attempted throughout his reign to secure the provisioning of the city, in water particularly. To this end, he initiated a vast program of irrigation works, then decided to simply re-establish the city on a new site on the banks of the Yamuna. This was the new city of Fīrūzābād, in the center of which he had the royal citadel, or Kotla Fīrūz Shāh, erected. Notwithstanding, he did not neglect other cities, ordering the pools of Iltutmish and ʿAlāʾ al-Dīn in the heart of "old" Delhi to be overhauled. The second of these basins, today known as the Hauz-Khas, owes the lion's share of its present-day appearance to the repairs made at Fīrūz Shāh's instigation in 1352, including the addition of a series of multistory buildings at the southern and western edges of the pool intended to house a madrassa and the tomb of the sultan himself, among other buildings.

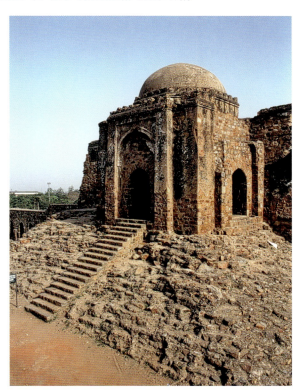

The Kotla Fīrūz Shāh

Within the new city founded by Fīrūz Shāh, the royal citadel stood on the banks of the Yamuna. The Archeological Survey of India, in its efforts to reconstitute the original disposition of the compound, which contains two major monuments in a relatively good state of conservation, has undertaken a thorough survey.[26] The first construction is a *baoli*—a well-cum-tank—which collected water as it seeped in from the nearby river, thus providing the inhabitants

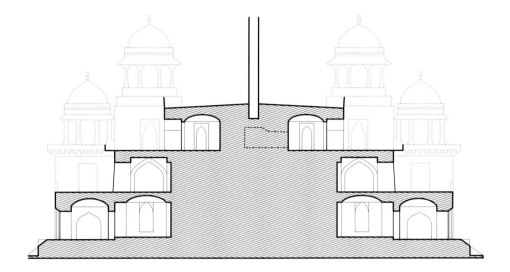

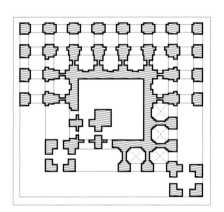 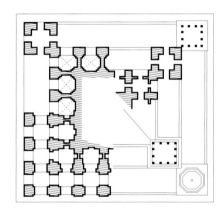 

Side view and plan of the two levels of the Lāt Minār, Kotla Fīrūz Shāh, Delhi, second half of the fourteenth century (after C. Tadgell and J. Hoag).

of the palace with drinking water. Galleries opening on to the interior of the well-tank ran over several tiers round the pool. A terrace ringed by balustrades topped the ensemble and presented two elegant *chhatris* (small pavilions with columns). Such an arrangement suggests that the complex might have been used as a pleasure garden and for taking the air.

Sometimes called the Lāt Minār because it stands next to the congregational mosque, the second building worthy of attention is a curious-looking, three-tiered pyramid, at the top of which towers a monolithic column. The column dates from the time of Ashoka, whose inscriptions it bears. While the function of the work remains unclear, it does seem to prefigure other palatial pavilions, such as the Pānch Mahal of Fatehpur Sīkri. Several historians of Indian architecture have dubbed this type of gallery-monument a *baradari*, without precisely defining its function. The building is arranged around a network of radiating galleries that communicate with the cells and whose elevation presents a staged pyramid organized around a massive central core. The corners of the first two levels supported pavilions of the *chhatri* type that topped solid towers. The structure must have allowed the air to circulate even to the innermost galleries, making it a pleasant shelter from the steamy and stifling banks of the Yamuna.

Little remains of the mosque that stood a few yards from this edifice, save the monumental staircase to the north of the building that led to the esplanade used for worship. The underpinnings of the earthwork have for their part been converted into cells. The terrace itself, originally girded with porticoes, encompasses a near square with sides measuring some 130 feet (40 meters) long. This leads to a prayer area where it is said Timur performed obeisance.

Pavilions, channels, and water storage
The inventory of monuments built by Fīrūz Shāh drawn up by historians features several pavilions that grace the edges of reservoirs. One such is the pavilion of Mahipalpur, on the road from Mehrauli to Palam, though there are three others, dotted about the Delhi ridge: the Kushk Mahal, the Mālcha Mahal, and the Bhuli-Bhatiyāri-ka-Mahal. Reserves of water in their immediate proximity betray an evident desire to develop irrigation, but they also exemplify another of the sovereign's passions: gardens. Official historians of the past attributed hundreds of gardens to Fīrūz Shāh, as the following passage illustrates:

> Fīrūz Shāh had a great passion for gardens and did much to embellish the plantations. He had one thousand two hundred gardens laid out in Delhi and its surroundings, restoring some thirty others founded by 'Alā' al-Dīn Khaljī.[27]

The majority of these gardens and reservoirs have since disappeared, but some of the more imposing constructions, such as the dam-bridge at Wazīrābād, have resisted the vicissitudes of time. Located at the extreme northern tip of the city of Delhi, this splendid construction served both as a thoroughfare and a method of controlling the flow of a *nala* (seasonal channel or brook). Not far from there stands a mosque with three domes that also dates from the reign of Fīrūz Shāh.

Historians of the sovereign also mention him as patronizing a great deal of irrigation work intended to make even regions at some distance from the larger watercourses arable. Among these there was the channel connecting the Yamuna to Hisār in the Haryāna, located more than 93 miles (150 kilometers) from the river. Re-dug on several occasions, this channel was used again in the seventeenth century by Shāh Jahān for his new capital under the name *nahr-e behesht* ("river of paradise"). Another channel collected water from the Kāli River in the Doāb—that is, between the Ganges and the Yamuna, dispatching it into the latter whence it flowed towards Delhi. What is certain is that Fīrūz Shāh did much to promote the region of Hisār—known as Hisār-i Fīrūza at the time.[28] His first task was to provide the city with the means of irrigating its arable land; he then went on to have a mosque built, whose courtyard is still adorned with one of those "pillars of Ashoka" that the monarch was apparently fond of erecting in the middle of his foundations.

The Hauz-Khas funerary complex
At the time of the Moroccan traveler Ibn Battuta's sojourn in Delhi, to which we have referred on several occasions, the pool created by 'Alā' al-Dīn Khaljī formed the center of an urban district dedicated to health and pleasure, so much so that it was dubbed "the city of joy." Fīrūz Shāh also chose to intervene on the disposition of the site, his reworking making it more serious, more reflective. With this in mind, at the southeast corner of the pool, he had a series of galleries punctuated by domes erected on the high earthworks that give onto the waters and lead to it down a flight of steps. The overall visual effect is one of serene harmony, although not without a hint of austerity. The center is occupied by the sultan's mausoleum, topped by the grandest of the cupolas, towards which the two wings converge, forming a right angle. The galleries are oriented north-south and east-west, each communicating with the mausoleum. In spite of the lack of epigraphic material to corroborate this finding, they have been identified as madrassas. Each gallery opens over two levels stretching across the front opening onto the pool, which is regularly dotted with balconies (*jharoka*) embellished with awnings or projecting eaves (*chajjas*). The imprint of indigenous palace architecture is perceptible in the design of a structure built up from units of columnated porticoes (*tibari*), bestowing a somewhat ethereal appearance. The presence of the mihrab directed towards Mecca expresses on the other hand an unambiguous commitment to dedicate the space to study and prayer.

The mausoleum, for its part, presents a square plan, on whose base a transitional octagon leads to a dome on squinches. The mural surfaces are for the most coated in mortar, masking building work of no more than average quality. Inside the monument, plant and geometric motifs painted on stucco in a style reminiscent of manuscript illumination decorate the squinches at the corners as well as the internal cupola, around the base of which runs an epigraphic band in Arabic.

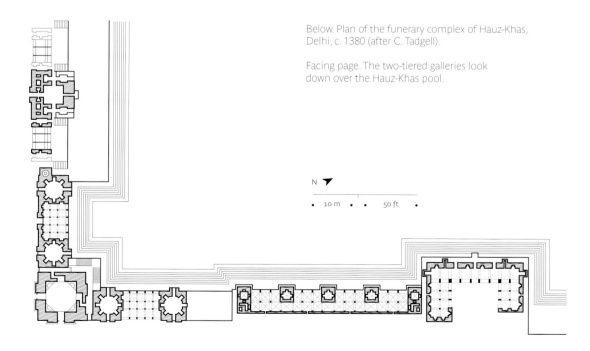

Below. Plan of the funerary complex of Hauz-Khas, Delhi, c. 1380 (after C. Tadgell).

Facing page. The two-tiered galleries look down over the Hauz-Khas pool.

Mosques and mausoleum of Khān-e Jahān Tilangānī
During the reign of Fīrūz Shāh, two noteworthy monuments that require more detailed examination were erected.

The Khirkī Masjid, or "mosque with windows," was probably built at the instigation of the grand vizier, Khān-e Jahān Tilangānī. It features a curious plan based on an elevated square measuring 184 feet (56 meters) down the sides; each corner is emphasized by a tower in the shape of a truncated cone, endowing the unit with a feeling of sturdiness. A projecting gate opens in the center of three of the façades, the main entrance being placed to the east. These impressive entries are flanked by solid "pseudo-minarets" that widen at the base. At the heart of the monument, the base is occupied by cells to which correspond on the floor above windows sealed off by *claustrae* from which the mosque takes its name. The prayer precinct is divided into twenty-five units, all of them square; the whole surface is covered with a roof comprising nine small domes per unit, except for four spaces forming "courtyards," which aerate and impart rhythm to the interior volumes.

Khān-e Jahān Kalān is also responsible for the Masjid of Nizamuddin, built in 1370–71 on a plan rather similar to that of the Khirkī Masjid. Virtually square, the mosque also features four "courtyards," although the prayer hall lies off-center and the plan is asymmetric. Not far off stands the mausoleum of the grand vizier, today in a lamentable state of conservation and squatted by several impoverished families. The tomb of Khān-e Jahān Tilangānī was, however, arguably the first mausoleum of octagonal plan to be built in Delhi, and for this reason it constitutes a landmark in the history of local architecture. The monument is an octagon with massive walls alleviated around the periphery by an ambulatory supported on pillars that forms an anteroom for the eight entrances topped by as many small domes, while the funerary hall is for its part capped with a large cupola.

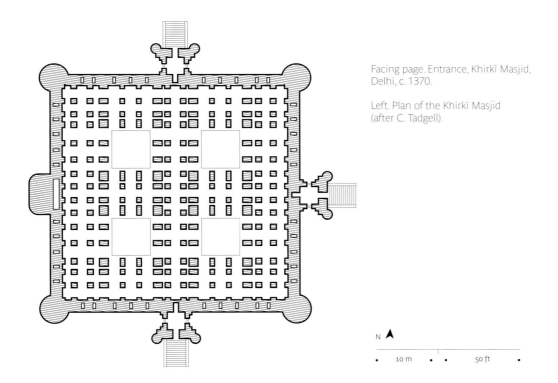

Facing page. Entrance, Khirkī Masjid, Delhi, c. 1370.

Left. Plan of the Khirkī Masjid (after C. Tadgell).

The establishment of Fīrūzābād on the banks of the Yamuna thus constituted a turning point in the history of the city. The integration of the river into the life of the city improved irrigation, facilitated trade, and reduced transport costs.

The economic links forged between the capital and local countryside that supplied it with foodstuffs of all kinds proved instrumental in a boom unprecedented since the foundation of urban Delhi. The increasing wealth of the sultanate, however, assumed proportions that aroused the envy of invaders who were soon encamped at the borders of the state. When Fīrūz Shāh died in 1388, a tussle over the succession broke out that weakened the power of the throne. Timur made the most of the disorder, invading the north of India and marching on Delhi. There he faced the army of Mahmūd Shāh, the rival of Nusrat Shāh in the struggle for power, defeating him decisively. While the sultan fled to seek refuge in Dhār with one of his faithful subjects, the governor of Mālwa, Dilāwar Khān Ghauri,[29] the capital was duly sacked:

> On that day, Thursday, and all the night of Friday, nearly 15,000 Turks were engaged in slaying, plundering, and destroying. When morning broke on the Friday, all the army, no longer under control, went off to the city and thought of nothing but killing, plundering, and making prisoners. All that day the sack was general. The following day, Saturday the 17th, all passed in the same fashion and the spoil was so great that each man secured from fifty to a hundred prisoners, men, women and children. There was no man who took less than twenty. The other booty was immense in rubies, diamonds, garnets, pearls, and other gems; jewels of gold and silver; *ashrafis*, *tankas* of gold and silver of the celebrated 'Alai coinage; vessels of gold and silver; and brocades and silks of great value. Gold and silver ornaments of the Hindu women were obtained in such quantities as to exceed all account. Excepting the quarter of the *saiyids*, the *'ulama*, and the other Moslems, the whole city was sacked.[30]

Mahmūd Shāh regained the throne of Delhi from 1399 to 1413, but he now governed a state whose territory hardly exceeded the area immediately around the city. In 1414, the governor of Multān, Khizr Khān, grabbed power and founded the Sayyid dynasty (1414–51), but for two centuries Delhi lost its position as a great Indian metropolis. Not only did the massacres and destruction attendant upon the sack of Delhi by Timur deal a fatal blow to the city, the defeat also halted the extension of its political power dead in its tracks. One of the most flagrant manifestations of its waning influence was the deportation of many of its artists and craftsmen to Samarkand. Meanwhile those who did stay behind, finding themselves deprived of patrons, emigrated to the new courts springing up in the sultanate's former provinces.

The situation on the eve of Timur's invasion
Up until 1398, however, the sultanate of Delhi had been enjoying a period of sporadic but rapid economic growth that culminated under Fīrūz Shāh and which was attended by the strengthening of its political might. News of the prosperity thus spawned traveled far and wide. The flames of the constant threat of invasion were fanned in turn by the skirmishes that kept on breaking out along the borders of the sultan's territories. In parallel to the sovereigns' assertion of authority, their architectural achievements left a visible imprint on their epoch; over the long term, the emergence of an architectural style can be observed which, although still devoid of unity or system, nonetheless exudes originality. Technically speaking, these ambitions were materialized in stone,

forming, as we have outlined, a clear distinction with the brick structures promoted by invaders from the Iranian world. The formal repertory is for its part a fusion of typically Islamic elements with borrowings from indigenous aesthetics. The Persian arch and the dome on squinches, hitherto unknown in the region, thus affirm the Muslim dispensation of the new power, but builders also found room in the edifices they endowed with such personality and meaning for stone lintels, for *chajjas* and *chhatris*—all forms inherited from the pre-Islamic traditions of the subcontinent. In consequence, after an initial period that had essentially been content to juxtapose elements from disparate identities, during the sultanate era, as reign followed reign, these stylistic combinations became increasingly refined. This era was thus the prelude to the emergence of a cultural personality that, paradoxically, the fatal blows struck by foreign invaders perhaps made possible to elevate to the sublime as the capital rose from its ashes following the sack of Timur.

The Sultanate of Delhi from the Sayyid Dynasty to the Mughals (1414–1555)

For the sultanate of Delhi the period between the ascension of the Sayyid dynasty and the seizure of power by the Mughal Akbar was one of turbulence and disorder. The consequence of this lack of overall state control was a discontinuous urban fabric that could no longer plan for settlements around its core structures or ensure stability of development. On the architectural plane, the lion's share of the remains that have survived come from the funerary monuments scattered about the capital. Their function is of course itself an unconscious illustration of the transient nature of the ascendency various rulers gained at the head of an empire that now lay in tatters.

After the sack of Delhi by Timur, Mahmūd Shāh II, the last of the Tughluqs to occupy the throne (1399–1413), strove to get a firm grip on the affairs of state, but soon encountered the resistance of Khizr Khān, once, by the will of Timur, governor of Multān, and shortly to be the founder of the Sayyid dynasty, a line that claimed descent from the Prophet.

Though Timur had since withdrawn his forces, the Sayyid Khizr Khān, the scion of a venerable Arab family who had settled in Multān, continued to pay him tribute. Although enjoying plenary powers after 1414, he even swore allegiance to Timur's successor, Shāh Rokh, who reigned over Samarkand and Herat. This refusal to adopt the title of sultan or to mint currency in his own name is better seen, not as servile vassalage, but as an effort to keep the fear of the terrifying invader alive and thus bathe in the reflection of its awesome power.

In 1421, Khizr Khān was succeeded by Mubārak Shāh II, who did assume the royal title with the approval of the military aristocracy, but over a territory pared down to the minimum and whose forces were concentrated on the garrisons of Lahore and Multān where they were faced by unremitting assault from the neighboring sultans of Jaunpur, Gujarāt, and Mālwa. Mubārak Shāh was assassinated in 1435 and replaced by Muhammad Shāh, who exercised power from 1435 to 1446. Bereft of energy and vision, Muhammad Shāh was a clumsy and unscrupulous ruler. In 1440, he in turn was confronted by Sultan Mahmūd Khaljī of Mālwa. Imprudently appealing for assistance from his powerful feudal lord Bahlūl Lodī, it was the latter's power base within the state that grew with each succeeding victory, earning Lodī new fiefdoms at every turn. In 1446 Ālam Shāh took over at the head of the kingdom, but his total ineptitude soon became glaringly obvious; by 1451 the balance of power between involved forces had led inevitably to his abdication in favor of Bahlūl Lodī. Bahlūl Khān Lodī descended from an Afghan tribe long established in Punjab, where he initially rose to be governor of Sirhind, and then of Lahore. He then ascended to the throne of Delhi where he remained from 1451 to 1489, a period during which he sought to give fresh luster to the tarnished reputation of the sultanate. His actions were crowned with success and, reversing a decline that had seemed inexorable, he eventually managed to seize the kingdom of the Sharqī sultans of Jaunpur.

His son Sikandar attained power in 1489. Until 1517, he, too, continued to harass the nearby Rājput principalities from Āgra and retake the territory the sultanate had lost. It was that city, however, which he chose as his capital, because it was a base better adapted for military forays. However, by the time Ibrāhīm II became ruler—for a period that lasted to 1526—a new phase of waning power had begun, and once again the integrity of the kingdom came into question. Enemies of the sovereign at the very heart of the court thus called on the Mughal Bābur, a distant descendant of Timur then reigning in Kabul, who overthrew the last of the Lodī at the battle of Pānīpat in 1526.

Yet it was not during Bābur's brief hold on power from 1526 to 1530 that the hallmark of the Mughals was to be stamped onto India; even his son Humāyūn held power only from 1530 to 1540, before being dethroned by an Afghan tribal chief, Shēr Shāh Sūri, who then occupied the throne from 1540 to 1545. Unlike Humāyūn, whose reign was distinguished by no major political or architectural achievements, the feats of the usurper who succeeded him were as remarkable in the administrative as in the military field. Totally overhauling the government, he also breathed new life into the art of architecture, a domain his predecessors had left to founder over the decades. His talents as a statesman and his powerful personality were firm foundations on which to build a lineage, but his descendants were not of the same stuff, and they failed to prevent the kingdom being retaken in 1555 by Humāyūn with support from the armies of Persia, where he had taken refuge during his exile. A year later though, Humāyūn died in an accident and bequeathed the throne to his son, Akbar, through whom the authority of the Mughals over the subcontinent was to grow more entrenched, giving rise to one of most dazzling civilizations in the history of the entire region. It was, moreover, under Akbar's aegis that the Mughal style acquired its true personality, particularly in the realm of architecture.

The Sayyid (1414–51) and the Lodī (1451–1526) dynasties
The architectural heritage of the Sayyid dynasty in Delhi

Mahmūd II, the last Tughluq, died without heir in 1413. Although his courtiers recognized the legitimacy of Daulat Khān Lodī to the succession, their protégé was promptly thrown into prison by Khizr Khān, who thus usurped the throne of Delhi. The dynasty he founded was backed by the Timurids from Central Asia, with whom he forged an alliance, and was to number four monarchs. In between the exuberantly creative episodes of the previous and subsequent eras, these sovereigns presided over a period of relative artistic inactivity: during this colorless and melancholic parenthesis, the urban fabric was left fallow and the architectural prestige of the capital was enriched with no remarkable palatial or religious buildings. The construction of a number of mausoleums can, however, be indubitably ascribed to this lineage, some of which—in particular those of Mubārak Shāh and Muhammad

Mausoleum of Muhammad Shāh Sayyid, Delhi, 1446.

Shāh—are relatively significant monuments. They subscribe to the tradition of the earlier, octagonal-type mausoleum, taking as their model the Tughluq mausoleum of Khān-e Jahān Tilangānī that some refer to as a "tomb with baldachin."

The Sayyid era also bequeathed a series of mausoleums planned around squares, whose principles as regards elevation are quite different from those of their octagonal cousins. All four façades are adorned with blind niches over two or three levels suggestive of true floors, and open broadly through archways with doors with a horizontal lintel placed on consoles. The corners of such buildings are flanked by pinnacles (*guldasta*), silent guards of the dome topping the funerary hall. The denizens of these tombs cannot always be identified; certain authors have proposed that the octagonal tombs were destined for sovereigns, while those organized around a square plan served for the nobles of the court, but there is no conclusive evidence for this assumption.

Kotla Mubārakpur (1435)

The funerary complex whose centerpiece is the octagonal mausoleum of Mubārak II (r. 1421–35) initially occupied a vast compound opening to the exterior through monumental gates—today only the one to the south remains, sheltering a mosque. It bears the name of Kotla Mubārakpur and the site is practically confined to the mausoleum itself, now strangled in the heap of modern constructions around it, an outcome of the unthinking urbanization of the district over recent decades. The lower reaches of the edifice are ringed by a gallery pierced by three openings per side. In each corner, the octagon is shored up by battered buttresses. Three doors, the largest of which lies to the south, lead to the funerary hall, while the western side is continuous so as to allow room for a mihrab. The dome surmounting this room features a low, broad cupola standing proud on a sixteen-sided drum, crowned with a lantern allowing in the daylight—a true innovation in the architectural landscape of Islamic India. For its part the drum bristles with pinnacles emphasizing each of its sixteen corners.

On the roof, toward the center of each side, the outline of *chhatris* stand like muffled stone bells. Although the space of the funerary hall is far from claustrophobic, there persists a sense of ponderousness and constriction caused by its lack of verticality in comparison with its footings. The edifice, would, however prove to be a model for the monarch's successors—its influence could still be perceived, with minor adaptations, at the time of Akbar, in particular in the mausoleum of Adham Khān, built in about 1562.

The mausoleum of Muhammad Shāh (1446)
This monument, intended for the memory of the Sayyid sovereign Muhammad Shāh (r. 1435–46), now lies buried in the midst of the Lodī Gardens. Its general appearance is in keeping with that of the successors of Mubārak Shāh, but its lines and proportions exude genuine harmony. It testifies to the more refined implementation of the stylistic principles developed: the mausoleum stands on an impressive earthwork delimited by a square enclosure; the octagon of the funerary hall is ringed by a gallery of similar form, each side of which sweeps into three archways. Such suppleness contrasts with the solidity of the inclined buttresses thickening the corners. A *chajja* (or awning) borne on consoles scampers round the entire building, delicately underlining the transition to the upper reaches of the edifice reached by a low parapet that serves as a barrier at the edge of the roof terrace. *Chhatris* can also be seen standing at the center of each side of the octagon. All sixteen corners of the drum supporting the dome brandish a pinnacle—as at the preceding mausoleum—but there is no lantern to bring daylight into the interior of the cupola at the top of which a large floret or lotus flower opens its mineral petals to the winds.

The Lodī dynasty
When Bahlūl Khān Lodī seized power in 1451, he laid the foundations for a period of some seventy-five years during which the sultanate of Delhi gradually recovered much of its former prestige. The first monuments of this new era were not particularly impressive in terms of scale. This is the case with the mausoleum of Bahlūl, whose reign came to an end in 1488, and who was inhumed beside the *dargāh* of Chirāgh-i Dihli. He reposes in a simple square funerary room opening on three sides through arcades, while the fourth, with its mihrab, serves as the *qibla* wall, the whole capped by a central dome to which four other cupolas of smaller size underscoring the corners give a sense of perspective. The extrados of the arcade is circumscribed by a series of quotations from the Koran, while stucco medallions adorn the spandrels. The whole is suffused with a sense of sobriety in marked contrast with the creative freedom that the founder's successors—Sikandar Lodī in particular—display in the buildings they were to finance in both Delhi and Āgra. This architecture immediately precedes the arrival of the Mughals and prefigures many of its stylistic features.

The baradari *of Sikandra*
It is to Sikandar Lodī that we owe the 1495 construction of a pleasure pavilion on the outskirts of Āgra, in a suburb that then took his name. The term *baradari*, which means "twelve doors," designates an open building, laid out with corridors and cells, creating an aesthetically relaxing and charmingly playful ambiance, although the bond with palace life was not quite broken. The Sikandra example conforms, however, to a strict plan which became a model for the genre.

The building's red sandstone walls take their place within a square plan of approximately 118 feet (36 meters) down the side, the same configuration appearing on the façade: nine arcades, including two wider than their neighbors, lay delicate stress on the openings in the volumes of varied depth that define the recesses and passages of the monument. The construction, moreover completely vaulted, is calculated according to a principle of radial symmetry allied to an east-west axis that penetrates the construction, and which is visually reinforced by two entryways emphasized by preceding flights of stairs. The puzzling if rigorous plan reinforces the obvious intention to avoid hierarchizing the various interior sectors of the layout. In what is a lighthearted gesture of defiance, the roof terrace leading to the staircases fires off a salvo of towering *chhatris* above the main doors and the corners of the pavilion. In 1613, under the Mughals, and while the mausoleum of Akbar virtually opposite the *baradari* was being completed, the function of the building was changed to house the tomb intended for Maryam Zamāni, wife of Akbar and mother of

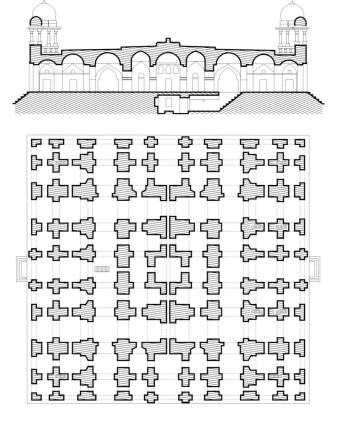

Side view and plan of the *baradari*, Sikandra, 1495, reworked in 1613 (after J. Hoag).

Jahāngīr, although the new function did nothing to modify its structure. This type of architectural organization, which aims to arrange the space without precedence, appeared in earlier monuments: for example, in the two levels of the Lāt Minār at the Kotla Fīrūz Shāh. Similarly, the rigorous symmetry presented by the *baradari* also prevails in certain Rājput palaces, as in Gwalior or, later, during the Mughal era, in those at Orchha or Datia in particular. At that time, a taste for pleasure pavilions inspired the construction of buildings in Fatehpur Sīkri, such as the Pānch Mahal, instigated by Akbar.

These constructions develop an aesthetic of repose and should be compared to the countless gardens Sikandar Lodī had planted around Āgra, testifying to the progressive adoption of a philosophy of easy living by the Muslim elites of the subcontinent.[31]

The Mān Mandir of Gwalior
This name designates the palace of the fort in Gwalior, built at the time of Sikandar Lodī but for Maharaja Mān Singh, a Hindu sovereign who reigned between 1486 and 1516. Although not essentially an Islamic construction, the monument is a prime example of how artistic contacts and crosscurrents could transcend the religious and political spheres, whatever their particular obedience. The architectural ideas, as much in the plan as in formal terms, were to provide inspiration for the originators of several

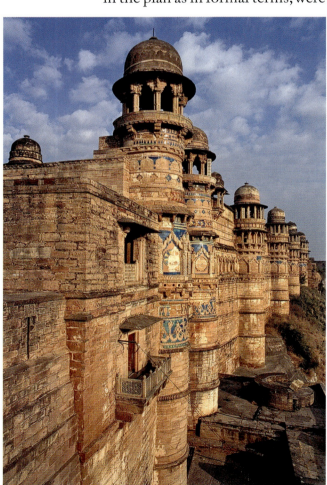

Mughal constructions, such as the Jahāngīrī Mahal of the Red Fort in Āgra. The builders of the Mān Mandir, moreover, made considerable use of ceramic decoration in an ornamental glazed inlay of turquoise, yellow, and green that embellishes the mineral severity of the façade. Most striking is the astonishing frieze of ducks passant in the middle—luminous yellow on a turquoise ground. Beneath the crenels, a yellow and blue mosaic with tigers and banana trees embedded in the sandstone alternates with stone bas-reliefs depicting elephants. Finally, in between the two registers, a band of blind niches composes a harmonious ensemble that relies on the clash between the turquoise rock and the ceramics. Color also explodes in the central courtyard of the palace, albeit to a lesser degree; the compositions there are a headlong juxtaposition of geometrical patterns and stone reliefs above the openings they serve to underscore.

Left and facing page. Mān Mandir, Gwalior, India, late fifteenth century; left: façade over the ramparts; facing page: one of the interior courtyards.

Few subsequent Mughal palaces boast such an integration of color into their ornamentation, with the exception of the fort of Lahore to which we shall return in detail later. Perhaps the origin of such a profusion of ceramics in the Mān Mandir stems from the impact of the contemporary decoration on monuments in the sultanate of Mālwa located slightly more to the southwest, and whence Muslim craftsmen might have been enticed by the rajah to his building site. In any event, this taste for touches of bright color resurfaces, be it more discreetly, at the Rājput palace of Orchha, built in about 1600, in that of Datia, built in 1620 and the fort at Ranthambor, that fell into Mughal hands after the siege of Akbar in 1569, only to be recaptured by the Rājputs on the death of Aurangzeb.

The mausoleum of Sikandar Lodī and other monuments in the Lodī Gardens
Sikandar Lodī (r. 1489–1517) is buried in a mausoleum located within a vast square compound. A monumental gate marks the entrance on a terrace introduced by a pair of corner *chhatris* whose base—also square—is set upon four stone pillars rising to a delicate roof emblazoned by monochrome enameled ceramic tiles. Even today, the rich cobalt blues and tactile chromium greens still glow in the company of some dazzling yellow and vibrant turquoise neighbors. The whole enclosure teems with "guardian" corner towers, while around the external circumference small-sized cells have been hollowed out to offer accommodation to travelers who find themselves without a roof. The west side of the internal flank of the perimeter features a sober if rudimentary mosque wall; only then does the octagonal mausoleum surge into view, of a plan similar to that of Sayyid, with its lines of three arcades to each side, its inclined buttresses, its *chajja* and its parapet with merlons. The *chhatris* that would have once done the rounds on the roof terrace have since disappeared. The interior decorations afford considerable scope to the exuberance of glazed ceramic ornamentation. On entering the building, each side of the octagon is clad in panels forming blind arcades whose frames and spandrels are awash with ceramics of every hue and encrusted with stucco rosettes, while echoes of this surging color is answered at level of the dome drum. Volumes, materials, and colors are fused into a chromatic variety reminiscent of the view through a kaleidoscope.

From the same era—or virtually the same era if judging by the style—the Shish Gumbad, or "dome of glass," stands encamped on its square plan some 820 feet (250 meters) from the preceding monument. The name derives from the frieze of glazed ceramic tiles alternating monochrome turquoise and cobalt-colored surfaces with which it is decorated; these are combined with unexpected stretches of painted interlace patterns enriched by turquoise and cobalt epigraphic decorations on a white ground. The craftsmanship of these ceramics remains untutored, but such a repertoire is extremely exceptional in the India of the sultanates, though "blue-and-white" tiles are to be found in the mausoleum of Jamāli-Kamāli. The intended recipient of this mausoleum remains unknown to this day, but the building has structural links with another building, the Kāle Khān-ka-Gumbad, dating to 1481—during the reign of Bahlūl Lodī—located in the South Extension district.

Facing page top. Overall view of the Bara Gumbaz mausoleum and mosque, 1494.
Bottom. Shish Gumbad, Lodī Gardens, Delhi, fifteenth century.

Another mausoleum of square plan, named the Bara Gumbad, or "Great Dome," rises in the Lodī Gardens some fifty meters from the Shish Gumbad, and contiguous to a mosque dating to 1494 in the reign of Sikandar Lodī. The terrace of this tomb features a prospect of five archways of unequal breadth that dramatize the prayer space; slightly narrow, the two farthest out are followed along a still low curve by two intermediate examples gathered in like shoulder pieces and ornamented with a double extrados. The central arch, with its dressing of segments of red sandstone and triple extrados, is a towering flamboyant affair, projecting mildly and penetrating into the *chajja*. The three porches at the center similarly extend vertically into the cupolas at their summits. The mosque is in addition liberally laden with stucco ornaments, in particular epigraphic bands and arcade motifs (at the level of the mihrab and corner squinches, for example). Counterbalancing the mosque, another hall opens onto the terrace through arcades. On both sides of the mausoleum, the cells form a *mehmānkhāna*, or "guest house," acting as a bridge between the mosque and the other building. The mausoleum itself boasts a terrace in the center of which stood a dais probably intended to receive the body of the deceased, whose identity—like that of person who commissioned it—remains unknown. The access to the terrace is gained by way of a U-shaped staircase of remarkably balanced proportions.

Below and facing page. View of the façade of the prayer hall and details of decoration in the mosque of the Bara Gumbaz, Delhi, 1494.

The Moth-ki-Masjid (c. 1505)

The merit for building this construction belongs to Miyān Bhuwa, who was, before his disgrace, minister for Sikandar Lodī and then for his successor, Ibrāhīm.

Located in the South Extension, this monument, whose name means "mosque of the chickpea," stands on a platform excavated into cells reached down a flight of steps from which the majestic portal offering access to the courtyard appears. Five richly ornamented stucco arcades open up to reveal the depth of the prayer hall. The decoration of the entire construction is generated from a two-color principle that opposes the gray quartzite of the basic masonry to the dark-hued blaze of the red sandstone, embellishing various zones, such as the central arch in the prayer hall, above which enfold the plump curves of three cupolas. Finally, to each side of the hall, a corner tower with two levels of arcades endows the monument with the surprising aspect of a composite if refined fortification. In the words of J. Marshall, the mosque displays "a freedom of imagination, a bold diversity of design, an appreciation of contrasting light and shade, and a sense of harmony in line and color , which combine to make it one of the most spirited and picturesque buildings of its kind in the whole range of Islamic art [in all India]."[32]

Entrance to the prayer hall, Moth-ki-Masjid, Delhi, c. 1505.

Because of its subtly decorated mihrab, its pendentives with stalactites (*muqarnas*), and its (few remaining) enamel tiles, this monument may be considered as the seed from which some of the earliest Mughal mosques sprung, such as the Jamāli-Kamāli and the mosque in the Old Fort (the Purana Qila), built under Shēr Shāh in 1541.

The Jahāz Mahal and the Rājon-ki-Baoli

On the edges of Iltutmish's pool and not far from the Qutb Minār in Mehrauli, stands a somewhat amusing monument. Embedded within the rectangular proportions of the Jahāz Mahal, or "boat-palace"— it appears to float on the waters next to it, or at least to emerge from the surrounding moat—lies an inner courtyard decidedly broader than it is deep. Placed between an entrance pavilion and the western wall, it is preceded by a series of archways that perhaps delimit a prayer hall, since a mihrab stands framed in its center and buttresses cinch the monument's four main quoins in a bold manner that hints at "pseudo-minarets." Evidence for a religious function for the edifice recedes, however, when one reaches upper sections that display the extravert personality of an imposing *chhatri* overflowing onto a terrace dominating an arched access to the east side, as if to highlight the focus of radial projections that also terminate in somewhat more modest *chhatris* above each corner of the building (although one of them has been destroyed), as well as in the center of the wall facing the entrance. All are decorated, or rather drenched in the greenish blue of turquoise tiles evocative of an aquatic fairyland suspended in time and space. In the same village of Mehrauli, nearly 1,312 feet (400 meters) from the *dargāh* of Qutb Sāhib, the Rājon-ki-Baoli, or "*baoli* of the stonemasons," is a splendid deep stepped tank divided into four levels. The entire perimeter of the first is ringed by an arcade gallery.

Also in the immediate vicinity, a small oratory mosque, together with a *chhatri*, shimmers on a terrace. The *chhatri* is decorated in turquoise tiling and, on a slab of red sandstone bears a carved inscription dating from AH 912 (1506 CE), indicating that it was erected during the reign of Sikandar Lodī.

The rule of the first Mughals

Contrary to a commonly held opinion, the victory of Pānīpat in 1526 did not spark a geopolitical and artistic disaster for the subcontinent. Bābur's arrival in the Indian arena, although it did mean that the first Mughal piece was being placed in the jigsaw of cultures and powers in the region, actually amounted to something of a boon. His tastes and family traditions inclined this fifth-generation descendant of Timur towards his ancestral lands and their capital, Samarkand. Born in Fergana in 1483, Bābur succeeded his father at the head of the small Central Asian principality at the age of eleven, but was forced, in spite of tenacious resistance, to yield before the Uzbek tidal wave and take refuge in Kabul in 1504, where a junior offshoot of the Timurid dynasty still held sway. If he only acquiesced with reserve when a faction among Ibrāhīm Lodī's courtiers urged him to join their cause. He defeated the Lodī before going on, in 1527, to crush a confederation of Rājput princes in Kānwā on the outskirts of Āgra. These victories laid before him a territory and an administration that he neither knew nor could govern—a state of affairs that limited any influence he might exert, all the more so since he died four years after his conquest, leaving to his son Humāyūn a throne with an uncertain future.

The gardens of Bābur (1526–30)

Bābur's four-year reign was too brief for his successes as a military conqueror to be given concrete form as buildings, all the more since the sovereign wielding power over Āgra, the then Indian capital of the kingdom, remained at heart more attached to Kabul where he was to be buried. The Babri Masjid of Ayodhya is one of the few monuments that can be attributed to his brief reign. Legend has it that this mosque was erected at the very spot where the god Rāma was born. This reputation explains why, at the conclusion of a prolonged and fanatical campaign, a group of Hindu extremists leveled it in 1992, erecting in its place the Ram Janam Bhumi, a temple commemorating the birth of the god. This event sparked terrible reprisals: in 2002 a train containing Hindu pilgrims returning from the temple was set alight resulting in dozens of deaths, an atrocity avenged in turn by thousands of Muslims being slain in the ensuing riots. The archaeological excavations instigated by the government in an effort to calm the waters and determine the true religious origin of the site have so far failed to produce convincing results.

While Bābur's architectural interventions proper were few and far between, the same cannot be said for the gardens he was instrumental in introducing into the subcontinent. The "memoirs" monarch's are singularly revealing of his ideas on the subject. Founded on the Timurid models with which he had become familiar in Central Asia, they were structured around principles of order and symmetry deploying "running waters" (i.e., channels), avenues, and parterres meeting at right angles.

Bābur inspecting works in his garden, the Bāgh-e Wafā, in what is today Afghanistan, in a painting illustrating a Persian translation of his memoirs, late fourteenth century. Victoria & Albert Museum, London.

This is what Bābur says of benefits ascribed to the gardens he planted in his newly conquered territory:

> One of the great defects of Hindustan being its lack of running-waters, it kept coming to my mind that waters should be made to flow by means of wheels erected wherever I might settle down, also that grounds should be laid out in an orderly and symmetrical way.... Then in that charmless and disorderly Hind, plots of garden were seen laid out with order and symmetry, with suitable borders and parterres in every corner, and in every border rose and narcissus in perfect arrangement.[33]

While Bābur outlines the rules to be respected for the successful design of a garden with relative clarity, the many details he mentions in his descriptions seldom allow the actual plan to be precisely identified. He seems to have preferred evoking the décor surrounding the garden, and even more readily the flowers and plants that embellish it. In Gwalior, for instance, he lingers over a variety of oleander:

Rahlm-dad has planted great numbers of flowers in his garden, many being beautiful red oleanders. In these places the oleander-flower is peach, those of Guallar [Gwalior] are a beautiful, deep red. I took some of them to Agra and had them planted in gardens there. On the south of the garden is a large lake where the waters of the rains gather; on the west of it is a lofty idol-house, side by side with which [Iltutmish] made a Friday mosque.... Rahlm-dad has made a wooden pavilion in his garden, in the Hindustani fashion ... somewhat low and shapeless.[34]

The gardens of Āgra
When Bābur initially conquered the city of Āgra in 1526 he must have invested the original Red Fort, which, as indicated by the vestiges from the Lodī epoch still visible, already represented the focus of power. He had further works carried out (he mentions the intervention of stonemasons on several occasions), and also kept busy planning and planting gardens on the banks of the Yamuna. The first problem he confronted—selecting a suitable terrain—stemmed from the region's lack of relief. The monarch would surely have preferred soft undulations or foothills leading down to the river, rich in springs whose waters he might have tamed into fountains, sprays, channels, and waterfalls, with tiered terraces that would have afforded prospects to all sides down to some nearby slope. In the end, however, he had to accept the dull reality of the riverbanks and set up his garden on what is probably the site of the current Rām Bāgh. Subsequent interventions by Jahāngīr unfortunately prevent us establishing meaningful correlations with the wealth of detail Bābur provides about the works he commissioned, as in the following extract:

> One of the great defects of Hindustan being its lack of water ... we crossed the Jun-water to look at garden-grounds a few days after entering Agra. Those grounds were so bad and unattractive that we traversed them with a hundred disgusts and repulsions. So ugly and displeasing were they that the idea of making a Char-bagh [*chahār-bāgh*] in them passed from my mind, but needs must! As there was no other land near Āgra, that same ground was taken in hand a few days later. The beginning was made with the large well from which water comes for the Hot-bath, and also with the piece of ground where the tamarind-trees and the octagonal tank now are. After that came the large tank with its enclosure; after that the tank and *talar* [portico] in front of the outer residence; after that the private-house with its garden; and after that the Hot-bath.[35]

The garden of Dholpur
Unearthed by Elizabeth Moynihan in 1978, the chief interest of this garden derives from the fact that it constitutes one of the few commissions of Bābur that has come down to us without significant alternation.[36] Prior to the arrival of the conqueror, the site comprised the dam erected by Sikandar Lodī we evoked above, as well as a garden, which Bābur may well have regarded as too rudimentary for his taste. Ongoing excavations and surveys undertaken on the spot have revealed a well, several polylobate pools, a network of runnels, a mosque, and a hammam; an organic plan, however, or even its bare bones have proved impossible to convincingly identify or reconstitute. In consequence, there can be no decisive affirmation that it was a

genuine *chahār-bāgh* (quadripartite garden) or even that it conformed to any kind of design based on axial symmetry. Bābur himself supervised the alterations made and he dealt with their progress in his memoirs, as in this note from 1528:

> As it was not found high enough for a house, Ustad Shah Muhammad the stone-cutter was ordered to level it and cut out an octagonal, roofed tank. North of this tank the ground is thick with trees, mangoes, jaman (*Eugenia jambolana*), all sorts of trees; amongst them I had ordered a well made ... its water goes to the aforenamed tank. To the north of this tank Sikandar [Lodī]'s dam is flung across [the valley]; on it houses have been built, and above it the waters of the Rains gather into a great lake. On the east of this lake is a garden; I ordered a seat and four-pillared platform (*talar*) to be cut out in the solid rock on that same side, and a mosque built on the western one.[37]

Initially Bābur was interred in a garden on the banks of the Yamuna, perhaps at the Bāgh-e Eram (a name deformed into Rām Bāgh). Several years later, his remains were, in accordance with his wishes, transferred to Kabul and inhumed in a garden that still bears his name. There he reposes on the terrace of a tiered garden in a tomb far more modest than those of his descendants. For a long time it was comprised of a simple slab and a stele before Shāh Jahān ordained the tribute of a marble balustrade and a mosque to be added to his ancestor's burial place.

The tomb of Bābur situated in the garden of the same name in Kabul, Afghanistan; extensively restored, the openwork marble screen is a further embellishment from the time of Shāh Jahān.

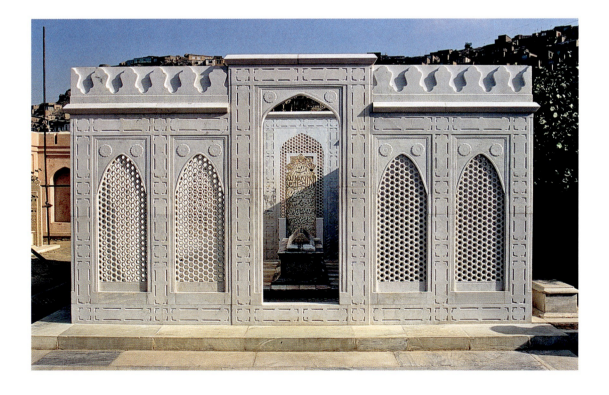

The first reign of Humāyūn

Chroniclers report that with his last words Bābur advised his son Humāyūn to refrain from hostile action towards his brothers. If the new sovereign did his best to respect his father's dying will, this particular counsel proved fatal, in the sense that in hesitating to take the measures necessary to counter the divisive intrigues of his family undermined the foundations of his power, eventually leading to his enforced flight in 1540 from a coup engineered by Shēr Shāh Sūri. Moreover, the number of monuments subsisting from the ten years of Humāyūn's first reign as sultan is extremely limited. The histories record that in 1533 he had founded a new city named Dinpanāh (the "refuge of religion") on the site of Delhi, but this citadel is presumed to have been leveled by Shēr Shāh after his coup d'état and replaced by the current Purana Qila ("Old Fort"). The ostentation of Humāyūn's court had his many toadies dipping their pens in purple ink, but their accounts give little indication that he shared his father's fervor for gardening or his son Akbar's architectural enthusiasm.[38]

Nevertheless, one contemporary, the historian Khwāndamīr, did praise the inventiveness and creativity of the sultan, which led to some intriguing choices and ingenious constructions. Humāyūn is thus meant to have ordered the building of boats to bear him along the inland waterway from Delhi to Āgra, which he had decorated with a colorful bazaar of well-stocked booths simply to add variety to the lengthy journey. Humāyūn is also thought to have come up with the idea for a collapsible palace, whose fantastic appearance is thus described:

> Each time it was desired, it could be transported in separate parts to any terrain. Ladders leading to the upper floor were provided so they might be opened or closed at will.[39]

Beyond the demolished citadel and his weird imaginings, some buildings do survive, testifying to our monarch's first reign.

The mosque and mausoleum of Jamāli-Kamāli
Sheikh Fazl-Allāh (also known by the name of Jalāl Khān) was a poet and mystic who, before passing away in 1535, exerted considerable sway under the successive authorities of Sikandar Lodī and the first Mughals. By 1528, he was building the mosque and mausoleum that bear his penname today: the Jamāli (to which is added the "doublet" Kamāli).

On the lofty mosque's façade featuring five grand arches, local gray quartzite stonework sets off the faintly glowing embers of the red sandstone and the snowy white marble. In the center, an avant-corps flanked by two truncated pseudo-minarets flirts with the boldness of an *iwan*, duetting with the main dome that corresponds to it in front of the mihrab. The side archways are for their part trimmed with a triple extrados, whose profile is more refined than those at the Bara Gumbad Mosque. *Chajjas* (canopies, awnings) and a parapet probably embellished the no longer extant upper reaches, while the corners of the *qibla* wall are stiffened by octagonal turrets. The expanse of the prayer hall displays relative sparseness around a principal mihrab in red sandstone that subtly enhances the impression of refinement occasioned by the squinches in the quoins on the finely worked lateral domes.

In its final appearance, the monument provides a transition in which the Lodī style of the Moth-ki-Masjid recedes and the more definitive lines that structure the later mosque of the Old Fort come into firmer focus. Of square plan, the mausoleum seems to want to retreat into its exuberantly ornamented interior; the painted ceiling thus reminds one of an enlarged illumination from a prince's manuscript, unrolling trails of palmettes of a dominant red and blue tonality; the walls are adorned with motifs of blind arcades created by a tile mosaic of cobalt blue and yellow, above which run epigraphic cartouches in stucco over which run verses penned in Persian by the deceased. Under the pentice girdling the exterior, square tiles painted in blue and white serve as metopes. They are remarkable for their unusual if somewhat rough-and-ready facture, rather like an echo of those that glint on the facades of the Shish Gumbad in the Lodī Gardens.

Nila Gumbad and Sabz Burj
The mausoleums bearing these names stand near what today constitutes the funerary complex of Humāyūn. The Nila Gumbad ("blue dome") owes its name to its predominantly blue ceramic cladding. It was believed that it was erected in the early seventeenth century, in spite of topographic indications attesting to a construction prior to the mausoleum of Humāyūn. It is structured around a "Baghdad octagon" (that is, alternately four large and four small sides), sheltering a square funerary hall topped by a single dome. The decoration of the façades is confined almost exclusively to patterns in enameled tile mosaic, following the example of those decorating the *qibla* wall of the tomb of Ataga Khān (1566–67) in Nizamuddin, and that which later, and on a larger scale, adorns the mausoleum at Āgra known as Chini-ka-Rauza.

As for the Sabz Burj (literally, the "green tower"), it is a small mausoleum lying at the intersection of the avenues of Mathura and Lodī, whose plan once again is that of the Baghdad octagon. It features no inscriptions to clarify the circumstances surrounding its construction, but its uncluttered lines and its elevation free of *guldastas* (pinnacles), *chajjas*, and *chhatris* immediately suggest the Central Asian affiliation from which sprang the architectural idiom of the first decades of the Mughal period.

Above. The mausoleum of Sabz Burj, Delhi, second half of the sixteenth century. The cobalt blue of its dome is the result of a twentieth-century restoration.

Facing page. The mausoleum of Shēr Shāh Sūri, Sasarām, Bihār, India.

The Sūri parenthesis, before the return of the Mughals (1540–55)

It was from the far-flung base of Bihār—to which he had been appointed governor by Bābur—that Shēr Shāh Sūri ventured out to overthrow Humāyūn in 1540 and found a dynasty of his own. Above and beyond his reforms of the government and economic organization of the territory, it is surely the statesmanship and charisma of the founder of this line—one which spent little more than fifteen years at the helm of the sultanate—that explain how such major pieces of architecture saw the light of day within such a short time span. They focused primarily on Sasarām where the princes of the family were to be inhumed, and on Delhi, which once again was to recover something of its lost supremacy.

Mausoleums at Sasarām

When, for a brief period, Sasarām (in the present-day state of Bihār) found itself on the brink of becoming the capital of the Sūri line as they pursued their meteoric political rise, it was scarcely more than an overgrown village. For this purpose, three mausoleums were erected intended for the remains of the ruling family, each the brainchild of the architect Aliwal Khān.[40] Built in 1535 for Hasan Khān, Shēr Shāh's father, the most venerable rises on an octagonal plinth in the center of an enclosure entered through a monumental gateway. It differs little in general appearance from preexisting Lodī models—save for the expanse of the drum supporting a majestic

central dome featuring *chhatris* clustering round each of its eight corners. Another beneficiary of the inspiration from the tombs of the Lodī, but indicative of a more ambitious conception, is the mausoleum of Shēr Shāh, a monument immediately striking for its exceptional setting, floating like a flawless pearl on the waters of an artificial lake measuring 1,401 feet (427 meters) down the side. A further extraordinary characteristic is its unusual dimensions since it possesses an external diameter of 249 feet (76 meters) for a height of 148 feet (45 meters). A vast avant-corps in the form of a cube alleviated by a dome surges forth rather like a security entrance. This leads to a bridge giving access to the tomb, a lofty octagonal barrel whose walls rise in the center of a square terrace, its corners bristling with *chhatris*. Each side wall of the mausoleum is draped with a three-arch arcade that parades calmly around, while, like timeless sentries, the *chhatris* at the base of the arrises of the octagon echo those guarding the corners of the dome drum. As it rises above the water's edge, the building's upswept curves, punctuated by *chhatris* over several levels, impart a pyramidal thrust. Sixty-six feet (twenty meters) in diameter, the funerary room rises ninety feet (27.5 meters) to the ridge of its single-shell cupola. In general, the decoration on both sides is sober, although it is richer on either side of the mihrab along the *qibla* wall. Still dressed with the beautifully dense yet soft gray of the Chunar sandstone in which it is built, it was probably initially decked out with touches of color, either in the form of painted decorations or ceramic tiles, traces of which can still be made out at the level of the *kangura* ("battlements"). Finally, though, the mausoleum presents a curious and probably involuntary discrepancy between the fundamental square plan of the

Left. The mausoleum of Arawal Khān, Sasarām, Bihār, seventeenth century; entrance to the complex.

Facing page. Overall view and ambulatory, mausoleum of Hasan Khān, Sasarām, Bihār, 1535.

building and its subsequent elevation that has been "corrected" by a rotation of some eight degrees. If at the outset this must have resulted from a miscalculation when laying the underpinnings, it sets the monument as it is reflected in the scintillating waters of the lake quivering almost imperceptibly, thus accentuating the feeling that it is in fact little more than a slowly emerging mirage. Lastly, Sasarām can also pride itself on the mausoleum of Salim, son of Shēr Shāh, who died in 1552. Similarly ensconced on an island in the middle of a manmade lake, it aimed to exceed the gigantism of the final resting place of the incumbent's father, but remained unfinished.

The Old Fort of Delhi
The perimeter of the Old Fort (the Purana Qila) takes root on the supposed site of the legendary Indraprashta, as described in the epic of the *Mahābhārata*. Excavations undertaken by the Archaeological Survey of India have revealed vestiges dating from the Maurya period (c. 300 BCE) to the beginning of the Mughal era, today displayed in a small museum within the precinct of the fort. It was on this zone—so densely covered that it resembles a palimpsest—that the town of Dinpanāh, founded reportedly by Humāyūn, had begun to be built before being razed on the order of Shēr Shāh.

The great walls of the fort encompass an irregular space of vaguely oblong shape that snakes over a mile. The corners and west flank are studded with towers, offering a counterpoint to the three enormous gateways punctuating stretches of the walls of irregular length to the north, south, and west. To the east, this complex looks over the Yamuna whose untrustworthy flow protected it from the heart of the city, though over the centuries its course has wandered to within a dozen feet of the fort. Standing two stories tall, the gateways boast *chhatris* at their summits.

The north entrance, adorned with a motif of a man fighting wild beasts engraved in the marble, is named the Talāqi Darwāza ("Forbidden Gate"), but the reason for this is unclear.

The west gate—the only one in use nowadays—is dressed in severe red sandstone plaques, enriched with notes of black, yellow, and white rock, in particular in the form of hexagrams, while the balconies on the upper reaches and the cornices show traces of a sumptuous ceramic decoration of colored cut tilework, the most characteristic being the cheerful friezes of flowers. A handwritten inscription in ink mentions the name of Humāyūn, in all probability because it was contemporary with this monarch's return to India. As for the southern gate, it is dubbed Humāyūn-Darwāza, as it afforded a breach out to his mausoleum; it also bears, however, the marks of graffiti in the name of Shēr Shāh, dating to AH 950 (1543–44 CE). Finally, cells were excavated along the internal face of the outer wall, though only a small number of constructions testify to the original purpose of these outworks.

The mosque of the Old Fort
When he decided in 1541 to build this monument, Shēr Shāh Sūri probably did not imagine he was about to create a mold that would not only fix for all time features inspired by the immediately preceding mosques (the Bara Gumbad in the Lodī Gardens, the Moth-ki-Masjid, and the Jamāli-Kamāli Masjid), but more

Facing page and below. View of the façade and detail of the inlaid decoration in the mosque of the Purana Qila ("Old Fort"), Delhi, c. 1541.

importantly refine them and thus pave the way for the elegant balance and delicately shimmering forms of the Mughal style.

Typically for sultanate architecture, the prayer hall directly connects to the preceding terrace through a series of five arches. The whole building is clad in gray stone, though the façade features slabs of white marble and red sandstone accentuating the preeminence of a central opening that already exceeds its neighbors in dimensions and which is festooned in florets. The dynamic elevation of the main archway delimits a field containing a panel in the middle of which is embedded a second arcade topped by a minute *jharoka*. The whole area is entirely encrusted in a geometrical pattern that opposes in remorseless regularity the muted glow of sandstone to the smooth, luminous chill of marble, underlined by clean-cut fillets of black stone. Patently, the meticulous workmanship of this mineral inlay offers a foretaste of the celebrated Mughal decors of a somewhat later period.

The positioning of the mihrab in the inner space also benefits from special care: the polychrome mosaic cut-tile embellishment diffracts the vast dome drum into geometrical patterns and frames of blind arcades. The internal face of the cupola features a composition painted with motifs from illuminations, unfortunately in a sorry state today. The mihrab, in contrast, opts for the understated juxtaposition of white marble with black stonework. As at the Moth-ki-Masjid, there is no minaret to offer an impulsion to the heavens. The external face of the *qibla* wall swells slightly outwards and leans on quasi-cylindrical buttresses that splay out towards the base, just where the hollow space of the mihrab excavates the wall within. It is also flanked by galleried corner towers that aerate its mass, tempering the mystic intimacy of the place with a note of harmony.

Above. Mihrab in the prayer hall of the mosque of the Purana Qila, Delhi.

Facing page. Arcades in the prayer hall clad in sandstone, quartzite, and white marble, in the mosque of the Purana Qila, Delhi.

Shēr Mandal
To the south of the mosque of the "Old Fort" is a strange octagonal pavilion over two floors whence spouts a graceful *chhatri*. Enthroned between two Persian archways, the monument, called Shēr Mandal, is encased in plaques of red sandstone underscored with marble. The plan of the second level is cruciform. The lower reaches of the ceramic lining are decorated with painted stucco.

Based on the notion of the cultural subservience of Muslim India with regard to the Persian or Central Asian worlds, this monument has traditionally been seen as bearing the imprint of Safavid Iran. In fact, no Iranian pavilion truly resembles it; if influences did percolate to here, they probably provided pointers rather than fuelled imitations. Constructed under Shēr Shāh, the pavilion might perhaps have served as Humāyūn's library, and in any case it was here that the sovereign is supposed to have met his end after falling down a staircase.[41]

The Shēr Shāh Gate and the mosque of Khayr al-Manāzil
On the other side of the road separating them from the Old Fort, there remain vestiges of a huge gateway erected on Shēr Shāh's initiative and which once formed part of the enceinte running around the city that the sovereign had built at the foot of the citadel. It is erected essentially in red sandstone and is thus sometimes described as the Lāl Darwāza ("red gate"). Some authors are of the opinion that it belonged to the same protective ring as the gate known as the Kabuli or Khunin Darwāza standing near Kotla Fīrūz Shāh.

The Khayr al-Manāzil Mosque was erected in 1561 beside the gate of Shēr Shāh at the instigation of Māham Ānaga, one of the future sultan Akbar's nurses. The monument flares out into a five-arch arcade, the central one echoing the cupola whose dome curves gracefully round the space enclosing the mihrab, while its walls allow glimpses of a glazed ceramic dressing. Overall, the mosque is handled in a more

Facing page. Mosque in the funerary complex of 'Issa Khān, Delhi, 1547.

Above. The mausoleum in the funerary complex of 'Issa Khān, Delhi.

traditional fashion than in the sultanate style from the first half of the century and eschews the challenges in design and ornamentation that constitute the audacious reigns of the line of Shēr Shāh Sūri and the onset of Mughal splendor.

The funerary complex of 'Issa Khān

This architectural complex was built in 1547 for a general who had served in the army of Shēr Shāh Sūri and then of his son Islām Khān (r. 1545–54). The great entryway breaches the northern sector of a broad octagonal precinct, the center of which features a tranquil garden. In the center—in a haven created by a second, low-lying belt of a park—is the similarly octagonal mausoleum, a fusion of rotundity and verticality. Each side of the building brings light to the gallery encircling the funerary hall with supple lines of three arcades opening beneath a *chajja* running round the lower edge of the upper register. On the roof, the central dome sits atop a polygonal drum, the corners marked with pinnacles, orchestrating a roundelay of eight *chhatris*, one to a side, as if suspended in a timeless dance. Openwork stone screens close off the funerary hall allowing shafts of sunlight into its mysterious interior—except at the west end harboring the mihrab and the southern side, which contains the entrance door.

A mosque nestles against the enclosing wall, opening on the terrace through a trio of arches. To the right of the central archway rises a majestic dome framed by *chhatris* perched on the two side arches. The architectural forms and decorations of the complex are deployed in voluptuous homage to the Lodī style, which here indulges its languor for one last time.

Mausoleums of Adham Khān at Mehrauli and Muhammad Ghaus at Gwalior
The central interest of these two monuments lies in the fact that they are prime illustrations of the transitional style between the Lodī period and the trends that will govern the architectural revival instigated by Akbar and his successors over succeeding centuries. The son of Akbar's wet nurse Māham Ānaga and boasting the rank of army general, Adham Khān had provoked the anger of the sovereign, who had him thrown from the top of the ramparts of the fort at Āgra. On her son's downfall, the mother of the courtier from Akbar's innermost circle was wracked by grief and soon expired. In 1561 the sultan decided to build a mausoleum worthy of containing their remains.

The octagonal building nestles in the heart of an octagonal compound studded with corner towers. A gallery, receiving daylight on each side through three arcades, runs like an ambulatory around the funerary room, though the passage to the higher register is not marked by *chajjas*. The interior space of the hall, vast and singularly spare, creates a sober, self-contained volume whose coherence is not without a kind of rugged nobility. Though dating from after the return to power of the Mughal dynasty, the monument asserts its clear affiliation with mausoleums from the Lodī era, though dispensing with some of the liberties in ornament taken by the more daring buildings from which it takes its inspiration.

Muhammad Ghaus, who helped Bābur conquer Gwalior, bathes in a reputation for saintliness, explaining why the tribute of a mausoleum was bestowed upon him and erected in the aforementioned city in 1564. In its original formal lines, the building intertwines borrowings from the Lodī era with ornaments taken from the repertory of Gujarāt, as will be seen later. Each face of this square structure, bolstered at the corners with galleried towers topped by *chhatris*, is chiseled with expertly carved and delicately convoluted *jalis* (openwork stone *claustrae*), inserted into rectangular panels in the form of arcades or lunettes. Finally, a *chajja* stands on elegant consoles, running around the summit of the wall and marking the break between the different registers of the building. The square mass of the funerary hall rises up to the cupola and is framed with *chhatris* at the corners, conferring a rather pyramidal aspect.

Facing page. The mausoleum
of Adham Khān in Mehrauli, Delhi, 1561.

Above. The mausoleum of Muhammad Ghaus,
Gwalior, 1564.

Partial assessment on the eve of the Mughal artistic explosion

The mausoleum of Humāyūn, which was begun at the same time as the two monuments described above, was the first to manifest a fundamental rupture in the architectural styles of the Indian subcontinent. The shift in the Delhi sultanate to the splendor of the Mughal masterpieces was, however, less rapid than is sometimes credited; initially the latter were to coexist for a time with constructions of a more backward-looking conception. They were, moreover, the fruit of a rapid concentration and reinforcement of the political power in the hands of its sovereigns beginning with Akbar, allowing them to acquire the architectural tools necessary to realize their ambitions—the latter were to a large extent rooted in the legacy of the dynasties that had preceded the new masters of Delhi. In effect, these rulers shared their predecessors' propensity to marshal local, pre-Islamic construction techniques and decorative processes, and adapt them to potentially alien Muslim models. Yet, inventiveness and expertise also inspired genuinely Indian styles and, as the centuries passed, an Islamic identity specific to the region was forged. Furthermore, this process was far from occurring only along the mid-reaches of the Yamuna. The fragility of the sultanate of Delhi following the sack by Timur presented an opportunity for other independent sultanates to flower, all of which made attempts to affirm their own personality, in politics as well as in the arts, enriching—each in its own way—the expression of Islam in India, all the while deepening the imprint of Muslim culture on the region's social, economic and political texture in the broadest sense.

It is this cultural and creative effervescence that we will now seek to address.

Facing page. Claustra (or *Jali*), mausoleum of Hasan Khān, Sasarām, Bihār, India.

Above. *Jali*, of the mausoleum of Muhammad Ghaus, Gwalior, India.

THE INDEPENDENT SULTANATES

Facing page. Staircase in the Ashrafi Mahal, Māndu, India, mid-fifteenth century.

Pages 98–99. The entrance pavilion to the Ashrafi Mahal; in the background, the entrance to the Jama' Masjid, Māndu, India.

Pages 100–101. Mihrab, Jama' Masjid, Bījāpur, India, c. 1576.

Pages 102–103. *Jali* in the prayer hall of the Sidi Sayyid Mosque, Ahmedabad, India, 1572.

When the sultanate of Delhi crumbled, many local potentates, benefiting from the deliquescence of the central government, seized the opportunity to affirm the independence of once vassal provinces. The destinies of these fledgling states were each very different, in terms of longevity geographical size, and political sway. Notwithstanding, all of them, following the example of their unseated suzerain, sought to give material form to their newly acquired glory in an architectural boom that was expressive—in varying doses—both of the resumption of local traditions and the marshaling of foreign artists or models, in particular from Persia, Egypt, and Iraq.

In this manner, throughout the fourteenth century, the more far-flung and generally prosperous regions with strong personalities gradually unyoked themselves from the sultanate of Delhi. Among the first to rebel against the central administration, Bengal gained its freedom as early as 1336, when a first line of sultans threw off the authority of Delhi and took over the province. One will have to wait until 1576 before the Mughal Akbar could subdue this vast region. Still, even before the collapse of the sultanate of Delhi following the sack of the city by Timur, Kashmir (1346–1589), the Deccan of the Bahmanids (1347–1527), Gujarāt (1391–1583), and then the Sharqī sultans of Jaunpur (1394–1479) also founded autonomous entities. In its turn, Mālwa, too, managed to struggle free of the empire—but only after having first given sanctuary to the fleeing sultan of Delhi—giving rise to the kingdom that was to hold sway over this area of central India from 1401 to 1531.

Each of these emergent powers expressed its individuality through the promotion of constructions whose sometimes disorderly originality is nothing if not striking and testifies to an evolution in style—from incipient to increasingly refined to fully rounded—which resulted in undeniable masterpieces. For these states, however, the period was one of consolidating their identities. Thus, they often absorbed foreign influences solely as a vehicle through which to express more directly their underlying local cultures, while pressing economic demands and relative political isolation also obliged the new territories to use indigenous architectural models. Thus, Sindh and Bengal build mainly in brick, whereas for their part the sultanates of central India expressed their identities in stone. Invariably drawing to a greater or lesser extent on local artistic traditions, the variety of formal and decorative idioms adopted testifies to the surge in creativity that affected these societies. When the Great Mughals restored the authority of Delhi over these states, a wave of stylistic standardization smoothed over these regional variations, though this did not prevent the borrowing of certain features specific to sultanate architecture, such as the "Bengal roof," for instance.

Alexander receives the envoys sent by Darius. Illustration from a *Khamsa* by Nezāmī executed for Nusrat Shāh, sultan of Bengal, in 1531. British Library, Or. 13836, f. 21b.

Bengal (1336–1576)

It was in the late twelfth century that the military campaigns conducted by Ikhityār al-Dīn Muhammad Khaljī finally sucked Bengal into the orbit of the sultanate of Delhi. Gaur (Lakhnāwati) thus became the Delhi principality's chief outpost in the region, though it remained doggedly resistant to overall control. In point of fact, after the death of Balban in 1287, the governors of Lakhnāwati enjoyed a broad measure of autonomy. After being reined in briefly by Ghiyāth al-Dīn Tughluq, shortly after his death the population rose up once more and asserted its independence. The subsequent establishment of a stable Muslim sultanate brought with it a significant wave of conversions among the more impoverished layers of the local Hindu society that goes some way to explaining the density of Muslim occupation in this area even today.

Unified under the aegis of Shams al-Dīn Ilyās and his dynasty, which reigned from 1345 to 1487, both arts and letters developed apace in Bengal, while industries such as textiles made major strides—from the early fifteenth century in particular due to a boom in trading and diplomatic links with China. It was at this juncture that the port of Chittagong experienced an expansion that reflects a steady rise in the volume of transactions with the Far East. The line of the Ilyāsids was extinguished when Abyssinian guards grabbed power for a few years, only for the Sayyid 'Alā' al-Dīn Husayn Shāh to succeed in establishing a more stable authority in 1494 that his descendants kept in place until 1539. At this date, Bengal was invaded by Shēr Shāh Sūri, who established a government that survived through his successors for about thirty years, only for Akbar to bring the region back into the Mughal Empire in 1576.

The monuments marking the history of the sultanate may be divided into three periods. The first includes buildings built between the Islamic conquest and the 1340s. This evolved into a second phase corresponding to the transfer of the capital to Pandua (1340–1440). The last period is illustrated by the monuments of Gaur built between 1442 and the Mughal reconquest of 1576. The most venerable monuments are concentrated in the district of Hooghly, in Chota Pandua, and in Tribeni, while the architectural heritage of the last two eras are exemplified in the district of Mālda, around the confluence of the Ganges and the Mahānanda, nearly 220 miles (350 kilometers) north of Calcutta. A relatively restricted stretch of land there contains the ruins of Lakhnāwati, the capital of the Pāla and Sena rajahs before the site was overrun by the Islamic city of Gaur, and, slightly to the north, the city of Pandua, both—successively—capitals of the sultanate.[1]

The path to Islamic cultural assertion in Bengal

Monuments from the first two periods referred to above mirror the rise to prominence of the Bengali powers liberated from the chains of vassalage and keen to forge an identity of their own. Very few buildings representative of this initial phase have survived, however, and those that have are in a parlous state or have been severely altered by subsequent transformations. For this reason, the ancient capital of Lakhnāwati yields little more than shapeless vestiges. The most representative legacy of this period of culture is to be found today on the sites of the towns of Chota Pandua and Tribeni in the Hooghly district. The second stage of this progress towards an indigenous architectural personality is illustrated solely by the Adina Masjid at Pandua, while the Eklakhi mausoleum is the single survivor from the interregnum during the line of Raja Ganesha.

The Friday mosques of Tribeni and Chota Pandua
An inscription preserved on the Friday mosque in Tribeni attests to the fact that the monument was founded in 1298 by Zafar Khān, but sadly most of its surviving and visible remains are no more than significantly later interventions—with the notable exception of the odd pillar, probably of Hindu origin. Within its oblong plan, the edifice presents ten domes over a pair of naves, with, around the largest of these, five mihrabs arranged in twos.[2] The construction of the Friday mosque in Chota Pandua dates to the mid-fourteenth century; the building survives in a severely degraded state.[3] Arguably the template for the Adina Masjid, the monument rises on a rectangle of roughly 230 by 43 feet (70 by 13 meters), surprising proportions that imply that the prayer hall was broad but extremely shallow. The walls and the arches are made of brick set with basalt pillars taken from nearby temples. The *qibla* wall is equipped with no less than twenty-one mihrabs; the central one features particularly rich ornamentation. It is flanked by a stone *minbar* that seems to prefigure the one in the Adina Masjid.

In the immediate vicinity of this monument stands a curious minaret, or "victory tower," rising 120 feet (36.5 meters), whose construction may date to around 1340. Though the ratio between its height and diameter leaves something to be desired in terms of elegance, its tiered structure implies it that it must have been inspired by the Qutb Minār in Delhi

The Adina Masjid, Pandua (1375)
The Ilyāsid chose Pandua as the capital of the sultanate of Bengal. When Sikandar I (r. 1358–90) had the Adina mosque (the Friday Mosque) erected there, it was meant to mark a focal point for the new metropolis. Begun in about 1364, the works were completed some ten years later, as authenticated by an inscription dated to the month of Rajab 776 of the Hegira (December–January 1374–75).[4] The monument boasts rather sizable dimensions, with a courtyard extending 402 feet (122.4 meters) embedded in a rectangle measuring 507 by 285 feet (154.5 by 87 meters): in this manner, it constitutes the largest and most imposing mosque in Bengal. A succession of forty arcades, unfortunately partially in ruins today, extends over the width of the plan, while three sides of the courtyard are occupied by porticoes with three aisles. The center of the prayer hall, five aisles deep, features a broad *iwan* measuring 71 by 344 feet (21.5 by 105 meters) for an approximate height of 51 feet (15.5 meters) that introduces straight into a majestic mihrab, together with a large-size stone *minbar*. The *qibla* wall is studded across its entire width with secondary mihrabs, all enchased in five-lobe arches and surmounted by tympana all decorated differently. The dressed ashlar of the lower reaches of the monument remains admirable, but the upper

Pages 108–109. Adina Masjid, Pandua, India, 1375. *Qibla* wall with tympana decorated with terra-cotta and a squinch.

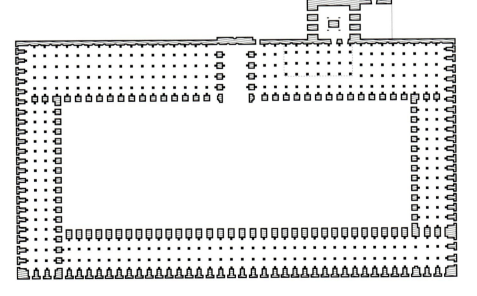

Above. View of the prayer hall, Adina Masjid, Pandua, India, 1375.

Facing. Plan of the Adina Masjid, Pandua, India.

108

Above and facing page. Carved decoration on the *qibla* wall and mihrabs, Adina Masjid, Pandua, India, 1375.

zones, as well as the vault of the *iwan*—in brick—are extremely dilapidated. The best conserved, however, is the gallery located to the north, designed for the use of women only (the *zenāna*). Its painstaking carvings are of singular beauty, in particular at the level of the principal mihrab, and constitute an original blend of indigenous elements—now shorn, however, of all figurative elements (i.e., the motifs such as the *suraj mukh* ("sun face") at the top of the arch and the *hansa* ("sacred goose") on the dado)—and consciously Islamic contributions, such as the Arabic inscriptions, the "arabesques," and the lamps. The sole representative of the intermediate phase of Bengal sultanate architecture, this remarkable building prepared the terrain for the third stage in the emergence of Muslim identity in the region, considered by many to be the most brilliant.

The mausoleum of Eklakhi, Pandua (c. 1425)
This strange pile, whose name means "the mausoleum that cost a lakh of rupees" (i.e., one hundred thousand), is supposed to house the remains of Jālal al-Dīn Muhammad Shāh. Son of a major Hindu landowner whose name was originally Raja Ganesha, the ruler, having converted to Islam, drove out the Ilyāsids and governed the whole region from 1414 to 1432.

The exceptional character of the tomb initially derives from its highly individual architectural idiom, as well as from the fact that it was to be adopted as the prototype for many later constructions that drew inspiration from its groundbreaking originality.

Below. The Eklakhi mausoleum, Pandua, India, c. 1425.

Facing page. The Dākhil Darwāza, Gaur, India, c. 1465.

A square structure of seventy-six feet (twenty-three meters) along each side, it is underlined by corner towers and capped by a dome forty-six feet (fourteen meters) in diameter. Each of the four façades has a door allowing access to the funerary hall organized around an octagonal plan. These entryways combine pointed arches and lintels, following the example of Tughluq architecture, but these techniques are here deployed in a construction built exclusively in brick. For its part, the decoration features terra-cotta juxtaposed with ceramic tiles that are found only as vestigial remains, but which nonetheless present lively and varied plant motifs, including finely executed large rosettes and trails.

The monuments of Gaur or the architectural maturity of the sultanate

At the end of the interlude inaugurated by Jalāl al-Dīn Muhammad Shāh, Ilyāsids returned to power, making ancient Lakhnāwati the capital again in around 1442 and renaming it Gaur. The city's renewed dynamism resulted in a series of monuments illustrating the maturation of architectural language in the state of Bengal, as exemplified by some inventive and intelligent constructions combining harmonious structural forms with proficient methods of decoration.

The Dākhil Darwāza (c. 1465)
An impressive pile constructed entirely out of brick, the Dākhil Darwāza ("inner gateway") was probably built in the reign of Bārbak Shāh (1469–74).

It is a massive structure with a façade 75 feet (23 meters) across, 113 feet (34.5 meters) deep, and 59 feet (18 meters) tall. Its proportions and imposing aspect give it the appearance of a triumphal arch; this is tempered, however, by the sense of movement imparted by the flanking towers and the entry pylons set alternately forward and back. Although dilapidated today, when they were still

topped by their domes the towers must have originally turned this monumental gate into a wave of hemispherical or pyramidal domes, creating a splendidly rhythmical and fluid effect.

The Tantipara Mosque (c. 1475)
Incorporated into a rectangular plan of 72 by 44 feet (22 by 13.5 meters), this building presents a balanced façade organized around two horizontal registers underscored by the addition of a band of five arches. Each field of the wall set within a pair of openings is punctuated by two blind niches flanking a cornice. The treatment of the surfaces features carved terra-cotta trim teeming with rosettes and plant patterns. The prayer hall is defined by two aisles supported on stone pillars parallel to a *qibla* wall. The ornamentation of the recesses on the façade is echoed in the treatment of the five mihrabs, with the largest in the center. A monumental inscription probably from this mosque—and today in the British Museum—dates to 1480.[5]

Other monuments in Gaur
The jewel in the crown of the reinstated dynasty of the Ilyāsids, their capital Gaur, naturally accumulated a host of fine monuments between the last quarter of the fifteenth century and the 1530s. The Lotan Masjid, for instance, erected in around 1480, is characterized by a glorious cladding of glazed ceramic. The architectural accomplishments of the sultanate at this time favored this type of decorative material, and it recurs on the Fīrūz Minār, raised in around 1488, a bold combination of "victory tower" and turquoise "minaret," from the top of whose imposing 84 feet (25.5 meters) distributed over five tiers the faithful were called to prayer. This Bengal-style tiling is readily recognizable and can be admired not only on the monuments themselves but also in examples in museums in Calcutta and London.[6]

Facing. The Tantipara Masjid, Gaur, c. 1475.

Above. The mausoleum of Fateh Khān in the Qadam Rasul complex, Gaur, c. 1657.

Below. The mausoleum oratory of Qadam Rasul, Gaur, 1530.

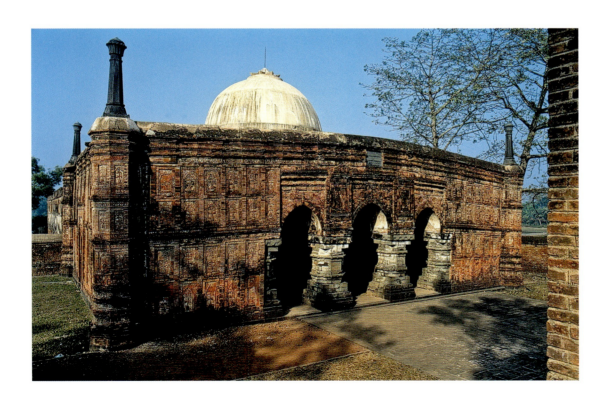

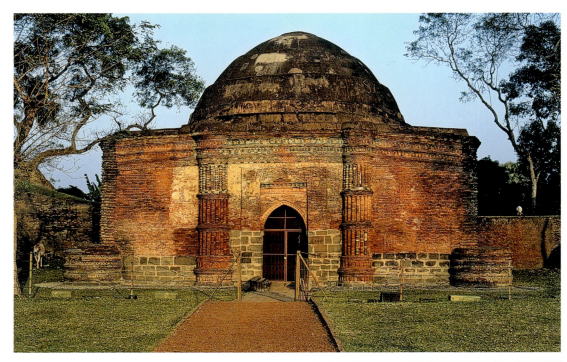

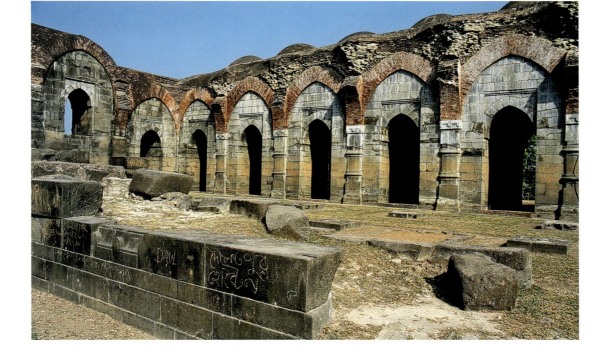

Facing page, top. Gumti Gate, Gaur, 1512.

Facing page, bottom. Chika Masjid, Gaur, constructed between 1415 and 1432.

Above. Bara Sona Masjid, Gaur, 1526.

Although in a sorry state today, the Bara Sona Masjid ("great golden mosque")—built in 1526—still possesses the exceptional dimensions that make it the largest mosque in Gaur. Eleven arcades stretch across the width of its rectangular plan. The first nave extends parallel to the *qibla* wall from which it is separated by magnificent piers opening on to the prayer hall itself; supported on stone pillars that further accentuate its majesty, it occupies a space three bays deep.

The Chota Sona Masjid ("small golden mosque," 1493–1519), similarly structured around an oblong plan, opens five arcades broad before plunging into a space three bays deep. The hemispherical domes dotted over the roof accentuate the impact of the one that rises above the central span, generating the form of a recti-curvilinear pyramid. The monument is dressed in stone delicately decorated with a range of carved motifs alternating or fusing reworkings of the indigenous repertory, such as the lotus flower, with assertions of Muslim identity, such as epigraphy, lamps, and mihrab niche motifs.

As for the mausoleum of Qadam Rasul, built in 1530—the conclusion of this intensely creative period—it is said to contain an imprint of the Prophet's feet, but the loss in clarity of its lines testifies to the onset of a decline of in Bengali artistic identity. Percy Brown is demonstrably of this opinion, referring to a structure that has "become flaccid and formless."[7]

Facing page. Brick-built squinches in the Chota Sona Masjid, Gaur, 1493–1519.

Top left and bottom. Enameled ceramic decoration, Gumti Gate, Gaur, 1512.

Top right. Terra-cotta mihrab panel decoration, Qadam Rasul, Gaur, 1530.

The monuments of Bagerhat, Bangladesh
In the fifteenth century, the city of Bagerhat, located where the Ganges meets the Brahmaputra, was known as Khalifatabad. Today in Bangladesh, it is thought to have been founded by General Ulūgh Khān Jahān, who is entombed there today. Its inclusion as a UNESCO World Heritage Site in 1985 is justified by several remarkable buildings, one exceptional example being the Sat Gumbaz ("mosque with sixty domes"), primarily because it is the largest mosque in the country.[8] Probably built around 1450, it features a rectangular plan of 161 by 108 feet (49 by 33 meters) and boasts no less than 77 domes (11 across by 7 deep), those over the wider central bay developing into a distinctive pyramidal form (*chau-chala*).

In the end, the architectural canon of Bengal at the time of the sultanate did not create what can be termed an undeniable stylistic coherence, but simply favored the emergence of certain characteristics. With some exceptions, such as the Adina Masjid in Pandua or the Dākhil Darwāza in Gaur, the monuments are of rather measured proportions, and even in the maturity of the period the size of the buildings remained within reasonable bounds. As a construction material, the region made wide use of brick, resorting to stone only when it could be recycled or for certain support units of especial decorative value, such as pillars in the most prestigious buildings. Following the example of countries in Central Asia, which also built in brick, Bengal saw the development of the art of the glazed ceramic tile

Below and facing page. Qutb Shāhī Masjid, Pandua, India, 1582.

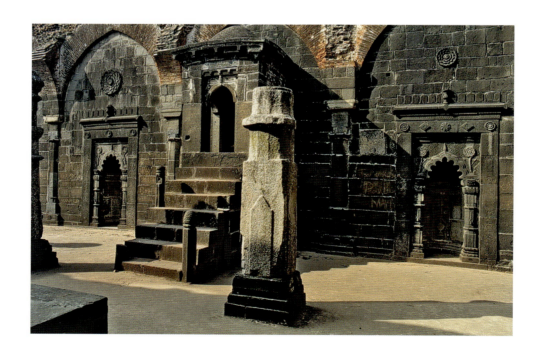

to protect as well as to adorn its monuments. Some regional specificities even found echoes beyond the limits of the territory; thus, a monumental gate built in Dimāpur, Assam, in the sixteenth century was obviously inspired by Bengali models. As the Mughals traveled, they took with them architectural references drawn directly from the achievements of this intensely if sometimes chaotically creative period; among others, the swelling, humped-back roof that often softens the lines of buildings in this region was to be exported under the name of "Bengal roof." One also thinks of the term "bungalow," borrowed from Hindustani and originally designating a type of low-lying dwelling in lightweight materials in what is simply a corruption of the adjective "Bengali."

Kashmir (1346–1589)

A remote, extremely compartmentalized and mountainous area, Kashmir succumbed to Muslim domination rather late in comparison with neighboring regions. It was indeed only in the fourteenth century, in about 1335, that an adventurer from the environs of Swāt named Shams al-Dīn Shāh Mirzā Swāti offered his services to the raja of Kashmir before grabbing power for himself in 1346. The lineage he founded remained at the helm of the country until 1561. Shams al-Dīn's reign, together with that of his four direct successors, marked a period of relative tolerance. In dramatic contrast, these rulers were followed by Sikandar Shāh, who ascended to power and reigned over the region with an iron rule from 1394 to 1416. Nicknamed Bot-shekan ("idol smasher") he seems to have been particularly fanatical, to the point that at his death, it has been alleged, only eleven Brahman families survived in the whole of Kashmir.

The apogee of the sultanate was reached under Zayn al-ʿĀbidīn, whose open-mindedness during his fifty-year reign (1420–70) was matched only by his undeniable scholarship. A great patron of the arts, he promoted not only architecture but also the translation into Persian of classic Sanskrit texts. Giving a considerable boost to

its economy, the sultanate witnessed the introduction into Kashmir of papermaking. As a supplier of one of the most prized papers in the whole Indian world, the region remained famous for this craft until the turn of the twentieth century. At the end of this period of glory and prosperity, the kingdom entered a tumultuous phase marred by political disturbances beyond the power of an ever-weakening central authority to quell; the ground was prepared for a takeover by the Mughal princes in 1585.

The independent sultanate of Kashmir has left us very few monuments; moreover, the climatic advantages and character of the region made it a favorite retreat for the Mughal emperors who later set their own seal on its architecture. Local buildings were traditionally constructed in wood, particularly deodar cedar, used especially as framing for the pyramidal roof that that is the trademark of Kashmiri monuments. In addition to its susceptibility to parasite attack, the wood was, of course, flammable and, over the years, vast tracts of the architectural heritage of the sultanate have gone up in smoke.

The mosques of Kashmir
The great Jama' Masjid of Srinagar was founded in 1385 and is representative of the fate of so many monuments of the region in that it suffered from devastating fires on no fewer than three occasions. The roof covering and frame are supported by three hundred pillars, each made from the trunk of a single tree, though only a few are original. The middle of the central courtyard is occupied by four brick *iwans* that open out onto the space. The mosque of Shāh Hamadān was probably also built in the late fourteenth century. The various reconstructions due to successive fires have clearly undermined the authenticity of the work.

Facing page. Mosque of Shāh Hamadān, Srinagar, India, founded in the late fourteenth century.

Below. Jama' Masjid, Srinagar, founded in 1385. *Iwan* opening onto the courtyard.

The mausoleum of Zayn al-'Ābidīn
The mausoleum of Sultan Zayn al-'Ābidīn, one of the most remarkable works of the period, was erected at the acme of sultanate civilization. The initiative for its construction—probably built over a former Hindu temple (a stone terrace in the shape of Greek cross)—is sometimes attributed to the sovereign's mother. The mausoleum itself is built in brick. It is organized around a central square within which the funerary hall springs from each of four branches of a cross. The solemnity of the monument is tempered by a consummately elegant Persian archway on one of these arms. The central hall is capped with a dome, with four smaller ones on each arm of the cross. The combination of the use of brick, of the theme of tomb-with-cupola, and the appearance of the Persian arch—all probably clad in a ceramic tiling—has often been ascribed to the influence of building superintendents from Persia, but the theory is weakened by the resolutely individual character of the edifice.

The paucity of vestiges of the architecture of the Kashmir sultanate makes it difficult to clearly define the salient features of the era. Nevertheless, arguably encouraged by the region's geographical isolation, one characteristic is certainly the use of timber in Islamic buildings employing local construction techniques. Its ruling princes, particularly Zayn al-'Ābidīn, were intent on generating a flow of trade which, at the pinnacle of its glory, rendered the sultanate permeable to foreign influences; these were surely absorbed by indigenous artists before the decline that heralded the arrival of the Mughal emperors.

Mausoleum of Zayn al-'Ābidīn, Srinagar, c. 1467.

The Sultanates of the Deccan

The Deccan is a vast entity whose coexisting but culturally diverse ethnic groups contrast with those of the Indo-Gangetic regions. The demarcation of this human landscape produced a complex situation that rendered the inclusion of the territory under the umbrella of a single political entity more than problematic. In fact, while Islam had long been present, the conquest of the Deccan by Muslim princes only truly got underway after the fall of Devagiri, the future Daulatābād, under the command of Alā' al-Dīn Khaljī. The completion of the Friday Mosque in that city—in 1318, if one credits the foundation inscription on the monument—resulted in this date during the reign of Qutb al-Dīn Mubārak Khaljī (1316–20) being adopted as the starting point of cultural influence by the invaders. Be that as it may, as the Tughluq dynasty progressed, ties between Delhi and the Deccan tended to loosen. Arguably, when Muhammad Tughluq ordered his capital to be moved to Daulatābād, he was thinking more of setting up a metropolis to link the northern capital of Delhi with the south, rather than of definitively transferring the focus of power. It may be that he also saw the process as a means of consolidating his authority over a restless region, dissatisfaction among certain strata of the administrative, religious, and military elites having if anything increased due to their enforced exile.

The friction generated by this episode paved the way for the building of the new capital in 1347 at the instigation of a general of obscure origins, Hasan Gangū. Pursuing the path of independence, this new strongman took the name Bahman Shāh, transferring his capital south to Gulbarga around 1350. For eighty years, the city remained the capital of a Bahmanid state that held in check nearly the entire Deccan until its fall in 1527. Its territorial unity, however, was over time to splinter into a number of emergent dynasties, such as the Barīdī (1504–1600), the 'Ādil Shāhīs (1490–1686), the Nizām Shāhīs (1496–1631), and the Qutb Shāhīs (1543–1687). Each lineage held sway over the area it controlled, radiating out from large towns such as Golconda, Bijāpur, and Bīdar, which were each endowed with the architectural attributes of a capital. The competition arising between these rival states was to be one of the factors that the Mughal Aurangzeb exploited when he annexed the greater part of the peninsula in a regained if now subject unity in 1687.

The Bahmanid sultanate (1347–1527) and its Barīd Shāhīs successors (1504–1600)

Holding power from 1347 to 1358, Bahman Shāh founded the dynasty that bears his name, establishing the earliest truly independent Islamic power in the region. His reign corresponded to an assertive phase in the existence of the fledgling state. Initially established at Daulatābād, a citadel on its rocky outcrop that could only be taken by treachery, as well as the symbol of the foreign conquest of the Deccan, the sovereign then transferred his capital to Gulbarga, which over succeeding decades was to become the jewel in the crown of a genuine homegrown Bahmanid kingdom. In 1401, the arrival of the Sufi Muhammad Gesu Deraz in the city signaled the onset of the religious figure's hold over the sultans, which was to last to his death in 1422. From 1425 to 1518, the capital was moved to Bīdar, the residence of the Barīd sultans, who rose to prominence under the last Bahmanids, prolonging their power beginning in 1518. Meanwhile, throughout the Deccan, other monarchs were founding states of their own.

Daulatābād and Gulbarga: the formation of a Bahmanid state
Daulatābād

The fortress of Daulatābād is a formidable symbol of the seizure of the Deccan by foreign forces. They had naturally been hell-bent on capturing the aerie so as to exert their authority over the area by way of military campaigns from the safety of its walls. The city is today located in the state of Mahārāshtra, a few kilometers from the famous carved caves of Ellora and the town of Aurangabad, founded many years subsequently. While the site can be regarded as the cradle of Muslim architecture in the Deccan, it also harbors many later monuments.

Today relegated to the dimensions of a village, the lower city is dominated by the impressive mass of the citadel standing on a conical hill topped by a rock face some

Below. Ramparts in the lower town, Daulatābād, India, with the entrance to the mosque; in the background, the Chand Minār, c. 1445.

650 feet (200 meters) high, which was altered by man so as to render its ascent as arduous as possible. A moat running around the base of the wall of the defensive complex offers further dissuasion, while the only access passage is surveyed by a barbican. The pile had already been highly effective before the Muslim conquest, but—as soon as the new power in the land seized it—it promptly set to work to make it capable of standing forever. At the foot of its bristling mass towering above the plain, a first enceinte of irregular form, whose widest point is no more than 3,280 feet (1,000 meters), contains edifices such as the Friday Mosque and the Chand Minār. This first sanctuary is in turn incorporated into another, larger compound.

The Friday Mosque has a square plan with sides of almost 246 feet (75 meters) and features a kind of an atrium opening onto a prayer hall; its satisfying proportions impart depth to a space whose organization is focused along the *qibla* wall. Pillars recycled from Hindu temples demolished nearby support a hypostyle volume—a partial explanation of why, as a reprisal perhaps, a multicolored statue of Burga has recently been set up in the very heart of the room.

Some 98 feet (30 meters) high, the Chand Minār is immediately striking: completely distinct from the mosque, it was erected on the other side of a thoroughfare serving both monuments. Its shape is characteristic, with three balconies that decrease in size—a reference to the corner minarets at the madrassa of Mahmūd Gāwān in Bīdar, which will be addressed presently. On the wall of the small oratory serving as the lower floor of the minaret, an inscription features a date of 1445 and the name of the patron, a certain Malik Parvez. The building probably used to be relatively colorful, as traces of glazed ceramic tilework attest.[9] In the heart of the fort is a very dilapidated pavilion dating probably from the substantially later period of the Nizām Shāhīs, around the second half of the sixteenth century. This is the Chini Mahal ("porcelain palace"), the name deriving from the graceful lines of its blue and white glazed ceramic decoration.

Gulbarga
Once the fortress of Daulatābād had fallen into their hands, the Bahmanid sovereigns quickly made Gulbarga the new capital of the state, thus implanting a symbol of their power in the heart of the Deccan.

This city plays host to one of the most spectacular mosques in all of India whose conception differs appreciably from that of the great mosques of Delhi, such as Quwwat al-Islām and Begumpurī, in that it is entirely roofed over. Built in 1367 and today enthroned in a virtually deserted citadel, it occupies a 213 by 164 foot (65 by 50 meter) rectangle that is impressive in its sheer scale. The prayer hall nestles in a U-shaped gallery comprised of a sweep of broad arcades generating remarkable curves and punctuated at all four corners with cupolas: the arched vault over each aisle falls almost to the floor. Far from feeling crushed, the projection of the arches over such a wide span confers on its generously proportioned volumes an intimate if uncanny majesty imbued with peace. It was a type of arch that made great inroads in many other monuments in Gulbarga. The volumes of the prayer hall are arranged beneath a curvilinear net of domes (seven wide by twelve deep), borne by a grid of pillars. A dome of larger size in front of the mihrab enhances the impact of the spiritual heart of the ensemble. The problem of lighting a roofed space is solved by the large windows piercing the external walls being discreetly sealed off by *claustrae* (except on the *qibla* wall).

Above. Ramparts of the citadel of Gulbarga, India, c. 1367.

Facing page. Plan (after J. Hoag) and view of the Jama' Masjid, Gulbarga, 1367.

This kind of covered mosque was more readily found in the cultural space of the Ottoman Empire than on the Iranian plateau, to the extent that some authors have regarded the monument as evidence of influences from the Ottoman world.[10] Notwithstanding, multiple-domed mosques are found in the Bengal, while the styles of the monuments in the Indian world are so distinct from those prevailing in Anatolia that any analogy seems coincidental.

Finally, there stands in Gulbarga the *dargāh* ("sanctuary") of the Sufi saint Muhammad Gesu Deraz, erected on his death in 1422. The mausoleum forms the hub of a wheel of monuments that the Bahmanid sovereigns and their successors extended over the years and offers a kind of précis of the evolution of architectural and decorative style in the sultanate. In this connection, the "Great Archway" decorating the main court of the sanctuary appears characteristic of the architecture of the 'Ādil Shāhīs in the seventeenth century, with its medallions decorated with heraldic animals.

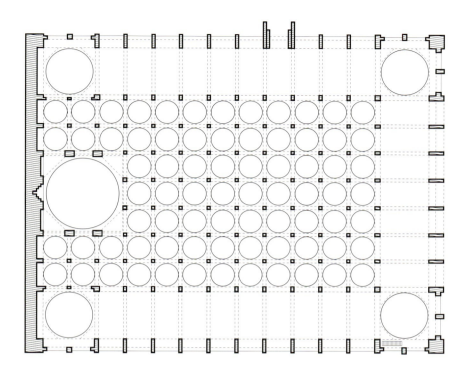

Bīdar: the rise of another capital city
In 1425 the Bahmanid sultans decided to transfer their capital to a new site sixty miles (one hundred kilometers) north of Gulbarga. This signaled the meteoric rise of Bīdar, a city that was to remain the greatest in the kingdom until 1518. The reasons leading to this shift in focus of power were rooted as much in internal conflicts among the ruling classes, which had made the atmosphere around the sovereigns unbreathable, as in the threats to the integrity of the sultanate issuing from a powerful rival kingdom, the Hindu Vijayanagar. Besides, the water supply, which at that time was as an important consideration as security in choosing an urban site, was easier to ensure in the new city. The capital of a prosperous state, the city attracted *affāqi*—or "emigrants" of Persian, Arabic, and Turkish origin—seeking to make their fortune and whose influence continued to grow throughout the Bahmanid era. These newcomers numbered a large contingent of Iranian monks who were at the root of the Shiite leanings of Islam in the Deccan. Today the ancient royal seat has become a provincial center in Karnātaka, yet one can still stumble across monuments of quality in many districts. The city is dominated by a citadel harboring vestiges of palatial buildings, while the lower city boasts the Friday Mosque and the splendid madrassa of Mahmūd Gāwān. The hallmark of the reigns of the Bahmanid princes (followed by their Barīd Shāhīs successors) is especially noticeable in the cemeteries containing many monuments commemorating their lives.

The fort of Bīdar and the palaces

Girt by ramparts, studded with bastions, and ringed by moats, the fort represents a redoubtable defensive unit. Greatly damaged when it was ransacked during the invasion led by the sultan of Mālwa in 1462, the enceinte has been renovated and later fortifications added. Like a great safe, the citadel protects the most venerable monument of the site, the Sola Khamba Mosque dating back to 1327, one of the oldest in the Deccan. The prayer hall opens through arcades onto a garden known by the name of Lal Bāgh.

The Takht Mahal ("palace of the throne") was thought to have been built during the reign of Ahmed I (1422–36). The complex was reached through a vast gateway on the western side, whose ceramic tile decoration featured the Shir-o-Khorshid (the "lion and sun" motif), a reference to the Iranian monarchy and one indication among many of the influence exerted by the migrants settling in the city during this period.

Facing page. View of the prayer hall, Solahkhambi Masjid, Bīdar Fort, India, 1327.

Below. The ramparts of Bīdar Fort, India.

The Diwan-e ʿĀmm ("hall of public audience") was a vast hall with columns, only the stone plinths of which survive—perhaps because the barrels were made of timber. The room was originally lined with extraordinary tile panels on which floral patterns alternated with geometrical motifs and calligraphic flourishes.[11] Finally the Rangīn Mahal ("painted palace") offers few traces of its original construction, since it was profoundly altered in the sixteenth century, during the rule of the Barīd Shāhīs. Its admirable interior is encrusted with mother-of-pearl, juxtaposing motifs from Hindu and Muslim repertories in the same location.

The madrassa of Mahmūd Gāwān
Mahmūd Gāwān was an adventurer from Gīlān, Iran, who arrived at the Bahmanid court as one of the horde of immigrants then flooding into Bīdar. After displaying his talents in several subordinate functions, he eventually climbed to the dizzy heights of vizier to Muhammad Shāh III (r. 1463–82). It was in 1472 that he erected the madrassa that bears his name. In this connection, it is worth stressing that, unlike in the Iranian and Central Asian cultural spheres, madrassas were comparatively rare in India. The building plan is clearly inspired by traditional Iranian models with a quadrangular structure delimiting a court opening into four *iwans* placed in the center of each side; the cubicles are arranged in the upper floor. The onion dome of the prayer hall is striking and perhaps the first example of the kind in India, though it seems to continue where other buildings of the same type in Timurid Afghanistan (such as the Gowhar Shād madrassa in Herāt, completed in 1438) left off. The substantial role allotted to a glazed ceramic architectural trim comes as little surprise; associated with the use of brick, such breadth of ornament offers a bold contrast with local traditions of construction that favor stone and carvings. This clean break, in conjunction with the references it deployed, probably betrays a desire to follow the lead of the masterpieces of Timurid architecture.

Facing page. The Mahmūd Gāwān Madrassa, Bīdar, India, 1472.

Above. Necropolis of the Bahmanids, Bīdar, fifteenth century.

The royal necropolises of the Bahmanids and the Barīd Shāhīs
The funerary architecture encountered in the royal mausoleums at Bīdar represents an advance over those found in Gulbarga. As decade followed decade, the domes in particular appear increasingly bulbous.

The oldest building in the necropolis is the tomb of Ahmed I. Starting from a square plan, the tomb is topped by a generous cupola on an octagonal drum, while arcades straddle the façades. The contiguous mausoleum of Ahmed II adopts a similar schema, enriched on the outside, however, by a wealth of glazed ceramic.

Approximately 3,280 feet from the necropolis stands another truly remarkable mausoleum. In point of fact, it does not contain a monarch, but the remains of a Shiite holy man, Khalil Allāh (died 1460). On an octagonal base, this monument, the Chaukhandi, features two rows of arches that once gave a dynamic impulse to a no longer extant glazed ceramic decoration. Within the monument, an ambulatory opens onto a square funerary hall.

A new necropolis to the west of the city houses the tombs of the Barīd Shāhīs sovereigns, who, as the Bahmanids gradually lost hold, became masters of the city. The mausoleum of 'Alī Barīd (died 1580) gave rise to a new style: set in a quadripartite garden (*chahār-bāgh*) and raised on a square plan, it has four wide doors and is capped with an onion dome.

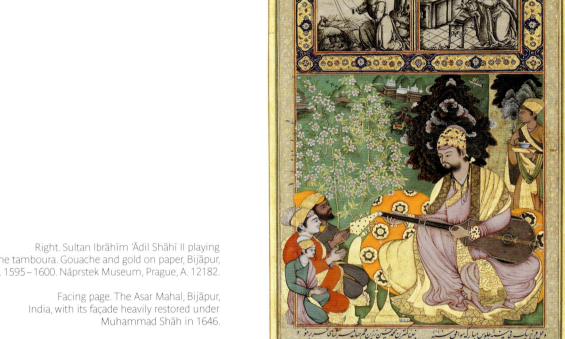

Right. Sultan Ibrāhīm 'Ādil Shāhī II playing the tamboura. Gouache and gold on paper, Bijāpur, c. 1595–1600. Náprstek Museum, Prague, A. 12182.

Facing page. The Asar Mahal, Bijāpur, India, with its façade heavily restored under Muhammad Shāh in 1646.

The 'Ādil Shāhīs and Bijāpur; or the full-blown originality of a capital

The dynasty of the 'Ādil Shāhīs was founded by Yusuf 'Ādil Khān (1490–1510), who at the outset had been no more than governor on behalf of the Barīd Shāhīs of the town of Bijāpur. In 1490, however, he proclaimed himself prince of the region and forged an alliance with the powerful Hindu kingdom of Vijayanagar against his onetime overlords. This bid for freedom was pursued by his successor, Ismā'īl 'Ādil Khān (r. 1510–34), who initially gained renown in battles against the Portuguese in Goa before routing the troops of Amīr Barīd (r. 1504–34) and establishing a new coalition with the kingdom of Ahmednagar. In extending its territory, the dynasty seems to have been opportunistic, playing the ambitions of its neighbors off one against the other and unscrupulously tearing up agreements on which the ink was scarcely dry. Thus, toying with the illusions of victory entertained by its "partners," the dynasty carved out a path to supremacy. The reigns of 'Alī 'Ādil Shāh I (1558–80) and then of Ibrāhīm 'Ādil Shāh II (1580–1627) mark the apogee of the kingdom, the crowning glory of the diplomatic skill and tactical flexibility of its sovereigns. Later monarchs were to run up against the Mughal expansion that first harassed then gnawed away at their lands, and the line faded into obscurity in 1686.

A reflection of the conceptual freedom and pragmatism that characterized this dynasty, the architecture of Bijāpur affirms itself as one of most resolutely original in the whole subcontinent. Isolated traces of buildings from prior to the ascendency of the 'Ādil Shāhīs, however, do survive. Through the works they financed or fostered, the spectacular style forged by the dynasty became a due reflection of their policy. From this context of impertinent creativity, there arose, for instance, an edifice as astonishing as the Gōl Gumbaz, one of the world's biggest domes.

The provincial period, or Bijāpur's stuttering start

Little architectural material today provides an idea of what Bijāpur must have been like before the 'Ādil Shāhīs seized power. Located within the citadel, the mosque of Karimuddin can be dated to 1320 thanks to an inscription and thus comes from a time when increasing Islamic power was marked by the use of spolia from Hindu temples. The Bahmanid period itself bequeaths works such as the mosque of the vizier Khwāja Jahān (1485), as well as one of the bridges spanning the moat around the citadel.

The first Friday mosque in Bijāpur, frequently referred to as the Old Friday Mosque of Yusuf, actually dates to 1513, and is thus posterior to the death of the aforementioned sultan. Placed on a high cylindrical drum, its single, large hemispherical dome emerges from a base decorated with petal-like forms. This sturdy and proud bloom foreshadows other major constructions, such as the Gōl Gumbaz.

'Alī I and Ibrāhīm 'Ādil Shāh II (1558–1627): the golden age of the dynasty

The lengthy reign of 'Alī I 'Ādil Shāh was marked by intense architectural activity. In 1565 the defenses of Bijāpur were completed by an imposing rampart 33 feet (10 meters) high and 33 to 39 feet (10 to 12 meters) wide, reinforced by a moat and counterscarp. Situated at the center of the city, the citadel is studded with towers and fortified gates. Around this urban core, other monuments sprung up in various districts, all reflecting the pomp of the central power. Within the citadel

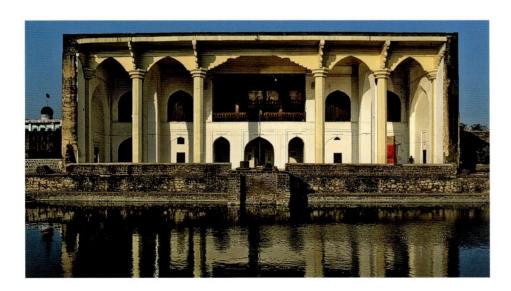

itself stands the impressive Gagan Mahal, an audience hall that opens boldly to the exterior through three archways, the two at the sides serving as worthy colleagues to the grandiose dimensions of the central arch. The spandrels of the latter are adorned with a characteristic decorative motif: a medallion borne on a double-ogee console whose shape verges on that of a fish. Even today in Hyderābād, one can still find this figure on banners deployed in Shiite processions in the month of Muharram.

The Friday Mosque (c. 1576)
The construction of a new Friday mosque started in 1576, while 'Alī I still held the reins of power, but the building was not completed; only the bases of the minarets are in place and the elevations were never erected. The lines of this monument, however, remain exemplary; their purity is unmarred by decorative overload. In the prayer hall, only the central archway whose curves soften the lines of the ample and spectacular courtyard is adorned with polyfoils and spandrels with medallions and accolades, as was common in prestige buildings of this era. The mihrab, meanwhile, richly ornamented in a style echoing manuscript illumination, lies on the same axis.

Below and facing page, above. The Jama' Masjid (Friday Mosque), Bijāpur, India, c. 1576.

Facing page, below. Mihtar Mahal, Bijāpur. Detail of the reveal in a canopy.

The pillars supporting the arches along the cornice at the summit of the prayer room boast a sequence of consoles which, in terms of size, alternate major and minor modes. The ensemble lacks a parapet or canopy, which probably could not be completed. The commodious space arranged in front of the mihrab, the *maqsura*, is capped by a dome borne by an ingenious vaulting system whose original conception issues from the octagon bearing the dome and from its pendentives. The selfsame process of transition from square to octagon reappears on a grossly inflated scale in the Gōl Gumbaz.

Monuments from the reign of Ibrāhīm II
The personality of several buildings erected at the time of Ibrāhīm II stems from their carved stone decoration that contrasts with the stucco on trimmed rubblework more usual in earlier times. In this connection, the mosque of Malika Jahān, built in 1582, is a prime example of the success of this new vehicle for creative expression. The domes emerge from a collar of petals, swelling proudly into a volume verging on a three-quarter sphere.

The Mihtar Mahal, similarly allotted to the end of the reign of Ibrāhīm II, presents something of a curiosity: it constitutes in fact the entryway to a small contiguous mosque and is built entirely in stone but replays forms and decorations characteristic of timber architecture. The balconies reeling under spectacular cornices surmounted by hoods are particularly revealing in this respect. Along the same lines, the consoles are carved in a rich and complex fashion, featuring friezes of ducks specific to the Hindu tradition.

Above. Mosque of the Ibrāhīm Rawza funerary complex, Bijāpur, 1626.

Facing page and pages 140–141. Mausoleum known as Gōl Gumbaz, Bijāpur, c. 1656.

The mausoleum of Ibrāhīm Rawza (1626)

This building was initially built for Queen Tāj Sultānā, the wife of Ibrāhīm II, but in fact conceals the remains of the sultan and his family. Lying amid a square enclosure 450 feet (137 meters) down the side, the funerary complex is incontestably one of the most refined works of architecture erected under the 'Ādil Shāhīs.

As if bearing an offering, a terrace—off-center and running down one side of the square compound—leads across to the mausoleum and the mosque facing it. Square in plan, the mausoleum features a double ambulatory proceeding round the square funerary hall and communicating freely with the outside through seven archways. Crimped around each corner of the monument are filled-in "pseudo-minarets" brandishing at their summits a three-quarter sphere in the manner of a *flambeau*. The front face of the consoles supporting the "awning" displays a cornice frieze, while to the right of each pillar on the arches stands a larger console corresponding to "minaret-like" florets of smaller dimensions at the level of the parapet. The three-quarter sphere dome in the funerary hall is bedecked with a ring of petals characteristic of the 'Ādil Shāhīs. The mosque opposite uses similar decorative elements, albeit differently arranged. The protective and intimate rectangular prayer hall—three bays deep—leads to the terrace through five arches. Once more, slender pseudo-minarets cluster around the corners of the building.

The end of the ʿĀdil Shāhīs: audacity and excess

The last three ʿĀdil Shāhīs rulers were Muhammad (1627–1656), ʿAlī II (1656–1672), and Sikander (1672–1686).

Peppered with a multitude of projections like so many architectural exclamation marks, the buildings sponsored by these rulers are frequently characterized by surprising proportional ratios that make use of squat or diminutive domes combined with oversized central archways. In this regard, the mosque of Mustafa Khān presents a gigantic central arch flanked by two narrower counterparts, forging an undeniable relationship to the façade of the Gagan Mahal, of which it looks like an "overcooked" version. The same doorway structure was used for the mausoleum of Shāh Nawāz Khān, where—following the example of many *pir* (Sufi guide) tombs of the time—the equilibrium between the various heights of the levels of the building is violently disrupted. As for the mosque and the tomb of Yaqut Dabuli, they let off a pyrotechnic display of aerial extensions (pinnacles and "pseudo-minarets"), but even these works—that seem to fix in stone the dynamism of a living entity—pale into insignificance compared with the staggering Gōl Gumbaz.

Gōl Gumbaz (c. 1656)
Of staggering dimensions, this mausoleum is the centerpiece of a funerary complex enriched with a *naqqāra-khāna* ("bandstand"), a construction that marked the entrance to the whole domain, together with a mosque and a hostelry, and was to be the final resting place of Muhammad Shāh (r. 1627–56). At his death, however, the building remained unfinished. Superlatives are unavoidable in any account of this

Above. Plan and side view, Gōl Gumbaz, Bijāpur (after C. Tadgell).

Facing page. Façade detail, Gōl Gumbaz.

exceptional edifice: the 144-foot (44-meter) external diameter of the dome is not only the largest in the entire subcontinent, it also vies in terms of architectural prowess with world-famous tours de force such as the domes of the Pantheon in Rome or the Hagia Sophia in Constantinople. The dome rests on a cubic space of 156 feet (47.5 meters) down the side, delimiting on the ground a unique, homogeneous space that exudes great majesty; a sizable apse faces the main doorway, breaking the static mass of the square base and filling visitors with mystical awe. All four corners of the monument feature seven-story octagonal towers topped with three-quarter sphere domes. The theatrical decoration of the external façades features three arches, the perspective effect of the middle one—broader than its lateral counterparts—being further enhanced by means of apertures. The uniformity of the elevation would seem severe were it not for the interplay among the volumes under the masterly cornice of consoles, prolonged upwards by a gallery whose lines are softened by arching bays capped by a crown of floret-shaped fleurons and pinnacles that extrapolate the energy released by the vertical axis. The cenotaphs in the funerary hall aid meditation, while a crypt dug out of the very foundations of the edifice shelters the royal tombs.

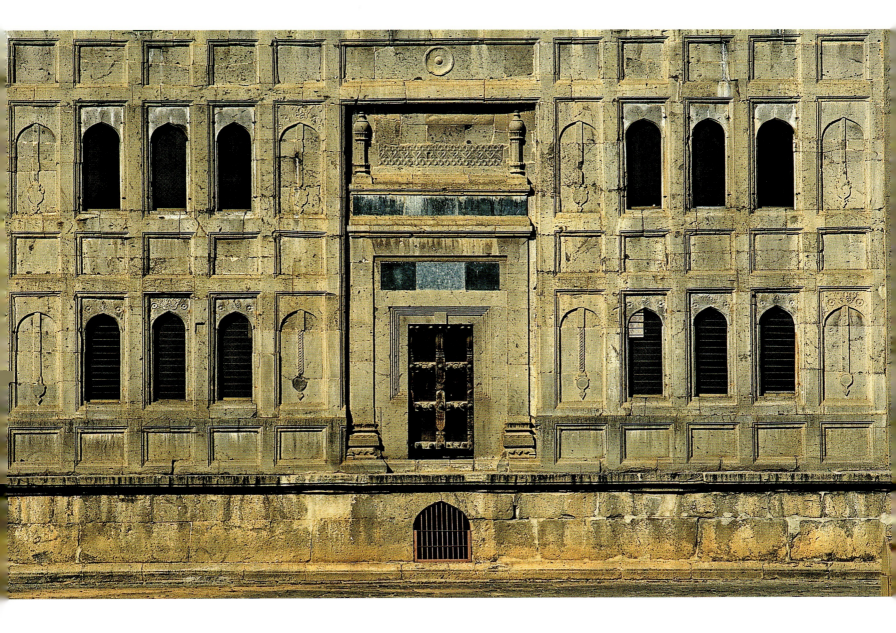

The Qutb Shāhīs (1543–1687)

In 1494 Qāsim Barīd appointed Qulī Qutb al-Mulk governor of the region of Telingāna, as well as of the fort of Golconda. After 1515, while still a vassal of the sultans of Bijāpur and Bīdar, Qulī Qutb al-Mulk—all the while completing the fortification of the citadel of Golconda—set off to retake the territories the Bahmanids had forfeited. By his death in 1543, due to his consummate military effectiveness, most of the eastern Deccan had been made subject to his rule. It was, however, during the reign of Ibrāhīm Qutb Shāh (1550–80) that the kingdom of Golconda reached its apogee. Ibrāhīm Qutb Shāh joined a coalition of sultans to defeat the troops of Vijayanagar, took the royal title, and extended his territory south of Orissa and as far as the kingdom of Berār. This expansionist push met with a backlash from the sultans of Bijāpur, with whom hostilities would flare up

sporadically. When, in the late sixteenth century, during the flourishing reign of Muhammad Qulī Qutb Shāh, these conflicts finally simmered down, the very lifeblood of the sultanate was already being drained by ceaseless Mughal raids. It was nonetheless on this sovereign's initiative that in 1591 the city of Hyderābād started its extraordinary ascendency that was to turn it into one of the most fabulous capitals in the whole subcontinent.

Golconda: the rigors of a martial capital

The reputation of Golconda was founded primarily on the famous diamond mines in the district that furnished gemstones for the ancient world. Once it became the capital of the Qutb Shāhīs, the city developed into the nerve center of a military-orientated state perpetually at daggers drawn with the powers on its borders that constantly threatened its independence. The sobriety and economy of the architecture that sprung up in that city are an embodiment of the defensive priorities of its pragmatic sovereigns, who basically equated town planning with fortification, and saw power as manifested in action rather than in ceremonial demonstrations.

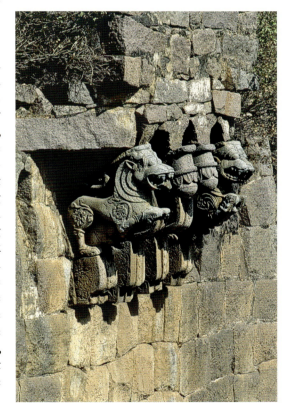

The fort of Golconda

As is typical, the capital is dominated by a citadel (Bala Hissar) whose needle-sharp fortifications bristle above a hill and rise 427 feet (130 meters). The lower city nestles in the heart of a system of ramparts with a perimeter of 1.6 miles (2.5 kilometers). In 1624 a new enceinte, the Naya Qila ("new fort"), was built up against the one in the city to complete a defensive outwork designed to ward off even persistent attack. Over an average height of fifty-nine feet (eighteen meters), the walls enclosing the urban core are pierced by eight specially strengthened gates; stuck with spikes to protect them against being rammed by elephants, the impressively massive teak leaves of the Fath Darwāza ("gate of victory") still stand today. Around one thousand feet (300 meters) to the west, the Bala Hissar Darwāza dominates the entrance to a second retaining wall that runs round the entire circumference of the hill. The thoroughfare connecting the two gates serves many public buildings, including markets, hammams, warehouses, and barracks. At the present time, unfortunately, these buildings are in a poor state of conservation.

Facing page and above. The fort of Golconda, India, overlooked by the small mosque of Ibrāhīm Qutb Shāh, and detail of carved consoles on the rampart.

Shortly before reaching the Bala Hissar Darwāza, a kind of triumphal archway offers a demonstration of the grandeur of the masters of this bellicose sanctuary, while a little more to the north stands a Friday mosque, founded in 1518 by Qulī Qutb Al-Mulk, who was assassinated within its portals some twenty-five years later. The Bala Hissar Darwāza was also important in being an access to the beating heart of the sovereign power—a point forcefully emphasized by the impressive stucco motifs of often martial connotations that decorate it, such as the lions adorning the spandrels. The citadel is reached up various stairways and as one ascends one glimpses to the left the many rooms of the palatial complex, now in ruins. At the top of the citadel, Ibrāhīm Qutb Shāh set up a small mosque, which dominates the panorama and remains the only monument on the whole acropolis to have been spared the vicissitudes of the passing ages.

The necropolis of the Qutb Shāhīs
Northwest of the city, the princes of the dynasty made plans for spaces for their tombs. In point of fact, only seven buildings of the twenty or so are authentic royal mausoleums, the other buildings being mosques and a hammam for cleansing the dead for burial, as well as pavilions and entryways. The whole nestles in a garden that enhances the coherence of the structure.

Above and facing page. Mausoleum of a Qutb Shāhī sultan in the Golconda necropolis, India, seventeenth century.

In keeping with the purposeful rigor of the architecture in the city, the design template for the mausoleums is based on repetition: for the majority, they stand over a square plan, the perimeter opening through arcades onto an ambulatory whence one reaches a funerary hall surmounted by a single, bulbous dome. Built in stone masonry daubed with stucco, these constructions were sometimes lined with glazed ceramic tilework. More imaginative, a few bold mausoleums undertook tentative variations from this basic structure, such as that of Yar Qulī Jamshīd (died 1550), which opts for an octagonal plan and a two-level elevation separated by a balcony—but here, too, the crowning glory is limited to a single onion dome.

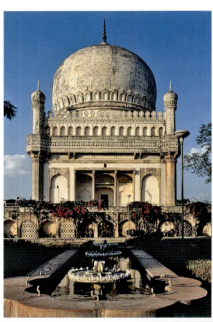
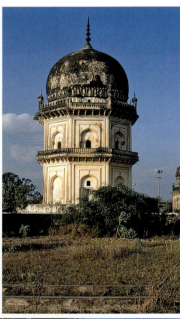
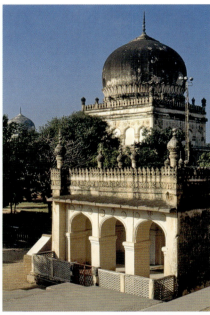

Facing page. Mausoleums and funerary mosque, Qutb Shāhī necropolis, Golconda, sixteenth–seventeenth century.

Left. The Jama' Masjid, Hyderābād, India, 1597.

Hyderābād: a mature capital

As the power of the Qutb Shāhīs line took root and droves of migrants from the country or abroad gravitated towards their states, it was clear that the city of Golconda was ill-adapted to such a surge in population. The trades exercised by the new arrivals were also alien to a government that had focused primarily on military and political organization and logistics. In 1591 the congestion in the city led Muhammad Qulī Qutb Shāh to found another town a few miles east of the iconic citadel: Hyderābād. The renown of that city was to climax a long time after the dynasty that laid its foundations had vanished from the face of the earth, when it was chosen in its turn as the dazzling capital of the Nizāms. The new city was moreover soon to extend its tentacles over the River Musi and stretch north, spawning squalid and downtrodden suburbs.

The era of Muhammad Qulī and the Chār Minār
During his reign from 1580 to 1612, the sovereign who founded the city erected many monuments that today structure its urban fabric. As the city crossed the river, the need arose to throw bridges, such as the Purana Pul, built by 1593, over its waters. Although these structures bear witness to the assumed grandeur of the sovereign in his new capital, none can be said to equal the imposing stature of the Chār Minār ("four minarets"), incontestably one of the most accomplished pieces of civil architecture in all India. It is a vast tetrapylon 98 feet (30 meters) down the side, flanked on all four corners by the towering 180-foot (55-meter) minarets that give it its name. Above arches that add a touch of buoyancy to some necessarily muscular underpinnings, the building is ringed by an outward-facing gallery. This is in turn topped by a second open balcony that looks like it is being yanked up; at the summit, the structure features a terrace bordered by *jalis*. To the west, like an offering on a silver platter, stands a mosque that echoes the huge entryway surmounted by a bulbous dome at the eastern side. In the immediate vicinity of the Chār Minār, the Friday Mosque was founded in 1597. The prayer hall façade displays unusual

The Chār Minār ("Four Minarets"), Hyderābād, late sixteenth century.

and highly elaborate combinations, with pointed and polyfoil arches, terminating in an openwork parapet of intersecting arches flanked by a pair of minarets with crownpieces of petals around their tops that ultimately sprout into two onion domes.

The later monuments: the dynasty's final flourish
The construction of the mosque known as the Mecca Masjid began during the reign of Muhammad, in 1617, but was completed only in 1693, when the region was already under the yoke of Aurangzeb. It appears as a monument of some size, with, at its base, a rectangle of 196 by 131 feet (60 by 40 meters) further enlarged by the apse-like mihrab. The volume of the prayer hall is encompassed by five three-bay aisles, each covered by a dome, except for the central arch that swells into an extensive vault. The façade is organized around a sequence of arcades topped by a cornice with consoles and ensconced between two minarets; heavy and squat, and seemingly squashed into the edifice, their galleried balcony leads almost without transition into the onion dome.

This monument stands next to a funerary enclosure in which several members of the Asafiya line (the Nizāms of Hyderābād) repose. The Toli Masjid was built in 1671, during the reign of Sultan Abdullah. Its proportions are more harmonious and it affords a more successful example of the late Qutb Shāhīs style, particularly its lively decoration and verticality. Just as admirable is the manner in which this outburst of energy still finds room for delicately worked corner minarets, as well as for intricately ornamented arcades and cornices.

The legacy of the architecture of the Deccan sultanates
As the hold of the Delhi princes slackened, precipitating the emergence of independent Muslim entities all over the Deccan, the many and varied ambitions of local potentates shattered the province into states, all forced to devote a substantial proportion of their energies to defending their little enclaves.

These princes would frequently use the pause between two phases of open hostility to enter into a policy of prickly alliance with their neighbors. This intrinsic instability is surely the source of the countless fortifications in this area of dramatic relief and full of vertiginous cliffs tailor-made for the construction of strongholds in which the various rulers might keep their little courts out of trouble.

The mistrustfulness of so many members of these dynasties whose meteoric rise was matched by their fragility was further exacerbated by saber rattling on the part of the rajas of Vijayanagar—constant irritants who ruled over a province with non-Muslim majority and who never entirely bowed to the sway of the sultans. Until the Deccan states progressively disintegrated under the weight of the Mughal empire, the glories of these sultanates—surrounded as they were by conflicts that might at any time menace their independence and forced to come to terms with the traditions of alien neighbors—were often short-lived, but, in architectural terms, their all too often illusory preeminence could be expressed equally in unbridled creativity or in the severest rigor.

The cultural originality of the region relative to the rest of the subcontinent can also be accounted for by contributions, more marked here than elsewhere, from immigrants from the Arab world, Central Asia, and Iran, and in particular from Shiism, to which the majority of these dynasties converted. The later dynasties of Mysore, followed by the nabobs of Arcot, were not afraid of taking their cue from these imaginative idioms, while even the architects of the British Raj were far from impervious to them.

The Sultanate of Gujarāt (1391–1583)

The vast region of Gujarāt was long a focus of considerable commercial contact between the subcontinent and the lands bordering the Gulf of Oman and the Persian Gulf. Its extensive coastline was fringed with ports from which goods were dispatched from India to the Arab, Persian, or African coasts—or to more remote destinations—and through which exotic products were imported into the subcontinent. Such exchanges ensured the province's enduring prosperity, all the more so since specialization in maritime trade was relatively rare in India. From an early date, the wealth the port accumulated inevitably attracted pillagers who followed in the wake of those who, under Mahmūd Ghaznī, had ransacked the temple of Somnāth and returned staggering under an immense hoard. The relative isolation of the territory and its links with neighboring powers, however, sheltered it from annexation until 1298, the date it was absorbed into the sultanate of Delhi after the victory of Alā' al-Dīn Khaljī over the reigning raja. Thus, throughout the fourteenth century, the region was governed in the name of the sultan of Delhi, before a governor named Zafar Khān, spurred on by the decline of Tughluq power, declared independence in 1391. His descendants ruled over Gujarāt until 1583, when the armies of Akbar launched a victorious campaign against the sultanate that was then relegated to the status of a province of the Mughal Empire.

Zafar Khān's grandson succeeded him as Ahmed I, founding Ahmedabad, the city that bears his name. As his reign went on, he was dragged into constant conflicts with his most important neighbors, such as the Hindu rajas of Gujarāt and Rājputāna, but also against the Muslim states in the region, which were flexing their muscles in Mālwa, Khāndesh, and the Deccan. The prestige of the dynasty culminated in Mahmūd Beghada, who exercised power from 1458 to 1511—that is, for fifty-three years. This sovereign also carried out numberless sorties against the rajas, before conquering Champaner, which he renamed Muhammadābād and subsequently took as the sultanate's new capital. In addition, the monarch signed an alliance with the Mamluks of Egypt against the growing power of the Portuguese, who nonetheless—after prizing Goa away from the 'Ādil Shāhīs—succeeded in settling in Diu, on part of the sultanate's territory.

The first fruits of Muslim architecture in the subcontinent date back to the monuments at Bhadreshvar, but the independence of the sultanate gave an unprecedented creative fillip to the region, the jewels in the crown being represented by the successive capitals of Ahmedabad and Champaner.

The emergence of buildings was little short of astonishing and clearly stamped with the seal of cultural "syncretism"; in all probability this was not unconnected with the ongoing habit of contact and concession that the commercial tradition of the country had entrenched in the region's inhabitants. Local artists could hark back to a splendid Hindu and Jain past with diverse decorative repertories and construction techniques, integrating them fully into the context of explicitly Islamic buildings. Hindu practices remained very much alive, moreover, as the rebuilding between 1263 and 1268 of the temple of Somnāth later destroyed by Mahmūd of Ghaznī testifies. It would not have been unusual for the same sculptors to work indifferently on sites for temples and mosques, their toing and froing further facilitating the permeability of various conceptual universes to techniques issuing from neighboring cultures and the exchange of their experiences.

From province to sultanate

The contacts of Gujarāt with Arab merchants had very early on favored the sporadic implantation of generally isolated Muslim communities, as had been the case at Bhadreshvar. Further accentuated by the surge in Muslim influence that resulted from the annexation of the sultanate of Delhi, from the very start of the fourteenth century the constructions of these various groups of believers fostered the emergence of an embryonic regional style.

Anhilawada (now Patan) is therefore significant; the onetime capital of the Solanki kingdom, which thrived from the tenth to thirteenth centuries, it was already teeming with monuments, including the iconic "well of the Rani," a magnificent *wāv* (or stepped tank), which a twentieth-century restoration has returned to its former glory. It was in this city that the Muslim conquerors of the region begun erecting the mausoleum of Sheikh Farīd in about 1300; it was an operation that consisted in converting a former Hindu temple into a tomb and adapting its symbolism. In the same vein, the Adina (or Friday) Mosque was erected with the extensive reuse of pillars purloined from various temples in the region, without much effort being put into their being originally or intelligently organized or integrated into the fabric of the new building.

While these initial stirrings of culture were handled somewhat awkwardly and marred by a certain roughness, they were counterbalanced by other, infinitely more effective monuments built during the same period such as the Friday Mosque at Bharūch, and more especially, the one in Cambay, built in 1325. In the fourteenth century, the city probably served as the chief administrative center of the province, which may account for the care taken over a construction whose delicate arches are reminiscent of the subtleties of line of the Jamā'at Khāna of Nizamuddin in Delhi, erected under 'Alā' al-Dīn Khaljī.

The reign of Ahmed I (1411–42): the assertion of Gujarati identity

For the sultanate of Gujarāt, the advent of Ahmed I signaled the onset of a period of ostentation that culminated in the foundation of Ahmedabad. Owing to the many famous buildings with which Ahmed endowed it, the prestige and name of this city is inextricably linked to its sovereign. The city is organized around the citadel (the fort of Bhadra) and the triumphal gate and Friday mosque, later supplemented by funerary monuments.

Tin Darwāza
Almost immediately after his accession to power, the sultan began constructing an enceinte to protect his city. Like a ring with its gemstone, the wall serves as a setting for a "triple gate" that leads to the heart of the urban space through three archways of unequal size, the broadest being a central arch whose majesty is underscored by engaged buttresses delicately worked into a shape like a minaret. A space fringed by a wall perforated by openings and topped by battlements forms the terrace, completing a building that was presumably designed to trumpet the might and glory of its prince.

The Friday Mosque of Ahmedabad
Completed in 1423, the mosque is noteworthy for its engaged minarets in front of the central archway of the prayer hall. Redolent of those that adorn the Begumpurī

mosque of Jahānpanāh in Delhi, they nonetheless present a lofty molded and carved decoration more reminiscent of the pillars of the temples of Somnāth than the sober, spare style cultivated in Delhi. One should underline the presence of recurring motifs in the decorative idiom of the art of the Gujarāt sultanate, including the trademark lanterns hanging from chains and trees extending oddly asymmetrical branches. In 1818, however, an earth tremor caused these minarets to partially collapse and they are sadly truncated today.

The volume of the five three-bay aisles in the prayer hall are divided into several levels by an array of 260 columns in pairs, the gaps between them affording various perspectives. If this disposition seems to take its cue from ideas similar to those that govern the design of the first phase of the Quwwat al-Islām in Delhi, in Ahmedabad the exploration of all three dimensions is decidedly more subtle and complex. This is most clearly the case with the tiers in front of the central archway in the prayer hall that make way for a space that—in the manner of a rotunda—rises as if by the power of inspiration up the entire height of the building to terminate in a dome. In spite of its rather rotund appearance and its floret finial, the dome derives from the

Above and facing page. View of the court and prayer hall, Jama' Masjid, Ahmedabad, India, 1423.

traditional processes used in Hindu temples with overhanging stacks of flagstones carved with a concentric pattern. The repertoire of the carvings, in particular on the minarets and in the small niches to either side of them, is inspired by the manner of the non-Muslim artists then working on religious sites in the region.

The successors of Ahmed I

From 1442 to 1451, Muhammad, the son of Ahmed I, took over at the head of the country, being succeeded by a son, Qutb al-Dīn, who ruled from 1451 to 1458. Both these sovereigns followed in the footsteps of the efforts of the city's founder, adding further to the network of monuments embellishing the capital and its near outskirts.

The funerary complex of Ahmed I

The immediate environment of the mausoleum of Ahmed I, who died in 1442, is prestigious indeed, since it stands a few meters from the mosque's eastern wall. It rehearses once more the square plan frequent for this type of monument, but adorns it with ample openings to each of its four sides, where a portico with pillars finesses the transition into the central space housing the cenotaphs of Ahmed I, his son, and grandson. The porticoes themselves are flanked by square rooms on the corners, intelligently combining the need for ease of circulation to the core of the building with the privacy visitors demanded. Finally, the work is capped by a central dome with four smaller cupolas on the corners.

A distance of some thousand feet (300 meters) separates the *qibla* wall of the mosque from the easternmost limit of the compound in which the buildings of the funerary complex stand. In the axis of the first two buildings—today on other side of a street—rises the Rani-ka-Hujra (literally, "apartments of the Rani"). It presents the form of vast square enclosure surrounded by a cruciform portico that confers solemnity on the open-air terrace containing the tombs of the royal wives.

The emotional vibrancy of the tomb enceinte has long since faded, and can only be regained through a conservation policy more energetic than that in use today.

The complex of Sheikh Ahmed Khattri "Ganj Bakhsh," Sarkhej
In 1446, during the reign of Muhammad Shāh, a hermit by the name of Sheikh Ahmed Khattri, the subject of great devotion and wielding considerable influence, died. The sultan resolved to mark his passing with a tribute worthy of the saintly gentleman's renown and erected in his honor a funerary complex at Sarkhej, a few miles southwest of Ahmedabad. The planned project included the siting, in the immediate vicinity of a large stepped tank (*kund*), of both a mausoleum and a mosque. The sultan's ambition was such that he did not live to see the work completed, but nonetheless it was here that later princes of the ruling dynasty chose in their turn to be entombed. Impressive in its rigor, the mosque occupies a simple and sober plan within a perimeter of 255 by 157 feet (78 by 48 meters), while the mausoleum, built on a square base 105 feet (32 meters) down the side, benefits from a carefully calculated play of light and shade by means of a screen-like structure that envelops a funerary hall borne on twelve columns. Around the lake a further group of buildings was erected, including a ravishing "summer palace."

Below. The royal mausoleum towering over the *kund* (pool), Sarkhej, India, mid-fifteenth century.

Facing page. The Saharwali Masjid, Champaner, India, late fifteenth century.

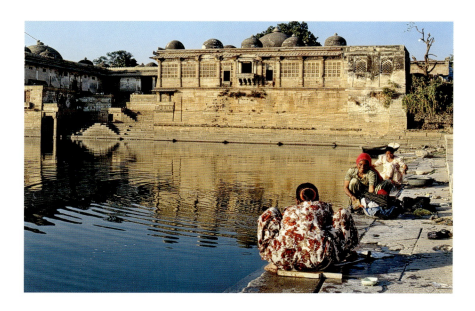

The reign of Mahmūd Beghada (1458–1511)

It was during the fifty-three-year rule of Mahmūd Beghada that the sultanate of Gujarāt reached its zenith. Setting up new monuments, the monarch continued the urban development of Ahmedabad, but more crucially, in 1485 he founded the town of Champaner, electing it as his capital, which it remained until being ransacked by the Mughal Humāyūn in 1536. The buildings of the period exemplify the full maturity of the architectural style of the sultanate, echoing the might of a state that for a time had gained the upper hand over the majority of its neighbors.

Champaner

The site chosen by Sultan Mahmūd for his future capital is located twenty-nine miles (forty-seven kilometers) northeast of Baroda. Tending to the exuberant and opulent, the city, safe behind its crown of ramparts, lies at the foot of a hill dominating the vestiges of an ancient Rājput fortress and a sanctuary.

Abutting the wall encircling the city, the small Saharwali Mosque dispenses with a courtyard. The prayer hall opens through a porch bolstered on either side by richly carved engaged minarets, while down the *qibla* wall there stretches a row of five mihrabs embellished with finely worked stone decoration. High up on the elevation, this rhythm is echoed by an enfilade of five domes, like so many clarion calls to glory.

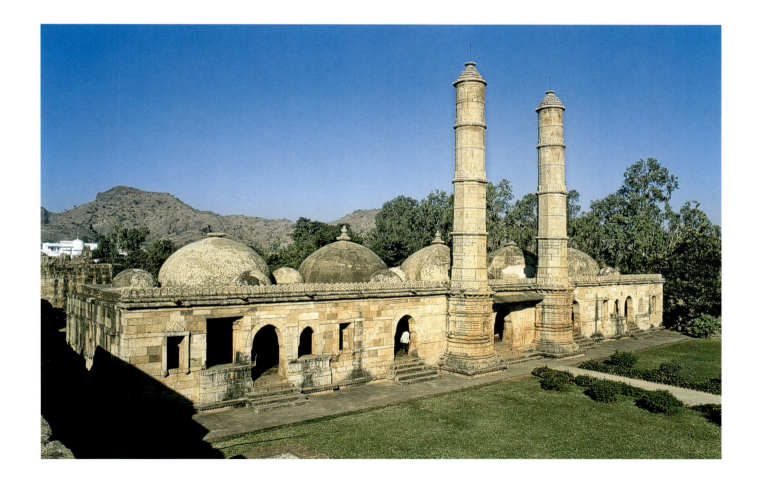

Above. The monumental entrance to the Jama' Masjid, Champaner, India, late fifteenth century.

At the other end of the city, the Jama' Masjid is remarkable for the sheer profusion of its attractions. The court of this masterpiece is reached through an elevated gate adorned with *jalis* screens delicately perforated with a vegetal and geometrical checkerboard pattern through which one glimpses the great drum flanked by two *chhatris* and a since vanished dome. The court front to the prayer hall opens in the center through a large archway framed by two minarets and overarched by a balcony. The volume of the hall is complicated, since two galleries of superposed columns supporting a central cupola extend within over several levels. Taken as a whole, this procedure increases the sense of space of the edifice through the generous role it allots to zones of diffracted light, reminiscent of the architectural conception of the Jain temples of Ranakpur that are contemporary with this mosque. The space in that part of the prayer hall to the right reserved for women seems as it were discreetly filtered through the finely chiseled *jalis*.

The writings of various visitors testifying to their admiration for this sumptuous ensemble of palaces and gardens that Mahmūd chose to make his principal residence and where he held court only deepen our regret that today the site has been reduced to little more than a heap of ruins.[12] One chronicle of the time records that "the princes possessed gardens teeming with flowers of all colors and fruits of all kinds," claiming in addition that an Iranian from Khorāsān "built a beautiful garden around a central tank, with jets water of various kinds and artificial cascades. . . . Never had such a garden been seen in Gujarāt."[13]

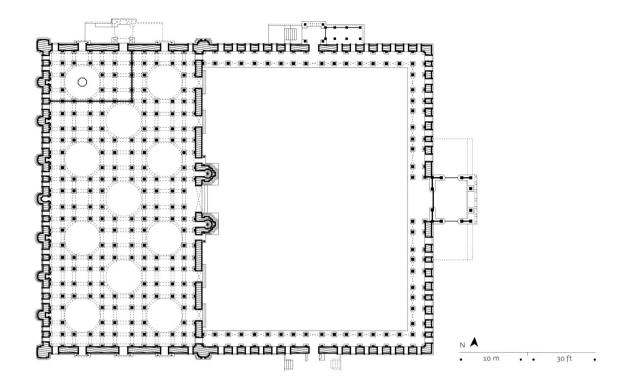

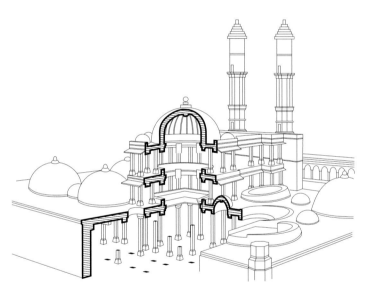

Facing and above. Plan and axonometric view of the Jama' Masjid, Champaner (after J. Hoag).

The task of reconstituting the appearance of the gardens as they then appeared is, however, an uncertain one. Lake Kankaria, south of Ahmedabad, certainly provides an example of a perfectly circular artificial pond, created in the mid-fifteenth century to adorn the royal residence located on a small island in the middle. This, however, can only give a hint as to the plantings and embellishments in palatial complexes; profoundly altered in the time of the Mughal Jahāngīr, the site today houses a zoo, an ornithological park, and various other structures that make it impossible to accurately picture the original design.

Above and facing page. The Jama' Masjid, Champaner, late fifteenth century. Decoration on the pillars in the entrance to the prayer hall. Views of the central cupola in the prayer hall and towards the mihrab.

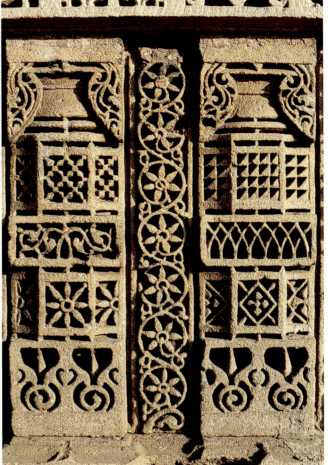

Above. Decoration on the pillars in the mosque and mausoleum of Dada Hari, Ahmedabad, India, late fifteenth century.

Facing page. The Wāv (well-tank with steps) of Dada Hari, Asarwa district, Ahmedabad, India, late fifteenth century.

The monuments of Ahmedabad

The magnificence in evidence at Champaner did not, however, mean that Sultan Mahmūd neglected the demands and prestige of his old capital.

The Wāv of Dada Hari

Built in the late fifteenth century, the spectacular reservoir (or *wāv*) of Dada Hari reemploys the kinds of architectural forms and techniques of water collection and conservation that had been mastered long before the Muslim conquest. In any event, the point in such a piece of civil engineering is, of course, less to make show of some novel style than to ensure a steady supply of healthy water to what was a rapidly growing agglomeration. Be that as it may, the galleries in four tiers supported on columns that lead to an octagonal well through which one reaches the water's edge are singularly impressive and undeniably bear the stamp of majesty. The water is just as accessible from the top of the well as down the flights of steps that descend by landings through shady arcades to the surface of the tank where the fresh air fostered a convivial mood among the townsfolk. The mausoleum and mosque contiguous to the tank are remarkable for the quality of their decoration.

Below. The mosque and mausoleum of Dada Hari, Ahmedabad, late fifteenth century.

Facing page. The Rani Sipri mausoleum, Ahmedabad, 1514.

The complex of Rani Sipri (1514)
Shortly after her death in 1514, the honor of a funerary complex was bestowed on Rani Sipri, Sultan Mahmūd Beghada's widow, which incorporates a mosque and a mausoleum. The density of Ahmedabad's urban fabric at the time made it in practice impossible to clear a sizable plot from among the gigantic monuments in the city center, leading to the construction of buildings of much reduced dimensions compared to earlier periods. The mosque and mausoleum here thus face one another to either side of a tiny courtyard. On the street side, the mosque greets visitors with an elegant double balcony that serves as a sort of prelude to the two bays of the prayer hall; on the courtyard side, the façade standing between two slender and graceful, but elaborately ornamented, false minarets is further enhanced by a portico.

A pendant to the mosque, the square-plan tomb sits behind a protective screen of *jalis* arranged in a chessboard pattern that does nothing to dissipate the mystery of a funerary hall borne on twelve columns. The curved elevation of the cupola terminates the work in a soft sweep, its traditional concentric entablatures further developed into an intricate carved decoration within the dome. The extreme delicacy and distinction that characterize the design and execution of this jewel-like monument are a prime example of the extraordinary refinement that must have prevailed in Gujarāt as the sun gradually set on the glories of the sultanate.

Above and facing page. Carved work in the Rani Sipri complex, Ahmedabad, 1514. Base of a pillar and panel with the "tree of life."

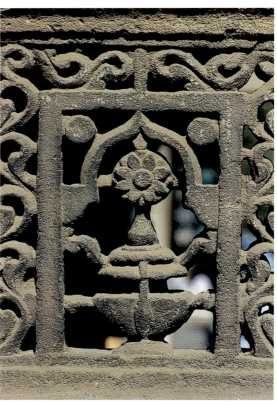

Above. Balcony in the prayer hall, Rani Rupmati Mosque.
Facing page, top. Decoration, Rani Rupmati Mosque, Ahmedabad, c. 1440.
Bottom left. *Jali* screen, Rani Rupmati Mosque.
Bottom right. Detail of a *jali*, mosque of Dastur Khān, Ahmedabad, 1486.

The late architecture of a declining sultanate

Mahmūd Beghada's successors too built tirelessly in Ahmedabad and Champaner, occasionally in a taste some describe as "decadent."

The mausoleum of the Nagina Masjid
The mausoleum of the Nagina Masjid was built in about 1525 and exemplifies the increasingly marked tendency to blend tried-and-tested techniques and decorative idioms with more novel forms. The building adopts a square plan in the form of a tetrapylon. The four arches are flanked by blind arches that seem to ricochet from façade to façade, and are topped by imposing consoles which probably supported an awning and a parapet, while the vestiges of a drum are the only evidence of the cupola that once vaulted the building. The most striking decorative detail, however, is located on the level of the jambs of the four doorways: carvings of great originality present variations on the theme of the plant—as much as in twisting rinceaux as in snaking creepers—all with a freedom of line that recurs only a few decades later, at the Sidi Sayyid Mosque in Ahmedabad.

The Sidi Sayyid Mosque
The Sidi Sayyid Mosque, built in 1572, is an astonishing example of architecture at the end of the sultanate. The plan is very simple, with the prayer hall leading to a court terrace through five archways; these arches do not extend into vaults and the roofing is articulated around corbelled domes that exploit the effect of the squinches in the corners. With windows visible from the outside, the *qibla* wall is worthy of especial attention. To either side of the mihrab, the openwork stone *jalis* were carved with singular freedom of line into plant motifs, such the "tree of life" with uneven branches framed by other species including palm trees. The whole composition is wonderfully balanced and is specially remarkable for its consummate liberty of execution—not only is it a prime stop on sightseeing tours in the city today, but reproductions of the panel often crop up in tourist haunts throughout the country.

The architecture of Gujarāt: a highly individual synthesis in the Indian world

Due to contacts built up over the centuries with the cradles of Islam through commercial links that proved of particular benefit to its appearance on its seaward side, Gujarāt was always likely to be one of the regions of the subcontinent most receptive to a type of creativity motivated by a desire to embody in art the identity of the ruling power and fuelled by the capacity of its populations to embrace a range of influences so as to forge an original cultural personality.

Detail on a claustra on the *qibla* wall,
Sidi Sayyid Mosque, Ahmedabad, 1572.

By establishing the area as a political entity, the sultanate was thus instrumental in setting in motion both these motors of culture and leading to the growth of an architecture affirming specific characteristics. If other territories in the Indian world certainly combined techniques or decorative idioms earlier than or parallel to those of Islam with the principles of construction and ornamentation promoted by reigning Muslim princes, in general these were in the last analysis more in the way of hybrids or rather haphazard overlaps. In the best case scenario and at the end of a certain amount of strain, a harmonious ensemble might eventually come out of such juxtapositions.

The openness to dialogue that economic conditions in Gujarāt had rendered imperative greatly escalated the cultural interpenetration spawned by the durable implantation of Islam in Indian societies. Rather than a fusion of styles and techniques—a term that invariably implies the partial loss of identity of at least one of the original protagonists—what is met with here is a process closer to authentic symbiosis. Thus, each cultural sphere (Islamic or otherwise) benefitted from the prosperity of the sultanate to affirm its own genius; artists and craftsmen would work indifferently and alternately on sites of mosques, Jain temples, and Hindu buildings, shuttling their expertise and experience from one to the other.

The originality of the style spawned by these principles was rooted in receptivity, generosity, and disinterested respect for the creative genius of one's neighbors that the "symbiosis" might transcend but never wholly overwhelm or undermine. Arguably this goes some way to explaining why Gujarati architecture exerted such an influence not only on monuments of nearby kingdoms, such as Khāndesh and Mālwa, but also on certain Mughal achievements—in particular during the reign of Akbar under whose aegis the sultanate was to be definitively attached to the government of Delhi.

The Sharqī of Jaunpur (1394–1479)

Following his campaigns in Bengal, Fīrūz Shāh Tughluq founded the city of Jaunpur, not far from Benares, in 1359. The city was an outpost on an eastern border that was always hard to secure, and, in this role, it represented an important link in governmental chain. As early as the end of the fourteenth century, however, a slave eunuch belonging to Mahmūd Shāh II Tughluq, Malik Sarwar, sallied forth to conquer Oudh. Promptly taking advantage of the spectacular decline of the Delhi sultanate during this period, he liberated the region from the central power and declared independence, proclaiming himself Malik al-Sharq ("king of the East"). With clearly dynastic intention, logically enough this was the title also chosen by his successors. The kingdom then expanded with the annexation of the Hindu cities of Kannauj, Ayodhya, and Bahraich, thereby placing the territorial integrity of the fledgling sultanate on a more stable footing. Mubārak Shāh, the adoptive son of the founder of the state and an African slave of Abyssinian origin, remained at the country's helm from 1399 to 1402, before his brother Ibrāhīm took over for a long reign that came to an end in 1440; it was his reign that saw the most glorious phase of the line. By the time Husayn Shāh, the last Sharqī sultan, was directing the state (from 1458), the sultanate's was already embarked on a steep decline, consummated in 1479 by the annexation of the region by the Lodī of Delhi.

It remains the case that the short-lived political limelight enjoyed by the Sharqī of Jaunpur was marked by a spectacular acceleration in architectural creativity, resulting in buildings implementing some truly extraordinary and unprecedented forms.[14] It is primarily the mosques of Jaunpur, the capital, that today testify to the dynamism that percolated down into other artistic disciplines: it may be assumed that the great Korans written in Bihārī script, a specialty of the sultanate period, in fact come from Jaunpur.[15]

The Atalā Masjid (1408)

The name of this mosque comes from a temple dedicated to Atalā Devi that previously stood on the very site selected for the new place of worship. Founded by Ibrāhīm Shāh, the building was enriched by much recycled material from its ancient Hindu predecessor, specifically the pillars now supporting the galleries; it already displays the original characteristics that are the particular trademarks of the Jaunpur style.

A square courtyard 177 feet (54 meters) along the side is ensconced among three porticoes over two levels and three bays deep; the arrangement of arches in each of these elevations is interrupted in the center by a soaring porch or avant-corps with dome; the north and south façades are characterized primarily by the balanced forces generated by this confrontation of rhythms. On the exterior, the rows of cells for accommodating travelers inserted round the porticoes and corresponding to the enigmatic volumes that frame the court also explore the interplay between light and shade.

The fourth side is dedicated to the prayer hall, whose front is emblazoned with a great *iwan* framed by others of more modest proportions and linked by a gallery. The overall disposition exhibits a family resemblance with the organization based on

The prayer hall of the Atalā Masjid, Jaunpur, India, 1408.

Above and facing page. Detail of carved ornaments and view of one of the main gates to the Atalā Masjid, Jaunpur, India), 1408.

courtyards with four *iwans* found in Persian mosques, but this relationship should not obscure the undeniable originality of the forms used here. One seeks in vain for the vertical zest of a minaret here: the central *iwan* is instead encased between the projecting and inclined planes of two massive and impressively majestic avant-corps reminiscent of the pylons in Egyptian temples. The ogee profile of the *iwan* archway is bordered by a trefoil frieze that refers, like the inclined planes, to certain features of Tughluq architecture. With its doorway topped by a lunette and its three rows of arcades, the central *iwan* performs the office of a screen in front of a cupola on squinches of almost the same height as the main arch, conferring a mystical sense of ascension on the hall that extends in front of the mihrab. Both secondary *iwans* are also topped by smaller domes, like timeless echoes of some cosmic glory.

While the material came to some extent from preexistent Hindu constructions, the decorative vocabulary is typically Indo-Muslim. Thus, rosettes and lotus buds inspired by the "indigenous" storehouse are joined by trails, bifid palmettes, cusped arcades, and interlaced geometrical patterns, while Arabic epigraphy—that indisputable signature of an aesthetic anchored in the heart of Islamic culture—runs riot over the decoration.

The Lāl Darwāza Masjid (c. 1450)
This edifice was originally integrated within a group of buildings financed by Bibi Raja, wife of Mahmūd Shāh who reigned from 1436 to 1458. It is the only one to have escaped from the destruction meted out on the other elements of the monumental complex, and in particular the palace that constituted its other main focus. Overall, the mosque is arranged following the principles that governed the conception of the Atalā Masjid. Three sides of its near perfect square are graced with a curving portico forming two aisles and connect imposing, centrally placed gateways, while the fourth side is structured around the prayer hall. The central *iwan* is certainly less lofty than in the preceding example, but the volume is harmoniously inserted between the compact, hieratic masses of two avant-corps reminiscent once again of "pylons." The archaic forms of stone columns lead to a prayer hall that, beneath the sturdy volumes of the cupola, gives on to a final room where the mihrab, with its triple arcade adorned with florets, together with the austere lines of the stone *minbar* that flanks it, seem almost crushed by the sheer architectural mass of the environment.

The Friday Mosque (1470)
The Jama' Masjid of Jaunpur, one of the most characteristic buildings in the style of the sultanate when its star was fading, was erected during the reign of Husayn Shāh (1458–79). It marshals the three by-now classic dome-capped monumental gateways around three sides of the courtyard to which they give access, while the wondrous prayer hall stands on the fourth side. The prayer hall features a broad arcade of so-called "Persian" arches and rises up over five tiers, folding out in the manner of a screen. Like a seamless melisma of stone and shadow, each level presents blind niches or galleries in the fashion of a clerestory. The arch itself is embedded between

strongly inclining avant-corps whose mineral solidity underscores the decorative impact of the stonework. The towering façade obscures the dome swelling above the prayer hall in front of the mihrab. Once again there is an astonishing absence of minarets—as if the powerful "pylons" formed by the avant-corps together with the cupolas are sufficient on their own to ensure the Muslim identity in the urban landscape.

Facing page. Prayer hall with mihrab and *minbar*, Lāl Darwāza Masjid, Jaunpur, c. 1450.

Above. Stairway and gallery, Jama' Masjid, Jaunpur, 1470.

Below. Plan of the Jama' Masjid, Jaunpur (after J. Hoag).

Page 178. *Iwan* on the courtyard, Jama' Masjid, Jaunpur.

Page 179. Vestiges of the Jhanjhri Masjid, Jaunpur, early fifteenth century.

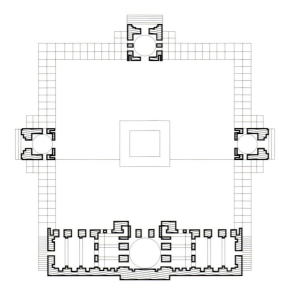

The legacy of the Sharqī of Jaunpur

In keeping with its image as an opportunistic dynasty that owed its power to riding its luck and to the intelligence or cunning of their unlikely leaders, the architecture of the Sharqī of Jaunpur is a cultural sponge that soaked up models furnished by the Indian or Muslim traditions, without, however, ever dissolving into them. Their theatrical monuments are like stage sets, but, while they proclaim the sultanate's pride and newfound freedom loud and clear, they can just as well plumb the depths of the soul. As if on the fringes of their era—and without ever imposing themselves as references in their historical environment—their value lies in occasional outbursts of energy and originality in what can be a standardized mental universe. While they were scarcely acknowledged by their contemporaries or their immediate successors, their influence was perhaps more enduring on the foreigners who encountered them several centuries later.

Epigraphy and openwork screens (*jali*), Jhanjhri Masjid, Jaunpur, early fifteenth century.

Facing page. The sultan of Mālwa observes the preparation of confectionary. Illustration from a treatise on cooking (*Ne'mat-nāma*), Māndu, c. 1495–1505. India Office Library, London, Persian Ms.149, f. 83.

The Sultanate of Mālwa (1401–1531)

For a protracted period, the province of Mālwa chaffed at a Muslim authority that was imposed on it only late in the day, following interminable and energy-sapping conflicts against the Rājput princes of Chitor and Ujjain. Following the victory of the army he sent to subject the region in 1305, ʿAlā al-Dīn Khaljī delegated his prerogatives to a governor who thus effectively became the representative of the sultan of Delhi in the area. Following the sack of the city by Timur, and while Dilāwar Khān Ghaurī occupied the governorship of Mālwa, Sultan Mahmūd Shāh II scurried off to the town where he sought refuge. In 1399 the sovereign finally returned to his devastated capital, but in a state sufficiently weakened for Dilāwar Khān to proclaim the independence of his stronghold two years later, and thus to found the first line of sultans of Mālwa, the Ghaurī. When he died in 1405, he was succeeded by his son, Hushang, who reigned until 1435. The procrastination which attended the succession of that prince, however, paved the way for a palace revolution at the end of which power fell into the lap of a onetime grand vizier, Mahmūd Khaljī, whose reign (1436–69) inaugurated in turn a dynasty bearing his name that remained at the helm of the province until it was overrun by the sultans of Gujarāt in 1531.

On several occasions, but without success, the sultans of Mālwa made a push to extend their territory towards Orissa; such saber-rattling opposed them to their Muslim neighbors—the Sharqīs of Jaunpur, the Bahmanids, and the sultans of Gujarāt—against whom they did not hesitate to forge sometimes incompatible alliances with Hindu princes. Be that as it may, the cultural life of the sultanate was rich and the stronghold of Māndu, the kingdom's capital, hides some architectural jewels behind its impressive enceinte. The imprint of its princes also affected the urban landscape of Chanderi and other smaller localities in the area, with monuments that reflect the style they promoted.

The Ghaurī in power (1401–36)

The dynasty first settled in Dhār, the sultanate's earliest capital. The constructions erected there display no great architectural ambitions and, moreover, their relics have failed to resist the ravages of time. They form a notable contrast with the joyous exuberance that courses through the buildings of Māndu, where Hushang transferred his power center after the death of Dilāwar Khān in 1405. The new capital was even called Shādiabad ("city of joy"). The new sovereign quickly ordered works to begin on a Friday mosque, as well as on his own mausoleum, but on his demise in 1435 building ceased. Two of his sons in turn then strove vainly to take up the reins of the state, but were forced to yield to the future sultan, Mahmūd Khaljī.

Above. View towards the *qibla* wall, mosque of Dilāwar Khān, Māndu, India, 1405.

Facing page. The prayer hall in the mosque of Malik Moghith, Māndu, 1432.

The mosque of Dilāwar Khān (1405)
The first Friday mosque in Māndu, where it is the oldest Islamic monument, bears the name of its founder and can be dated from an inscription. It embodies the seizure by a non-Hindu power of the ancient stronghold of Mandapadurga, whose fortress—complete with ramparts thirty or so miles long—is rightly considered one of the most imposing in the whole subcontinent. The building is of generous proportions, but its overall structure impresses neither by decorative refinement nor by any especial taste for architectural novelty. One finds a portico dividing on three sides a vast courtyard classically shut off by a prayer hall 105 feet (32 meters) long and 33 feet (10 meters) deep. Stone pillars in the local style—some reused and others specifically hewn for the building—support a space over four bays. The elevation remains a modest affair. Above and beyond its emblematic location, the Islamic character of the construction is declared only by the *qibla* wall, which features an ample central mihrab flanked by three secondary recesses to either side. The building lacks the minaret that might have made it a landmark in the urban fabric, but a staircase allows easy access to the roof from which the call to prayer was probably made, in imitation of a tradition dating back to the house of the Prophet in Medina.

The mosque of Malik Moghith (1432)
An inscription above the entrance attests to the fact that the building was founded in 1432; it bears the name of the father of Mahmūd Khaljī and is organized around a square courtyard fringed by galleries. Its style forms a link between the mosque of Dilāwar Khān, still rooted in indigenous artistic references, and monuments from the apogee of the sultanate built during the second half of the fifteenth century where novelty is the rule. The entryway with its columns standing proud ready to support a since collapsed dome is reached up a sprightly flight of steps. The base of the dome is still adorned with panels of pink sandstone encrusted with turquoise tiling that unfurl in geometrical interlacing that clearly refers to the turquoise stars that decorate brick constructions on the Iranian plateau—although the structural schemas and choice of building materials are in no way related to such references.

    The prayer hall plunges into four bays delimited by columns in an amalgamation of a pared-down local style with octagonal voids that interrupt the regular ordonnance and are spanned by arcades supporting three cupolas that serve to underwrite the unmistakably Islamic "lineage" of the monument. The niche-shaped turquoise tiles on the principal mihrab, as well as on its counterparts to either side, add a welcome touch of color to the *qibla* wall.

Above and facing page. The Jama' Masjid (Friday Mosque), Māndu, c. 1440. View towards the main mihrab and the women's gallery (*zenāna*).

The Friday Mosque and the mausoleum of Hushang
The initiative for constructing this complex combining a new mosque with a mausoleum intended to house his remains is attributed to Sultan Hushang himself, but it was completed under Mahmūd Khaljī. The association of these two monuments makes the site one of the most majestic in Māndu. The mosque, supported on an earthwork almost 16 feet (5 meters) high, stands on a quadrilateral with sides 320 feet (97.5 meters) long. The façade projects into an advanced entryway that greets visitors with a square hall topped by a dome. The base of the drum is decorated with bas-relief "sugar loaf" crenels; the interstices are encrusted with plaques of turquoise tiling. On the interior, the curved elevation of the dome volume springs from a narrow band of blue tiles in the shape of stars and rhombuses that parade above the bays. In front of the entrance door, a second opening leads to the courtyard of the mosque, itself the size of an agora and entirely enclosed by galleries pierced with arcades.

The prayer hall opens through eleven arches of the same dimensions that extend into a space five bays deep, a unity of proportions that confers a stately rhythm on the ensemble. Each group of four pillars is arranged into a square capped by a small dome. In front of the mihrab, the rhythm of the colonnades is interrupted to allow for the space called the *maqsura*, which is surmounted by a larger cupola on plain squinches. On either side, two cupolas of the same dimensions punctuate spaces over two levels: the upper reaches were probably reserved for female worshipers. For its part, the *qibla* wall accommodates a large mihrab whose black stone recess is set off by "sugar loaf" crenels carved out of pink and golden rock, fringed, like their harbingers on the entrance pavilion, with turquoise tiles. To the right of the mihrab, a superb stone *minbar* is crowned by a *chhatri* supported on S-shaped consoles in a discreet allusion to temple architecture. The *qibla* wall also forms the junction between the mosque and the precinct of the mausoleum of Hushang.

The funerary enclosure, however, disposes of an independent access with an entryway whose sober elegance is further enhanced by a stairway of six steps. This gives on to a court of the same dimensions as that of the mosque whose mystical presence is manifested by the profile of the mihrab emerging in the center of the wall. A portico defines a hypostyle prayer hall occupying the entire width of the western wall. Located on a square terrace of ninety-eight feet (thirty meters) down the side and served by a further flight of steps, the funerary monument stands in the center of the courtyard. The area is paved in a white marble, which also lines the entire visible surface, internal and external, of the mausoleum, its grandiose purity underlining the simple square plan of the building topped by a large central cupola around which gather four smaller domes.

The clean lines of the mausoleum, allied to the geometrical and chromatic unity of the volumes that structure it, have often aroused admiration, particularly on the part of the architects of the Tāj Mahal who even left some graffiti recording their visit on a doorjamb in the funerary hall.[16] This hall is defined by a forty-nine-foot (fifteen-meter) square, in the center of which is the stepped cenotaph of Sultan Hushang, flanked by several other tombs. The square space rises to more than twenty-nine feet (nine meters) before squinches convert it into an octagon that higher up further divides into a sixteen-sided shape supporting the drum of the dome. A frieze of small arched niches encloses the cobalt blue tiles at the base of the drum, adding a touch of bright but deep color to the mass of marble.

Facing page. The court in the Jama' Masjid (Friday Mosque), Māndu, with the domes of the prayer hall.

Below. Mausoleum of Hushang, clad entirely in while marble, Māndu, mid-fifteenth century.

The Khaljī sovereigns (1436–1531)

Even though, as has been seen, Mahmūd Khaljī grabbed the throne in a coup d'état, the reign thus inaugurated proved a prestigious era for the sultanate, attended by many victorious military campaigns and marked by a large number of brilliant pieces of architecture.

By the time his son Ghiyāth al-Dīn took power in 1469 for a lengthy reign (until 1500), peaceful prosperity was the rule—quite unlike the years of turmoil his embattled father had to face—to the point that historians have insisted on his reputation for disposing of a veritable army of servants. This period of plenty came to an abrupt end when Ghiyāth al-Dīn's son, Nāsir Shāh, had him assassinated to smooth his path to the supreme function which, however, this quarrelsome sultan was to exercise for only eleven years before being succeeded in his turn by Mahmūd II in 1511. It thus fell to the two decades of power under this last prince to watch over the end of the independent sultanate and its seizure by Gujarāt in 1531.

The architectural imprint the Khaljī dynasty was to bequeath to the Indian world was inaugurated by the manner in which it concluded the complex commenced by Hushang. Its sites then became more and more extensive, in keeping with the ambitions of a dynasty that—if judged by the political, economic, and military successes of its rulers—appear justified. This accounts for the splendid palatial complex of the Jahāz Mahal in Māndu, while other localities of lesser importance were adorned with constructions that rehearse or refine the salient stylistic features of the sultanate, at Chanderi, Sadalpur, and Kalyadeh, in particular.

The mausoleum of the Khaljī
The vast staircase to this mausoleum, also known as the Ashrafi Mahal, stands opposite another bold flight of steps leading to the entryway of the Great Mosque across the street; the two accesses thus vie for the visitors' attention, filling them with anticipation for the grandeur of the sites behind them. This strange mausoleum, now in a very ruined state, seems, according to the chronicle of Mahmūd Khaljī, to have been intended initially to function as a madrassa, so that the purpose of the building must have been modified at a later stage. The central space was probably

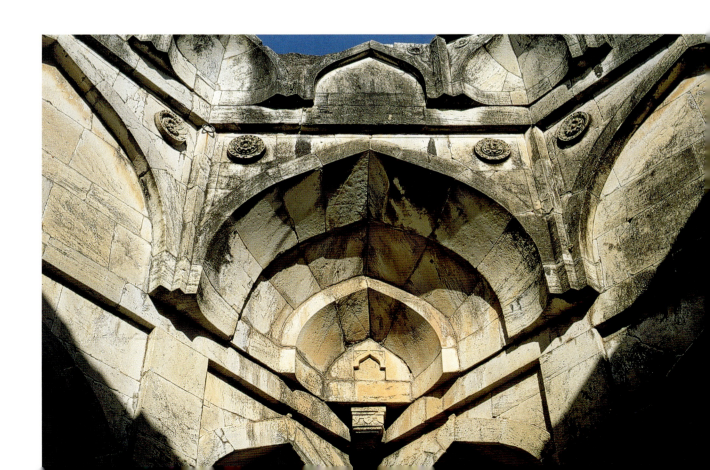

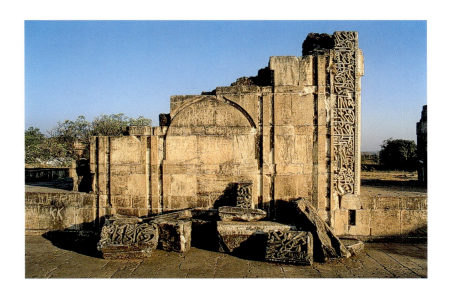

Facing page and above. The Khaljī Mausoleum, or Ashrafi Mahal, Māndu, mid-fifteenth century; squinch in the vestibule and vestiges of the funerary hall.

filled in and embanked to render it appropriate for its new function as a base for the subsequently erected mausoleum. Enthroned in the middle of the vast square that must have originally served as the madrassa proper, the mausoleum betrays the characteristics of its former vocation in ground-floor galleries whose cells seem to fulfill no discernable role in a funerary context.

The access stairs lead to a lofty gate from whence the dome has since vanished, but which still boasts a marble facing of astonishing opulence. At the center of the terrace, the square-plan funerary hall is ruggedly constructed in rubblework faced with marble and dressed with pink and yellow sandstone adorned with fillets in black stone. The ensemble would have further amazed us with a great dome of which only scant fragments survive, but whose vastness spoke volumes of the grandeur of the three Khaljī princes buried here in vaults signaled by gravestones. Historiographers of the time recorded the wealth of refinements that make the work so exceptional:

> Artisans and artists from Khorāsān and Hindustān assembled in the capital and in little time set to work. They did not spare any ornamentation. The four walls were adorned with designs in coloured stones—carnelian, jade, onyx, alabaster, black marble and still others. Persian artists made inscriptions of great beauty on the doors, on the walls and on the ceiling in *thuluth* and *muhaqqaq* characters with glazed tiles.[17]

Nothing remains of the ceramic decorations, but in places a handful of fragments of inscriptions inlayed in stone do hang on. On one of the rare stretches of wall still standing can be read an epigraph dating to 1605 stating how it was the Mughal Akbar who had the building restored. Finally, the site was dominated by a large tower at a corner that was inspired by the "minaret" and named at the time the "standard of Islam," although nothing more than the first few steps of the staircase remain visible at terrace level. The structure had not yet caved in when Jahāngīr staying in Māndu described it as a tower over seven floors with 171 steps leading to one chamber per level.[18]

The royal enclave and the Jahāz Mahal
One piece of architecture in Māndu amazes with its dreamlike, otherworldly quality: the palace complex, whose first foundation, according to the chronicles, dates to 1440 and was the work of Mahmūd Khaljī. The main building in this mirage-like reverie that juxtaposes palace and pavilions with the aquatic fantasy is today known as the Jahāz Mahal ("boat palace"), because of its long, languid profile that seems to hover between two large pools, the Kapur Talao to the east and the Munj Talao to the west. A text of the time demonstrates the prestige this peculiarly designed construction already possessed at the time:

> At the beginning of February in the year 1440, the king ordered the construction of the golden palace; from the depths of the basin named Munj-Talao, he erected—in stone cemented with mortar—pillars and tall arcades above which a flat roof was built. Artists from India and the Khorāsān joined the effort; this building of Shādiabad ["city of joy"] is such that it was called the "garden of India"; it can be compared with a second paradise.[19]

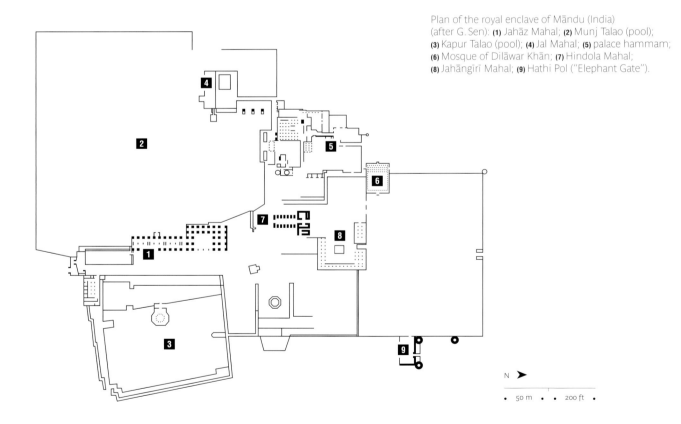

Plan of the royal enclave of Māndu (India) (after G. Sen): **(1)** Jahāz Mahal; **(2)** Munj Talao (pool); **(3)** Kapur Talao (pool); **(4)** Jal Mahal; **(5)** palace hammam; **(6)** Mosque of Dilāwar Khān; **(7)** Hindola Mahal; **(8)** Jahāngīrī Mahal; **(9)** Hathi Pol ("Elephant Gate").

Graced by the curves of "Persian" arches that impart a gentle and stately rhythm, the stone façade is scaled by a monumental staircase offering direct, if steep, access to the terrace. This is though probably a subsequent addition, arguably on the initiative of the Mughal Jahāngīr, who during his reign resided for seven months in Māndu, where he threw a marvelous festival he describes in his memoirs.[20] The variety in the stone employed exploits polychrome effects touched off by shimmering ceramic panel decorations that are in all probability the source of the name "golden palace," although only scattered fragments have survived.[21] The interior of the palace extends down a long gallery open though arcades down two sides. One end continues in liquid form reflected in a pool that spreads out in the shape of double floret, the perimeter being worked here and there into steps that offer an irresistible invitation to partake of the refreshing waters.

On both sides at the horizon, the terrace over the gallery bisects the light-footed geometry of two pavilions, each topped by a dome framed by two pyramidal roofs; the originality of this type of roofing is typical of Mālwa.

Opposite widthwise and to the center of the terrace, the delicate punctuation of a balcony and a square tower culminating in a dome stand tall over the façade. A small channel in the cornice at the eaves into which this hovering universe dissolves runs the length of the building, losing itself in flowing spirals and twists and draining into a basin in the shape of a multifoil mandorla. A mechanical system installed on the opposite edge of the terrace was devoted to supplying water to these bizarre pipes. Such runnels also appear at Kalyadeh, Champaner in Gujarāt and, during Akbar's reign, further beautifying the pavilion of Nilkhant in Māndu.

Below left. The Jahāz Mahal ("Boat Palace") viewed from the Jal Mahal, Māndu, 1440.

Below right. The central tower of the Jahāz Mahal.

Above and facing page. Nave in the main hall and exterior view of the Hindola Mahal ("Swing Palace"), Māndu, mid-fifteenth century.

The Hindola Mahal to the north of the Jahāz Mahal—the poetic "swing palace," so dubbed because of its sloping external walls—also allows for perambulations of a subtly enjoyable kind. Within, the arches in the splendid nave twist into an exquisite double ogee that terminates in balconies and galleries accessible up a ramp. Between this pavilion and the Munj Talao stands the Champa Baoli ("tank of the champak [flower]"), which owes its name to the scent of its waters. A two-tier terrace surrounds the building that features a lakefront façade from which a projecting half-octagon pavilion gazes out over a meandering channel. Such undulating forms recur in other palace gardens of Mālwa—in Sadalpur and Kalyadeh in particular.

To the northwest of the Munj Talao extends the Jal Mahal, a rectangular building articulated around a two-aisle gallery on the first level, whence a staircase ascends to a balcony. A footbridge in front of the palace conducts one to a terrace where frolics a basin in the shape of twelve lotus petals. This form reappears most notably in the Mughal gardens at Dholpur and Āgra; unlike their Mughal successors, however, the pools of this period are always equipped with steps to reach the waters below and are deep enough to permit bathing.

Chanderi and other sites in Mālwa
The sometimes unreal beauty of the sites of Māndu is so dazzling that it tends to overshadow the attention its princes lavished on other localities in the sultanate. In this connection, it was incontestably Chanderi that benefited most from the favor in which many sovereigns held the city—and not least Mahmūd Khaljī, who had a number of monuments erected for him there. Now rather deteriorated, the Kushk Mahal ("kiosk palace") affords a striking example in its exceptional proportions for its time; if accounts of it are to be believed, on its square base of 147 feet (45 meters) down the side the elevation was designed to rise to 7 floors—but it may be assumed that it was never actually completed.[22]

The Jama' Masjid of Chanderi was built after the model of its sister at Māndu, specifically reproducing the three-domed prayer hall, but in addition the construction integrated other telling influences, such as the consoles that support the canopy on the façade, patently inspired by Hindu temple architecture. The city also prides itself on two interesting mausoleums built in around 1450, identified as the Madrassa and Shahzadi-ka-Rauza, but even more intriguing is an enormous gate, the Badal Mahal, a resounding prelude to . . . no readily identifiable piece of architecture. After launching two forty-nine-foot (fifteen-meter) flanged "pseudo-minarets" designed to support, at the level of the road, an arched doorway topped by two horizontal registers decorated in flat-relief panels with motifs of niches and florets; its summit is crowned by a lunette delicately carved into an aerial *jali* that seems to hover in the azure sky. Less celebrated than the jewels of Chanderi, but no less inventive and refined, the massive stone ranges of the palaces of Sadalpur and of Kalyadeh lie across riverbeds, so as to benefit from a fresh influx of water when levels allow.[23]

The later monuments
The prosperity of the sultans of Mālwa during the dominion of Mahmūd Khaljī and his son Ghiyāth al-Dīn was not brutally curtailed after the latter's death. Indeed, the creative zest that then prevailed lingers on in constructions that draw their inspiration from the wellsprings of the style elaborated by artists and architects from the highpoint of the sultanate's existence. The captivating charms of this type of architecture were such that even after the fall of the sultanate, the new masters of the region continued to pay it the sincerest form of flattery.

The palace of Bāz Bahādur (1508)
Though explicitly attributed to Bāz Bahādur, this complex is rather significantly earlier than the reign of that prince (who ruled over the land between 1554 and 1561), since an inscription at the entryway ascribes its creation to Nāsir Shāh in 1508. The space is organized around a vast enclosure in which stands a quivering water tank, the Rewa Kund. The waters, duly filtered, supplied a well connected to a dam; they were then brought by machine to an aqueduct—traces of which are still identifiable—which conveyed them to the palace. This is accessed by a staircase of ample dimensions of a majesty that Versailles classicism would not have disavowed. There, a baffle entry serves an initial courtyard; to the north, a second esplanade boasts a string of porticoes running around the vast stepped pool in its center. Lively Persian archways provide a rhythmic impetus to the external northern front and embrace in their stony arms a two-level half-octagonal projection giving on to a quietly contemplative terraced garden. The balanced, supple interpenetration here between the plant and mineral worlds stops time in its tracks and summons up a bewitchingly simple and subtle harmony of forms and proportions.

The pavilion of Nilkhant
The description "blue gorge" given to this small pink sandstone pavilion comes from a moniker of Shiva—a telltale sign that prior to Muslim domination the place was once probably dedicated to the worship of that god. No remains confirm this hypothesis, however, and regrettably the building has been re-consecrated as a Hindu temple. The construction is limited to a simple *iwan* dominating a terrace and probably dating to the Mughal conquest of the region, as several inscriptions imply a date in the reign of Akbar. As shown by the absence of dwellings such, the place seems to have been designed so that visitors are able to contemplate for a moment the valley landscape lying at their feet. In the monsoon period, a waterfall shoots across the building, descending down a spiraling channel and collecting in a tank further down on the terrace. This water feature is clearly inspired by works from the sultanate period; indeed its emotional impact derives substantially from how its intimacy pays gracious homage to past constructions of the type.

Above. The palace of Bāz Bahādur, Māndu, built in 1508 under Nāsir Shāh.

The legacy of the sultanate of Mālwa

Perhaps it was to Mālwa's benefit that it was among the last of the larger sultanates to throw off the shackles of Delhi: it could thus draw on the riches of the cultures then asserting their identity in states nearby and even beyond the borders of the subcontinent, and thereby profit from their innovations, imbibing their creativity to build masterpieces of its own. The sultanate thus constituted a melting pot where various stylistic fusions reached maturity, as exemplified in the architecture built by its princes. Their legacy served both as a milestone and a springboard, not only for artists of the time, but also—a less frequent phenomenon—for their successors who were to further exalt the identity and universality of the Indian world in the splendor of Mughal architecture. Much more than a lucky coming together of local technical and decorative traditions with contributions from the Iranian, Arab, and Central Asian worlds, here both construction processes and ornamental idioms are imbued with a specifically Indian personality. By using polychrome stone and ceramic tilework, and deploying a careful amalgam of cultural references, and especially by establishing the conditions for a dialogue—satisfying to the imagination as much as to the mind—between stone, plant, and water within the enclosed and perfectible world of the garden as microcosm, the artists of Mālwa and their patrons sowed the seeds for the emergence of a genuinely Islamic India open to its environment, receptive to homegrown thought, and totally assured of its legitimacy and might.

THE GREAT MUGHALS AND THEIR HEIRS

Facing page. The Great Mosque, Fatehpur Sīkri, India, built from 1571.

Pages 198–199. The palatial enceinte, Fatehpur Sīkri; in the foreground, the Divān-e Khās; in the background, the Pānch Mahal.

Pages 200–201. Detail of the incrustations on the gate to the mausoleum of Akbar, Sikandra, near Āgra, India, c. 1611.

Pages 202–203. One of the screens (*jali*) in the mausoleum of Salīm Chishti, Fatehpur Sīkri, early seventeenth century.

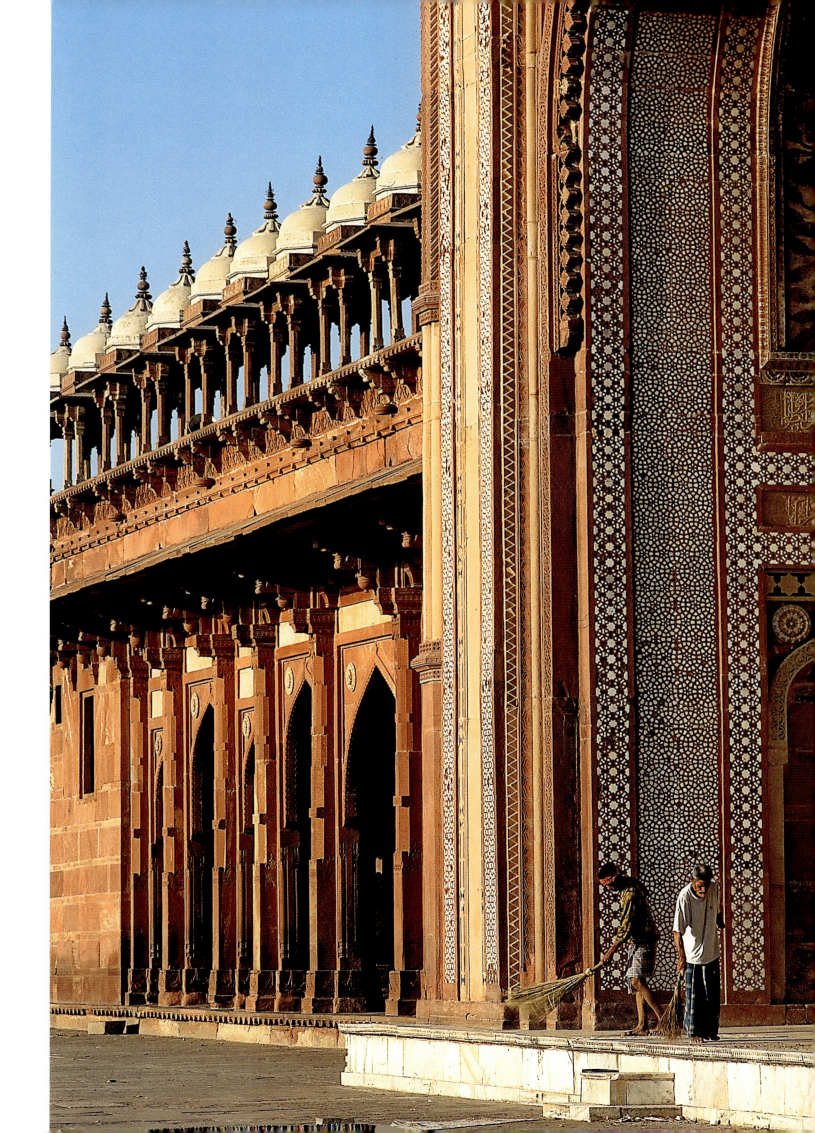

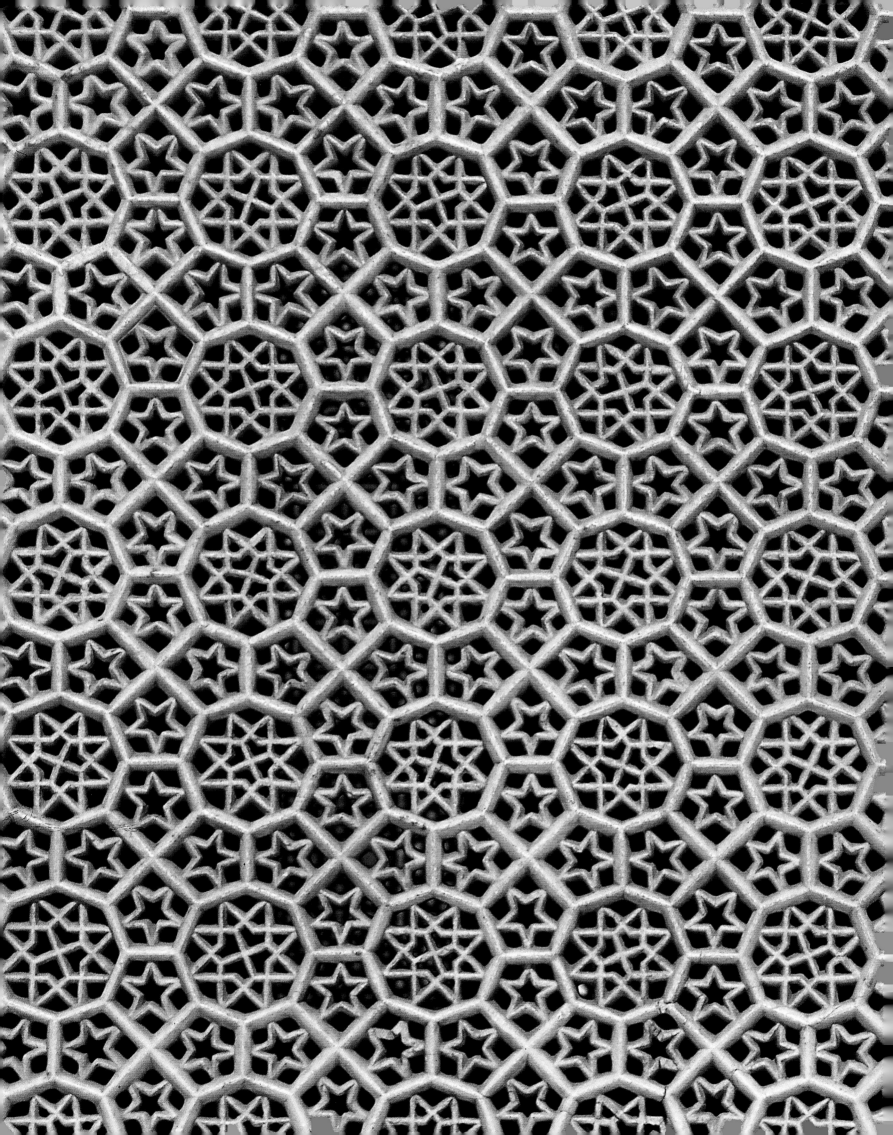

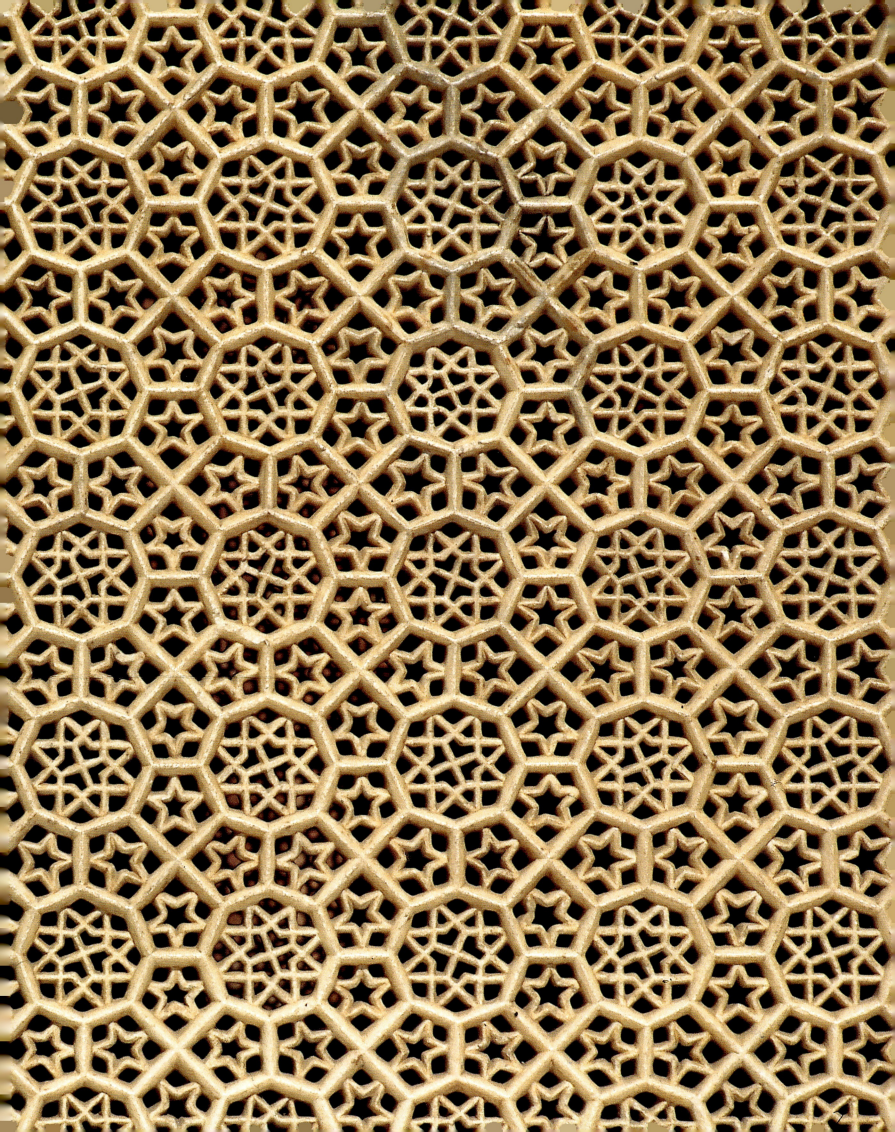

With Akbar, who reigned from 1556 to 1605, there began an unprecedented period of political solidity and an economic boom that gave impetus to the territorial expansion and cultural dominion of the Delhi sultanate. As the state increased its possessions and reinforced its control inside its borders and its influence abroad, this process accelerated under successive sovereigns up to Aurangzeb, further consolidating its power from 1657 to 1707. At the death of this last Great Mughal, however, the empire started on a slippery slope of decline, slowed only by periodic revivals in glory, until, in the wake of the Sepoy Mutiny of 1857, the descendants of those whom future generations will see as embodying the cultural prestige India were finally overturned.

Nonetheless, quite apart from the men themselves, the dazzling disproportion of their inspirations and the impressive technical quality of the works erected in their name continued dominate the imagination of artists and leaders alike. They were to remain the benchmark and model for a number of monuments, including contemporary ones, whose designs had their source in these masterpieces from the golden age of 1556 to 1707.

The Great Mughals, from Akbar to Aurangzeb

As soon as he acceded to the throne of the sultanate, Akbar began to reinforce his positions in the center and to the north, before launching an irresistible campaign against the independent Rājput states and Muslim kingdoms on his borders, including Mālwa, Gujarāt, and Khāndesh. Very quickly he invaded Bengal (1576), before securing control of the territories commanding the routes to Kabul and Kandahar, the latter becoming a bone of contention between the Mughal Empire and Safavid Iran until the eighteenth century. In 1589 he finally seized Kashmir, thus annexed to the Deccan. A skillful strategist and a remarkable politician, Akbar adapted the institutions of the sultanate to the new balance of power established by this chain of successes. Yet he was equally interested in religion, which he clearly saw could bind together populations with very heterogeneous cultures that his states now encompassed. He thus proceeded to lay down the foundations of a syncretic system called *Din-e elāhi* ("divine religion"), whose aim was to combine the principles of the Muslim faith with elements borrowed from other religions on the subcontinent. This drive to a unifying synthesis percolated through to the architectural designs he implemented, at Fatehpur Sīkri in particular.

Akbar's efforts were pursued by his successors Jahāngīr (r. 1605–27) and Shāh Jahān (r. 1627–57), especially within the limits of the kingdom proper, where the bonds of vassalage with regard to the Rājputs of Māwar and the Shiite sultanates of the Deccan had strengthened, but also with regard to relations with foreign powers. In point of fact, they did little to disturb the status quo with the Portuguese at their base in Goa and in their ports of call or the commercial links they maintained in the Bay of Bengal.

Shāh Jāhan sought to seize back the lands of his Timurid ancestors to attach them to India, dispatching a series of military campaigns to Balkh in Afghanistan (1647) and ending up encountering Uzbek troops, which drove him back, a defeat that seriously dented his prestige and represented an immense financial loss for him. When in 1657 Aurangzeb deposed his father and was crowned in 1658, he began a reign during which the Mughal Empire was to reach its maximum territorial extension, conquering most of the Deccan, before his death sparked the start of an unstoppable decline.

Akbar (1556–1605)

The monumental ensemble that best encapsulates the obvious rupture with the architectural practices employed in earlier periods we owe to the reign of Akbar: the mausoleum erected for this ruler's father, Humāyūn. This building, exceptional in terms of its design, plan, and lines borrowed partly from Timurid models, nevertheless has parallels in a series of constructions illustrating the search for a syncretic symbiosis between autochthon Hindu procedures and Indo-Persian elements. These achievements, whose high point is marked by the construction of the city of Fatehpur Sīkri, are an extension, on the artistic terrain, of the political and moral ideal of a fusion between what were, at the least, highly disparate religious, cultural, and social components that might otherwise have stirred up conflict among the monarch's subjects.

The funerary complex of Humāyūn

This milestone on the path to the acme of Mughal style appears in Delhi, not far from the *dargāh* of Nizamuddin and to the south of the Old Fort, where it replaces a large and ancient park, known as the "garden of the lady Bu-Halima." This unknown noblewoman is probably buried to the west of the complex as it stands today. The ensemble initially included a garden, a space arranged among various constructions and interconnected water systems. Nestling among the plantings, the mausoleum is joined by another tomb, known as that "of the Barber," as well as by several adjacent structures located outside the walls. The absence of a funerary mosque within the perimeter is, however, striking. The fact is all the more notable since they do appear in the mausoleums of 'Isā Khān and Afsarwāla that stand in the vicinity of the walls of the complex.

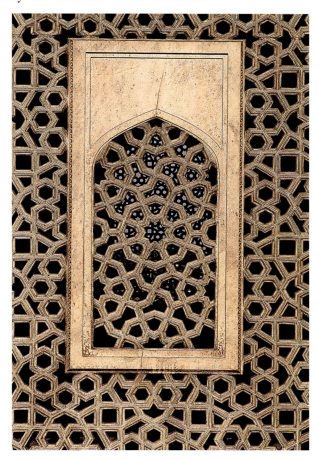

Jali in the funerary hall of the mausoleum of Humāyūn, Delhi, India, c. 1565.

The mausoleum

This monument, the construction of which began ten years after the death of Humāyūn, is a sumptuous pink sandstone building highlighted by white marble trimming and yellow ocher stone. It emerges from the center of a vast "Persian" garden or *chahār-bāgh* (literally "four gardens"), recently restored by the Aga Khan Foundation. Appearing as the ideal world towards which converge carefully staged perspective views from points along the periphery of a vast square compound 1,198 feet (365 meters) down the side, the whole is enclosed in high walls open to the west and south by two monumental gates. The garden is split into eight sections, each divided into four parterres; the isolation of each planting is disturbed by the babbling of a vast network of little channels running between the pools lazing among the avenues. Directly inspired by the Timurid art of Central Asia, these quadripartite spaces echo the description of paradise in the Koran: a garden traversed by four rivers of water, honey, milk, and wine. The funerary complex of Humāyūn remains at all events the oldest surviving Mughal garden still in use.

The mausoleum itself rises majestically on an imposing base of approximately 302 feet (92 meters) down the side, scanned by arched niches inclining towards vaulted rooms that serve as crypts sheltering many tombs from various periods. With its 180-foot (55-meter) long sides, the building of the mausoleum occupies a surface area equivalent to the squares in the garden. It is structured around four octagons embedding a fifth at the core of the edifice, corresponding to a central plan sometimes termed Hasht-Behesht ("eight paradises"), which usually occurs in the context of palace architecture, first in the Timurid and then the Safavid domains. The adoption of this architectural model (as well as the term Hasht-Behesht) in a funerary context, however, constitutes a first for the Indian world, as it is found neither in Iran nor in Central Asia. A broad arcade undulates gently over two levels of windows that modulate their ornamental melody along the whole length of the sandstone façades; the arch spandrels are dressed with six-branched stars, or "seals of Solomon," an apotropaic motif that protected many monuments of the period.

A double-shelled cupola in immaculate white marble projects above the central body to a height of 139 feet (42.5 meters), courted by a roundelay of little *chhatris*, their exuberance counterbalanced by four others of statelier size whose airy volumes rise up from the octagons on the periphery. The sense of vertical thrust is moreover accentuated by pinnacles (*goldastas*) extending from each corner of the building. The funerary hall is accessible only from the south; it houses a cenotaph, as the actual tomb lies in the crypt. The octagonal volume is articulated into deep arched recesses, blocked off by *claustrae* and immured within a flattened internal vault. Other princely cenotaphs are housed in corner pavilions, including those of two wives of the sovereign (Bega Begum and Hamīda Begum), Prince Dārā Shikōh, son of Shāh Jahān, and later sovereigns, such as Jahāndār Shāh (r. 1712–13), Farrukh-siyar (r. 1713–19), Rafīʿ-ud-Darajāt (1719), Rafīʿ-ud-Dawla (1719), and ʿĀlamgir II (r. 1754–60).

The initiative for constructing this mausoleum is frequently attributed to Humāyūn's widow, Sahiba Begum. It is, however, more probable that the expenditure incurred on the site, together with the conception of the monument, in artistic terms as well as in the political impact intended to be conveyed by its vast size, was actually assumed by the young Akbar, as a *pro domo* declaration.[1]

The design as a whole is attributed to Mirak Mirzā Ghiyāth, an architect in the Timurid tradition originally from Herāt. He designed not only the building, but also its gardens, enclosures, and the various constructions ensuring water supply and circulation.

The mausoleum of Humāyūn, Delhi, India, from 1565.

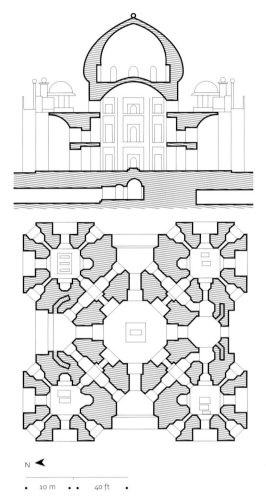

The entire site, designed at the outset as a pantheon for the Indian branch of the Timurid family, pays tribute to the great mausoleums of the dynasty, at Herāt and Samarkand. Hence the loans from the architectural vocabulary of Central Asia, such as the "Persian" arches and the central plan surmounted by a double dome on squinches. These, however, are successfully combined with local traditions that preferred pink sandstone and stone to brick, and marble dressing to ceramic tiles, not forgetting the contribution of elements quite unknown in the Central Asian sphere, such as the outburst of *chhatris* on the terraces. From the convergence of these disparate sources of inspiration results an original harmony which resembles nothing known in Iran or Central Asia. As is often the case with truly innovative masterworks, this edifice did not serve as a model for the tombs that came immediately after—those of Akbar and Jahāngīr—but the plan was reused by Shāh Jahān at the Tāj Mahal, where its perfection is elevated to the brink of the sublime.

Other monuments
Aligned with the axis connecting the southeastern corners of the tomb of Humāyūn with the garden enclosure, the elegant outline of another mausoleum stands in a wonderfully calm environment planted with trees. Its intended denizen is unknown, though popular legend has it that it contains the remains of the royal barber and his wife; one of the tombs bears the date AH 999 (1590–91 CE). The square plan of the monument is anchored in the center of a terrace, its splendid elevation projecting the energy of powerful, sober arches that spring from all four façades, the sole entrance on the south. Atop all this mineral tension stands enthroned a dome on a sixteen-sided drum guarded by four *chhatris* at the corners. The ensemble performs a gentle concert in gray quartzite and red sandstone, accompanied by muted chords of white marble trim.

Southwest of the garden enclosure, a building that looks like a caravanserai, known as the 'Arab Sarā'ī, served, if the rumors are to be believed, to house Arab prelates Humāyūn's widow sent for from Mecca. The eastern entrance to the building, which is still adorned with traces of gorgeous cut-out tile mosaic, is an addition from the time of Jahāngīr.

Above. Side view and plan of the mausoleum of Humāyūn, Delhi, India, c. 1565 (after H. Stierlin).

Facing page, left: The so-called Tomb of the Barber in the garden of Humāyūn, 1599. Right: The mausoleum known as the Afsarwāla, 1566–67.

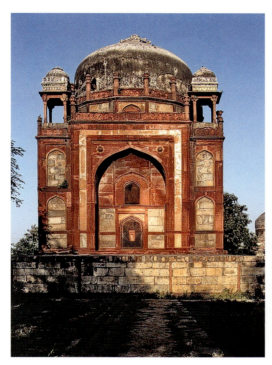
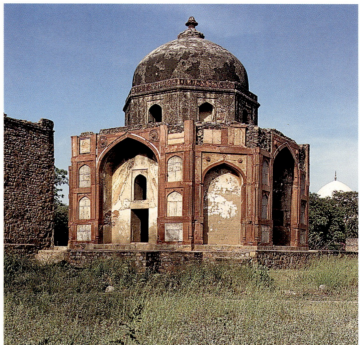

Between this latter monument and the entryway to the complex of Humāyūn, a sizable embankment underpins two buildings named the mosque and mausoleum of Afsarwāla ("the Officer"). Although one of the tombstones is dated, this personage remains an enigma. The mosque is built in rubble stone to which a few smatterings of colored stucco cling. From the terrace, the visitor is presented with the undulating perspective of three archways that signal the access to the prayer hall topped by a central dome. The mausoleum is set upon an octagonal plan capped by a double cupola on a narrow drum. It was dressed in a cladding—still visible in places—the lion's share of which was in a red sandstone whose intensity is wonderfully set off by the snowy marble.

The mausoleum of Ataga Khān (1566–67)
The *dargāh* of Nizamuddin is located near the mausoleum of Humāyūn. The sanctity of the site made it a favorite location for burial sites, including the monument of Ataga Khān, which deserves more detailed attention. This individual, the husband of Jiji Anga, one of Akbar's nurses, had the misfortune to be dispatched by the monarch's foster brother, Adham Khān. His tomb features an inscription dating its construction to AH 974 (1566–67). This aedicule of modest proportions encloses the tomb within a space measuring twenty feet (six meters) down the side and topped by a single dome. And yet, with its alternate bold pink sandstone and pure white marble emblazoned with elements of ceramic inlay in blue and green, it seems to shimmer like a jewel. The western flank of its enclosure, facing Mecca, was dressed in an imposing ceramic decoration in cut-tile mosaic that variegated blind niches reminiscent of mihrabs with a geometric pattern based on stars; this mural adornment is unfortunately badly deteriorated.

Āgra, Ajmer, and Allahābād

The first two decades of Akbar's reign were marked by intense building activity, especially with respect to palace structures. Āgra, Lahore, and then Allahābād duly received attention and were endowed with royal citadels; the great domains in the temporary "capitals" were complemented by other, less significant, constructions, such as the palace of Ajmer, the gardens of Kashmir, and the pavilion of Nilkhant in Māndu, to which reference has already been made.

The Jahāngīrī Mahal at the Red Fort in Āgra
During the early years of his reign, Akbar would often stay at the Red Fort in Āgra. The structures of this monument, from the fortifications to the royal residence, were profoundly altered by his successors, particularly Shāh Jahān. The building known as the Jahāngīrī Mahal escaped this fate, however, and is—contrary to what its name suggests—the last vestige of importance here to date from the reign of Akbar, who probably ordered its construction in about 1565, although the absence of inscription makes precise dating hypothetical.[2]

The building possesses a quadrilateral plan underlined by the corner towers that flank it. Those rising to the east are moreover embedded in the fort's outer ramparts. The principal access opens to the west through a monumental gateway whose majesty is further ennobled by a Persian arch with spandrels worked in a yellow rock with stone-encrusted Motifs; one can recognize the six-branched star, or "seal of Solomon," which already embellished the mausoleum of Humāyūn. A dogleg corridor passes from the vestibule to a central courtyard, whence one can take in at one's leisure

Below and facing page. The Jahāngīrī Mahal, Red Fort, Āgra, India. In spite of its name, it was probably founded by Akbar around 1565.

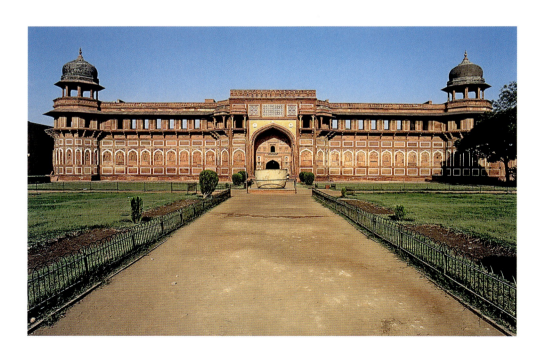

an overall architectural schema inspired, as were the majority of the decorative elements, by earlier Rājput palaces, particularly the Mān Mandir in Gwalior dating from the late fifteenth century. An inventory of these echoes from local repertories would include the corbels or consoles with pendentives supporting the lintels and the *chajjas* running around the courtyard embellished with a succession of carved reliefs borrowing—in simplified form—elements from the Hindu architectural vocabulary. The primary influence deployed in the central courtyard is countered by the *parti* adopted in the zones that open out onto the terrace overlooking the ramparts. Hidden behind a screen wall to protect them from prying eyes, the rooms overlooking the calm summits of this secluded haven, enlivened by discreet water features, are punctuated by decorative notes with a more exotic and pronounced "Timurid" accent; likewise the courtyard façades. Here, elaborate niches burrow into the core of cusped arches, whence emergent medallions, their contours painted with Motifs taken from illuminations. Elsewhere languishes a small fleuron-shaped pool, just like its predecessors from the reign of Bābur (in Dholpur, for example) or authentically Timurid forbears. The

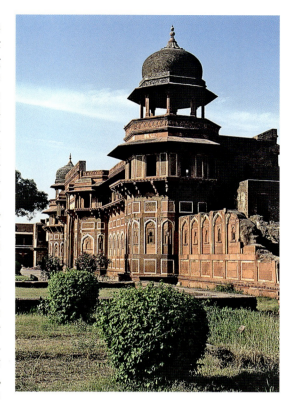

rhythm of the stone columns on the front to the terrace, finally, evokes the model of the wooden *tālār* ("precincts") that invaded so much of Central Asia and Safavid Iran.

The palace of Akbar in Ajmer (c. 1570)
The Sufi sheikhs of the Chishti brotherhood had exerted a dominating influence over the sovereigns since the Khaljī period, and Mughal monarchs did not escape the devotional traditions these saintly figures continued to inspire. Mu'in-ud-din Chishti thus came from Afghanistan in 1192, living, until 1233, in Ajmer, where the *dargāh* containing his tomb, which has become a major center for pilgrimage, is located. Tradition has it that the sovereigns themselves collaborated on the embellishment of the site and that Akbar, who greatly venerated the relatively tolerant message of the saint, endowed his burial place with a mosque (completed in 1571), which moreover he would visit every year.

On the same spot he also had a palace erected that forms a quadrilateral of 230 by 180 feet (70 by 55 meters) consolidated with corner towers not unlike those of Chambord in France, although the absence at that time of any contact with European monarchies means that the parallel is a sheer coincidence. The only entrance is underscored by a single monumental gate, with a hall and double guardroom, and is overlooked by a *jharokha* for the ceremonial appearance of the sovereign. This construction leads to a courtyard surrounded by a host of small rooms, while in the middle stands a rectangular *baradari,* each face of which opens to the outside through an *iwan* with columns and presenting rooms over two levels at each corner. The entablature of the *iwan* is borne on large consoles against which leans the *chajja* ringing the building.

The building that witnessed the meeting between Emperor Jahāngīr and Sir Thomas Roe in 1616 today contains the collections of a museum.

Allahābād

The fruit of several decades of work that came to a conclusion in about 1583, the massive fort of Allahābād stands on the northern bank of the Yamuna, near that river's confluence with the Ganges. The thick containing wall is pierced by three doors flanked with towers. In a fate that also befell its counterparts in Delhi and Āgra, the building has been occupied by successive waves of the British and Indian armies, which have left it in a rather sorry state.

Shāh Jahān also appreciably damaged the aspect of the monument, but a kind of courtroom does survive from the era of Akbar. It presents the form of a multipurpose *baradari* and is sometimes designated as Chehel Sotūn ("Forty Columns"), a figure less indicative of an actual number than of an image of abundance that is frequently appended to names of Iranian palaces. The pavilion is supported by pairs of columns—except at the quoins where they are grouped in fours—and the colonnade makes up a peristyle that thus runs around a central space from where there are delightful panoramas to all points of the compass. On the upper levels, an ample terrace nestles within an impressive *chajja* completed by an openwork parapet, while a second terrace, of cozier dimensions, is adorned with *chhatris* whose sides filter the light through delicate *jalis*. This fort also served as the stage for the rebellions of both Prince Salīm (the future Jahāngīr) and, in turn, of his own eldest son, Prince Khusrau. This latter, after having had his eyes put out and being incarcerated for the attempt on his father's life, died in 1622 and was inhumed in the city, in the grounds of the garden that bears his name.

Fatehpur Sīkri

With his piety and taste for spiritually edifying interchange, Akbar was in the habit of regularly consulting a Sufi sheikh named Salīm Chishti, who had retired to a hermitage in the small village of Sīkri twenty-five miles (forty kilometers) west of

Plan of the palatial compound of Fatehpur Sīkri, India (after H. Stierlin): **(1)** "stables"; **(2)** house of Bīrbal; **(3)** palace of Jodh Bhai; **(4)** house of Maryam; **(5)** garden of Maryam; **(6)** "hospital"; **(7)** Pānch Mahal; **(8)** Ankh Michauli; **(9)** Divān-e Khās; **(10)** Court of the Pachhisi; **(11)** garden; **(12)** Anup Talao; **(13)** Khwābgāh (dormitory); **(14)** pavilion of the Turkish sultana; **(15)** chancellery; **(16)** Divān-e 'Āmm.

Facing page. Arcades in the courtyard of the Great Mosque of Fatehpur Sīkri, India.

Āgra. In 1568 the sheikh announced to the monarch the imminent arrival of an heir whom his wife, Maryam Zamāni, duly produced the following year in the person of Prince Salīm—the future Emperor Jahāngīr. When the venerable sage died a few years later, Akbar resolved to honor his memory with a monumental mosque also capable of housing the tomb of the saint. Following his final victory over the sultanate of Gujarāt in 1573, Akbar decided to extend this first edifice, financing the construction of a new palatial city on the site and naming it Fatehpur Sīkri ("city of victory"). The city structure clings to a reddish sandstone ridge, prolonging its rugged stoniness along a northeast-southwest diagonal. Bordered to the northwest by an artificial lake, the city is girdled on the other three sides by a sturdy wall whose austerity is exacerbated by the severe-looking towers and reinforced gates with which it is peppered. In practice, for reasons that have yet to come to light—perhaps to do with an inadequate water supply—no sooner had it been completed than the site was completely abandoned, from the very start of the 1580s in favor of Lahore and settlements in Kashmir. The paradoxical advantage of this briefest of existences lies in the exceptional state of conservation of the palace complex and the Great Mosque, which has suffered relatively little degradation, compared with sites such as Delhi, Lahore, and Āgra, which Shāh Jahān altered substantially. Conversely, almost nothing of the urban structures peripheral to the palatial site remains, except for some poorly preserved residences once belonging to the nobility.

On the stylistic level, Fatehpur Sīkri represented a rupture with previous eras, in which the bonds of artistic dependence on Timurid references were loosened and more heed taken of properly Indian sources of creativity, especially in incorporating the highly original results of the architectural fusions underway in newly conquered Gujarāt. The result is a composite yet innovative array of buildings that ultimately embody the fanciful syncretism and conceptual freedom that Akbar was able to couple to a genuine rigor of execution. It is these qualities that today probably give the city an unexpected feeling of modernity that continues to fascinate contemporary architects and town planners.

The Great Mosque
Built in homage to Sheikh Salīm Chishti, the mosque was completed in 1571–72, shortly after his death. Sheltering in its courtyard the remarkable tomb of the saint, it is seminal as the prototype for Mughal great mosques.

Erected upon a quadrilateral of 541 by 436 feet (165 by 133 meters), its dimensions are awe-inspiring. It opens to the south through the Buland Darwāza, a gate of equally impressive proportions, its towering 135 feet (41 meters) further accentuated by the low-angle view enjoyed from the majestic flight of steps leading

up to it. It is adorned with several inscriptions, one from 1575 and another from 1601, commemorating a victory in the Deccan. The entryway is bordered by a scroll of text that marks the onset of the important role several later major Mughal edifices were to allot to monumental epigraphy:

> Jesus Son of Mary (on whom be peace) said: The world is a bridge, pass over it; but build no house upon it. Who hopes for an hour, hopes for eternity. The world is an hour. Spend it in prayer, for the rest is unseen.[3]

An array of some thirteen small *chhatris* flanked by pinnacles gives a disheveled aspect to the head of the gate, their round profile enlivening the straight-edge verticality of the entrance, while three other *chhatris* of larger proportions crown the whole piece in respectful equilibrium. An entryway generates a half-octagonal volume whose main front is encompassed over its entire height by a dynamic-looking arch, while on the returns a three-level arcade sets the scene for a rigorous elaboration of various architectural registers. Thus defined, the passage leads to a central hall inscribing a rectangle and is directly served to the

Above and facing page. The Great Mosque of Fatehpur Sīkri, India; Bādshāhī Darwāza and *iwan* of the prayer hall.

215 the great mughals and their heirs

Facing page, top: aerial view of the courtyard, Great Mosque of Fatehpur Sīkri;
left: the mausoleum of Salīm Chishti; right: the mausoleum of Islām Khān;
in the background: the palatial enceinte and the Hiran Minār.

Facing page, below and above: the mausoleum of Salīm Chishti, lined entirely in white;
above: general view and ambulatory in the funerary hall with *qawwāli* musicians.

longer side by three doors, while the lateral openings communicate on both flanks with the porticoes bordering the immense court that unroll in pious quietude the whole length of an unimpeachably linear space said to be able to contain up to ten thousand worshippers. Opposite the entrance called the Bādshāhī Darwāza ("Royal Gate")—probably originally the main entry—and thus corresponding to it on the west, the prayer hall extends from a slightly projecting central *iwan*. Beneath its largest arch, three doors conduct one to the hall topped by a cupola sheltering the principal mihrab. The mihrab is an elaboration on a sumptuous two-color theme in red sandstone and white marble, enriched by painted Motifs in the style of manuscript illumination. Two side domes add their note to the sovereign lines of this noble section of the edifice, supported as they are on curious triangular squinches at the quoins, carved as a stack of parallel horizontal moldings of decreasing size.

Although the construction of the mausoleum of Salīm Chishti opposite the Buland Darwāza started in about 1580, it was only finished in around 1606, during the reign of Jahāngīr. On a square plan of forty-nine feet (fifteen meters) down the side, it is entirely in white marble; sheltering behind a protruding porch and a portico, the funerary hall reposes beneath the corolla of a dome. Wrapping round the monument, the fluid lines of the *chajja* are enhanced by the slender, delicately carved S-shaped consoles supporting it. The shady ambulatory is illumined by a constellation of points of light subtly filtered through the spider's web of *jalis* that pierce the external walls. Another mausoleum, of greater size and in red sandstone, stands beside the first: it contains the remains of Islam Khān, governor of Bengal for Jahāngīr, and who also recognized the saintly Chishti as a spiritual guide.

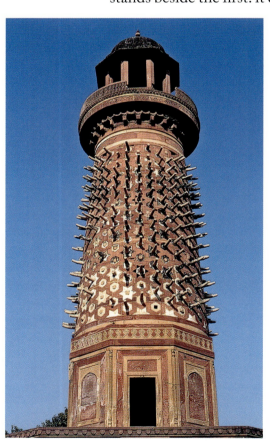

The palace enclosure

The path leading concentrically from the exterior to the core of this architectural spectacle of the arcana of power recalls a rite of initiation: through it, the select few were only gradually permitted into the presence of a sovereign whose talents and attributes were first diffracted and then reassembled into the often enigmatic forms of the various monuments of the complex. The closer one gets to the center, the more complex the structural forms become—as if they are designed to exemplify the

Left. The Hiran Minār, a curious tower bristling with fake elephant tusks, in the palace compound of Fatehpur Sīkri.

Facing page. The Divān-e Khās and the "kiosk of the Astrologer" in the foreground, Fatehpur Sīkri palace enceinte.

ultimate meaning of the individuals and functions they serve. The inner sanctum is entered through the main entrance set to the northeast. The solemnity of this entryway is underscored by the loggia topping it that would have contained a "brass band" (*nawbat-khāna*), before one emerges into a vast courtyard bordered by neat lines of porticoes where the hall for public audience (the Divān-e 'Āmm) would have been set up. The lines of the edifice are singularly sober and it forms a sort of elevated box with an entablature and a *chajja*. Like most buildings in the city, it was built in red sandstone. Its studied simplicity thus prepared for the effects marshaled in the various sectors devoted solely to the elite of the monarch's entourage. It is organized over two distinct perimeters: at the epicenter stands the court of the Pachhisi—from the name of a board game (*parcheesi*)—which affords access to the women's apartments.

The court of the Pachhisi
It is this haven that appears as the last stage in the palatial system, its heart of hearts, accessible only to the privileged few from the court of public audience. Here power is exercised in a manner as absolute as it is undemonstrative, the supreme master over a space where nature plays a role only in its tamed and mineral manifestation. Pavilions of oddly imaginative configuration are articulated round the court, their often mysterious functions distilling into this closeted world the essence of a parallel universe, at once disembodied and multifaceted.

The Divān-e Khās
To the north of the courtyard rises a curious building whose name translates as "hall of private audience." On a square base, it extends over two levels, with, on the floor above, a theatrical opening of a balcony with a very low balustrade in open-carved stonework supported on a pendant cluster of S-shaped consoles. The broad demarcation of a *chajja* marks the access to the level of the roof, whose corners are adorned with gracious *chhatris*. Inside, a single two-floor hall features a massive central pillar reminiscent of a totem pole. On it rests a circular platform, throwing out tentacle-like footbridges diagonally to all four corners of the room. Access to the floor above is made via staircases concealed in the walls. The inverted cone of a kind of giant capital comprised of superposed clumps of consoles hanging down crowns the pillar. Built in red sandstone, as are all the buildings on the site, the forms and techniques used in this monument borrow, however, from the timber constructions of Gujarāt. In spite of the name that has been attached to it, nothing precise is known concerning its true function. It has been simply presumed, without there being any definitive evidence to the effect, that the sovereign would take his place on the central platform during a private audience.

Ankh Michauli
This expression, which could be translated as "blindman's buff," designates a pavilion located facing the Divān-e Khās. Rather than being devoted to such childish games, however, the function of the building was more likely that of a repository, storeroom, or treasury. The interior walls are dug into recesses that some have supposed were sealed by a sliding stone slabs. In the central room, the fantastic animal carvings that swarm over the braces obliquely connecting

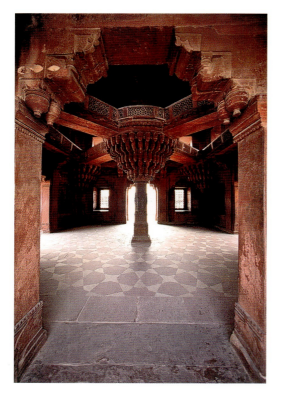

the corbels at ceiling level are inspired by a decorative repertory inherited from indigenous architecture.

In front of this building stands a curious aedicule baptized the "kiosk of the astrologer." It rises over a square plan enriched with exuberantly ornamented columns, particularly so at the level of the red sandstone consoles that morph into monsters totally at odds, once again, with the Islamic architectural canon. Perhaps this locale served as an observation post for the monarch since it overlooks the court of the Pachhisi. The central pavement is indeed arranged as a cruciform checker board characteristic of this game and legend states that when playing it the sovereign would use his women as pieces.

Anup Talao and the pavilion of the Turkish Sultana
The liquid mirror surface of the square pool named Anup Talao is set into the mineral immobility of the court to the south. As in a Hindu *baoli*, steps facilitate access to the waters, while footbridges arranged into the shape of a cross lead to a central platform with at its center a dais and bordered by an openwork balustrade in stone. This purely ornamental pool is located opposite the private

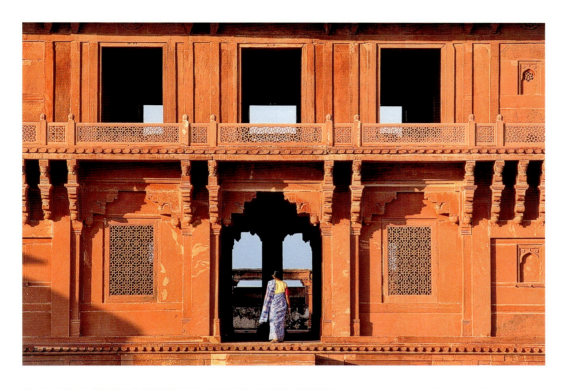

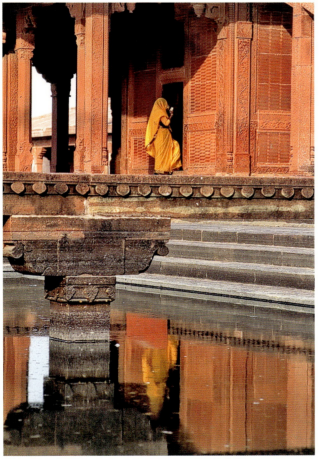

Facing page. The interior of the Divān-e Khās, with the startling column in the middle supporting a platform and walkways, Fatehpur Sīkri palace compound, India.

Top. The pavilion known as Ankh Michauli in the Fatehpur Sīkri palace compound.

Above and facing. The "pavilion of the Turkish Sultana" bordering the Anup Talao pool, Fatehpur Sīkri palace enceinte.

apartments of the sovereign. The platform occupying the center is linked to the memory of the musician Tānsēn, one of Akbar's favorite artists and the creator of the *dhrupad* genre of singing.[4]

At the northeastern corner of the basin, the pavilion known as that "of the Turkish Sultana" deploys charming proportions around a remarkable portico that transcribes in stone various motifs theretofore reserved for timber.

Originally, wooden *claustrae* served to enclose the space and the interior walls teemed with elegant animal or plant carvings, somewhat reminiscent of Persian miniatures.

Khwābgāh, the "dormitory"

The building occupying the south of the court and which is usually called a "dormitory," corresponds to the private apartments of Akbar (*khwābgāh*). A dais opened up from it to the courtyard front to allow the emperor to gaze down on the Anup Talao. The space that structures the building is a grand hall arranged on the ground floor that was probably once a library, implying that the recesses in the walls were intended to be used as shelves for the works with which Akbar surrounded himself. In any case, it certainly offers an insight into the cultural curiosity and intellectual open-mindedness of a ruler who even had Jesuits fetched from Goa to discuss theological questions and who was also interested enough in Hinduism to have the *Mahābhārata* translated into Persian.

A platform or podium adjoins the wall in a second room to the rear, framed by pillars elaborately carved with Motifs recalling those in wood. A window gave on the court lower down; from there Akbar would appear to his subjects during the ceremony known as the *darshān jharoka* ("the balcony where one shows oneself"), in what was a carefully coded manifestation of power. His successors, particularly Jahāngīr and Shāh-Jahān, were also fond of such ritual "revelations" of the sovereign.

The Pānch Mahal

One of its most original and iconic monuments of Fatehpur Sīkri lies to the west of the courtyard: the Pānch Mahal.[5] It spreads over five off-center floors of decreasing proportions, thus presenting on its southern side a nearly vertical stack of pavilions, looking, from summit to base, like a cascade of terracing tumbling to the ground in waves. The edifice, whose function remains hypothetical, may have been inspired by pre-Mughal *baradari* (Kotla Fīrūz Shāh or Sikandra, for example), and it can

Above. Detail of the carved two-plane relief on a jamb, "pavilion of the Turkish Sultana," Fatehpur Sīkri palace enceinte.

Facing page. The Pānch Mahal, or "palace of five stories"; in the foreground, the court of the Pachhisi, Fatehpur Sīkri palace compound.

be imagined that it would be pleasant to take the late afternoon or night air there. However, it was designed without any of those hideaways conducive to society that this type of construction usually afforded in rooms and recesses along its passageways; on the contrary, the total absence of walls or screens precludes intimacy. The ground floor features all eighty-four columns, a symbolic figure that certain authors consider as the result of multiplying the number of planets (seven) by the number of signs in the Zodiac (twelve). The first level is clearly the more refined, with its fifty-six columns with capitals in a plethora of different forms. On the last floor, a simple *chhatri* borne on four columns crowns the imaginative ensemble.

The women's apartments
Similarly organized so as to convey how regal might radiates throughout the cosmos, to the west of the court of Pachhisi are the buildings occupied by the female members of the sovereign's entourage. The mother of Akbar resided here, together with the aunts of the prince and his wives; legend has it that other figures such as his faithful minister Bīrbal also set up house there, but it hardly seems probable that a man would have been permitted to occupy a zone reserved for women.

The house of Maryam
The mother of Akbar, Maryam Makāni ("she whose place is the equal of Mary's"), is reputed to have occupied this pavilion, which is also known as the "golden house" because of its opulently painted décor. It may be however that one or other of the monarch's wives, such as Maryam Zamāni ("the Mary of her time"), mother of the future Jahāngīr, lived here instead. The vicissitudes of time have, alas, not been kind, often rendering the painted scenes decorating the walls almost illegible, but the north portico presents certain identifiable Motifs, such as an elephant fight on the pillars that emerges laboriously from the blur of paint. In addition, epigraphic cartouches of Persian poems in gold on a sky-blue ground adorn the stone beams. Scattered fragments were renovated in the early twentieth century, and one, terribly degraded, is meant to have represented an Annunciation inspired by European engravings.[6] A wall in the room adjacent to the portico serves as a frame to a large portrait, probably of the youthful Akbar. Finally, there is a painted composition in stars and geometric patterns in dazzling colors on the ceiling of the south-facing room.

The palace of Jodh Bhai
On its plan square, this vast construction, sometimes identified as a harem, was in fact designed as a collective dwelling, entailing a less personal approach in the details of its interior than in the residence described above. It derives its name from one of the Rājput wives of Akbar, a famous princess of Jodhpur. The prestige of its

occupants is underlined by the huge projecting portal at its entrance. Its tripartite façade opens in the center through a generously proportioned arcade decorated with a reserve whose austerity does not preclude a sober nobility, with a frieze of lotus buds fringing the intrados around the entrance door with a lintel on corbels, and some six-branched stars (or "seals of Solomon"), similar to those on the mausoleum of Humāyūn, adorning the spandrels of the arch. The sense of solemnity is further enhanced by deeply arching niches on both sides and by the way these extend along the upper register into balconies, and then, at roof level, into *chhatris*. Once through the door, one reaches an atrium with a guardroom, before a sort of baffle entry leads to the courtyard, the heart from which the various ranges of the building structure the circulation of its occupants: thus, to block off what were private domains, domed pavilions are encamped at each of the four corners, while in the center to each side advance porticoes overlooked by a *chajja* of protective aspect, each communicating with a series of apartments over two floors. On the upper reaches, two aerial *chhatris* elevate a building of an otherwise compact verticality, while a pavilion of oblong plan splashes, in refreshing contrast, the ruddy glow of the sandstone with a graceful roof of turquoise enamel tiles. Part of the building projects to the north of the palace of Jodh Bhai; called the Hawā Mahal ("palace of the winds"), in reference to its famous homonym at Jaipur, it corresponds to a side gate and is topped by a further floor whose apertures are ornamented with lace-like *jalis*. From there, a footbridge led to the small mosque known as the Nagina Masjid, reserved for the ladies of the court.

The "house of Bīrbal" and the "stables"
The building known as the "house of Bīrbal," from the name of the Akbar's Brahman vizier much vaunted for his wisdom, was more likely to have been used as a residence by one or more of the great ladies of the court. With its original and harmonious proportions, its plan is suggestive of two slightly off-kilter quadrilaterals one within the other, thus fusing the rigor of geometrical construction with an imaginative approach to composition. The ground floor is divided into six rooms densely decorated

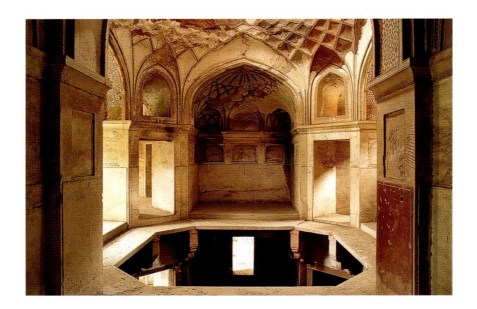

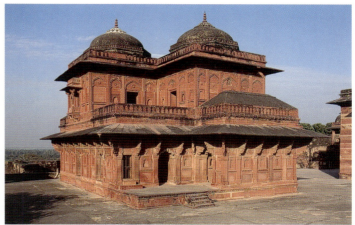

Facing page. View of the hammams, in the service area near the "stables," Fatehpur Sīkri palace compound.

Above and facing. The pavilion known as the "house of Bīrbal," with remarkable examples of carved decoration in red sandstone, Fatehpur Sīkri palace compound.

with splendid and painstakingly carved flat reliefs that make use of decorative models previously confined to woodwork exactly where they would have been expected to appear in that context: on the ceilings, doorjambs, and window dressings. The transposition of these Motifs into stone is indeed rendered more credible by the natural glow of the red sandstone employed. The story above is divided into four rooms, of which two are surmounted by domes, while the sunny openness of a pair of terraces adds the finishing touch to the building.

In the vicinity of the "house of Bīrbal" stand the "stables"—probably wrongly named, as it is simply inconceivable that such outbuildings would be sited to the rear of an enclosure reserved for women; surely the designers of such spaces would have taken into account the embarrassment that the boisterous behavior of the animals might cause the ladies of the court. In fact, this space would have housed the many personnel that the adequate functioning of the palace would call for, as confirmed by the presence of a hammam at the rear of the left wing of the building.

Jahāngīr Holding a Portrait of his Father Akbar, gouache and gold on paper, Mughal India, first quarter of the seventeenth century. Musée Guimet, Paris, no. 3676 B.

Facing page. Mausoleum of Akbar, Sikandra, near Āgra, India. Incrustations in red sandstone on the entrance gate.

Jahāngīr (r. 1605–27)

With a temperament sometimes described as muddled and readily taxed with indolence, dissipation, and feebleness, the reputation of Prince Salīm, who mounted the throne at the age of thirty-six with the name Jahāngīr, can hardly be said to be spotless.[7] At first blush, trapped on the one side by the overwhelming shadow of his father Akbar, who not only completely overhauled the power structure of the empire and conquered all before him, but was also a fine amateur theologian, and, on the other, by the dazzling renown of his son, Shāh Jahān, under whose dominion Mughal art attained heights compared to which all earlier manifestations pale into insignificance, Jahāngīr can appear a somewhat tepid figure. Coming between the two lengthy reigns of such eminent rulers, Jahāngīr would have been hard-pressed to emerge as a major force; prior to his accession, he had, moreover, champed at the bit on occasion, even making moves to start a revolt against Akbar.[8]

Notwithstanding, Jahāngīr was no disgrace, doing more than simply preserve the territorial integrity of the empire, and revealing in his memoirs a multifaceted personality with a supple mind, full of curiosity and intelligence for things cultural, and not devoid of originality. Where Akbar forged a solid framework that extended the structure of his power even into its artistic manifestations, Jahāngīr added a

physicality and sensuality that fed more than is commonly admitted into the sublime inspirations that Shāh Jahān applied with such admirable conceptual rigor in the artworks he commissioned.

The mausoleum of Akbar, which the emperor himself planned, was completed under Jahāngīr and constitutes the latter's most significant direct contribution to the architecture of his era. The most famous illustration of the art of this period is, however, the delightful gardens that flowered throughout the kingdom at his initiative, such as the Shalimar of Srinagar or Nishat in Kashmir. For her part, the sovereign's formidable wife bequeathed a remarkable series of buildings, including the funerary complex built after the Jahāngīr's death in Lahore, which also contains the remains of the queen and her brother, and especially the masterpiece that is the mausoleum built in Āgra for her father, I'timād al-Dawla.

Sikandra

Sikandra houses the mausoleum in which the great Akbar was interred. It is possible that construction begun during his reign, but the merit of having supervised the chief part of the works, completed in 1613, falls to his son Jahāngīr. His influence must have been all the more decisive in that he refers in his memoirs to the demolition of an earlier construction that he considered insufficiently eye-catching and to building activity being resumed on the basis of a wholly reconfigured design:

> When I was dignified with the good fortune of making this pilgrimage [to the tomb of Akbar], I saw the building that had been erected in the cemetery. It did not come up to my idea of what it ought to be, for that

Below and facing page. The mausoleum of Akbar, Sikandra, near Āgra, completed in 1613.

would be approved which the wayfarers of the world should point to as one the like of which was not in the inhabited world.... At last a certain expenditure was made until a large sum was expended, and the work went on for three or four years. I ordered that experienced architects should again lay the foundations, in agreement with men of experience, in several places, on settled plan. By degrees a lofty building was erected, and a very bright garden was arranged round the building of the shrine, and a large and lofty gateway with minarets of white stone was built. On the whole they told me the cost of this lofty edifice was 1,500,000 rupees, equivalent to 50,000 current tumans of Persia.[9]

These changes were wrought in innovative forms that stemmed from a blend of architectural and decorative principles. Impressively proportioned, the monument stands in the heart of an enclosure imbued with solemnity.

The park enclosure
For his final resting place Akbar had chosen a stretch of parkland of some 124 acres (50 hectares) founded, as its name implies, by Sikandar Lodī. It was there that the *baradari* in which Jahāngīr interred his mother, Maryam Zamāni, was built. In addition to this construction, the sector also contains scattered remains of gardens and residential pleasure pavilions, all in a sorry state now. The funerary complex stands at the heart of a practically square enceinte of approximately 2,230 feet (680 meters) down the side; the mausoleum is surrounded by a park subdivided into four plantings (a *chahār-bāgh*) by banked avenues decorated with gently flowing channels that widen out into basins at places along their course. Each avenue starts out from one of the four monumental doors of the enclosure and leads to the tomb. The entire structure of the park and mausoleum—including the absence of funerary mosque—is influenced by the site developed by Akbar for Humāyūn's remains.

The architectural forms employed are, however, quite unlike the elegant reserve prevalent in Delhi as they abandon themselves to a decorative fancy that flirts with the pyrotechnic.

The principal entryway to the site open to the south and called the Chār Minār already reveals a desire to impress with its large *iwan* archway covering the entire height supported on both sides by two flanking pieces set with arches over two levels. On the four corners, pure white marble minarets stand like lances or harbingers of light around the monument, evoking the Chār Minār at Hyderābād, completed in 1591. The façades are inlaid with floral curves and geometrical stone motifs whose color scheme is exceptionally refined. The sinewy yet graceful calligraphy is an example of the penmanship of 'Abd al-Haqq Shirāzi, a renowned artist from Shiraz who was later responsible for the epigraphic program at the Tāj Mahal.

One of the inscriptions, written in Persian, states the builders' ambition unambiguously:

> Hail, blessed space happier than the garden of paradise! Hail, lofty building higher than the divine throne! A paradise, the garden of which comprises hundreds of paradises.... The pen of the mason of the divine decree has inscribed upon its courtyard: These are the gardens of Eden, enter here and abide forever.[10]

The mausoleum

The monument radiates out from a square terrace of almost 328 feet (100 meters) down the side, its elevation comprising 5 levels of decreasing size with the whole culminating at a height of 72 feet (22 meters). On the ground floor, the masonry walls have been daubed with a blood-red wash and feature arcades along all four sides whose decorative economy sets off the exuberant *iwan* opening to the center adorned with red sandstone plaques encrusted with white marble like embers inlaid with ice. The most significant of the four opens to the south onto a hall that accesses a gentle slope leading to the crypt.[11] Galleries of red sandstone extend in stacks from the second to the fourth levels, their surfaces tapering as they rise to blossom the edge of the encircling terrace into *chhatris* whose formal variations catch the eye. Calm white marble dominates the fifth level, encased in its turn by *chhatris* that are placed like marmoreal fibulae at each corner of a terrace ringed with *jalis*. Their openwork decoration enhances the black-and-white marble pavement and gloriously floods in a subdued blaze of light the cenotaph in the center beneath a pavilion surmounted by three domes.

Facing page and above. Entryway in the form of Chār Minār ("Four Minarets"), mausoleum of Akbar, Sikandra, near Āgra, c. 1613.

Royal nomadism: Jahāngīr, from Māndu to Kashmir

The juxtaposition of such disparate architectural motifs prevents any feasible definition of the stylistic principles underlying Akbar's mausoleum. This is the same quandary that must have faced Jahāngīr in trying to forge artistic conceptions of his own in relation to his overwhelming reverence for the paternal image. The burden of such references seems to have been somewhat alleviated, when, as had become customary, the monarch set off to inspect his boundless empire. His epicurean nature soon turned these forays into something like a country jaunt that could last for months, depending on the season, the demands of the court, and the whim of the sovereign. He would, moreover, make the most of these wanderings to erect new buildings or renovate preexisting sites; these monuments of lesser importance proved to be more reliable markers of the king's taste for decoration playing on carnal layers, organic curves, and luxuriant and enveloping gardens.

Interventions in Māndu

From March 6 to October 24, 1617, the court first resided in Māndu, the ancient capital of Mālwa that the royal retinue took four months to reach from Ajmer. Jahāngīr used the intervening time to dispatch architects before him with orders to rehabilitate the site, as the following passage confirms:

> As before the arrival of the royal standards in these regions I had sent 'Abdu-l-Karīm, the architect, to look to the repair of the buildings of the old rulers in Mandu, he during the time the camp halted in Ajmer had repaired some of the old buildings that were capable of repair, and altogether rebuilt some places. In short, he had made ready a house the like of which for pleasantness and sweetness has probably not been made anywhere else. Nearly 300,000 rupees, or 2,000 Persian tumans were expended on this.[12]

During these interventions on the royal complex, the sovereign's emissaries often altered the preexisting architectural heritage; this was particularly the case with the addition of a monumental staircase to the terrace of the Jahāz Mahal. Furthermore, they also erected wholly new constructions.

The Jahāngīrī Mahal of Māndu

The palace built for Jahāngīr in Māndu had a monumental entryway called the Hathi Pol ("Elephant Gate"). Only the terracotta plinths of the sculptures of the august pachyderms that originally framed the doorway are still discernible. From a porch serving as a guardhouse, one reaches a first open space and then through to a vast parade ground on the southeast side of which rises a building with a balcony named the Nahār Jharokā ("Tiger Balcony") overlooking the esplanade awash with dazzling white marble; the figure of a tiger that presumably once adorned it has long since made off. From the Nahār Jharokā, a series of small vaulted rooms leads to a diminutive inner courtyard in the center of which played the refreshing waters of a pool. The spatial layout suggests that the monarch intended to follow the rituals initiated by his father designed to dramatize the appearances of the emperor; here, however, unlike at Fatehpur Sīkri, the space is more intimate and less resoundingly ceremonial.

The "house of Gadā Shāh"
It is probably during Jahāngīr's sojourn that other buildings were constructed whose remains are visible today, such as the "house of Gadā Shāh." Originally, the pavilion so named must have nestled in a garden of which rare vestiges survive. Opposite this first construction emerged the graceful outline of an octagonal kiosk, perhaps ornamented with a small pond. It seems that the "house of Gadā Shāh" was in fact an element in a more ambitious composition featuring a network of small buildings set in gardens among which danced refreshing waters murmuring between basins that gleamed in the light breeze; the whole ensemble is nowadays unfortunately in ruins. The pavilion itself features a square plan structured as a Greek cross opening into four units spread over two levels. On the floor above, the faded beauty of some female portraits in delicate or warmer tones executed in the imperial Mughal style still just cling to the walls.

The gardens of Jahāngīr

Kashmir had been retaken by Akbar; Jahāngīr, who particularly appreciated its climate and splendid scenery, repeatedly sojourned there with his court. It was there that the great royal gardens gave free rein to their bounty and creativity. Concentrated along the perimeters of Srinagar, they are enclosed in vast walls arranged in a square. The terrain of this mountainous zone is conducive to terracing, its regular levels being deliberately relieved by channels that sometimes flow languidly into basins and pools. Since these majestic parks amounted essentially to glorified camp sites, the only permanent constructions to feature among the plantings are an occasional pavilion or bench laid across the waters. The organization of the camp was closely regulated and demonstrably hierarchical: the lowest terraces served for the bodyguards, officers, and hoi polloi, the intermediate sections were used for public audiences, while the topmost plateau was reserved for the emperor's entourage—hidden from prying eyes, it also housed the harem.

The garden of the citadel, Hari Parbat
Akbar was responsible for the initial layout of the garden that lies in the heart of the citadel overlooking the lake. While staying in Srinagar, Jahāngīr resolved to restore it and render it still more impressive, as he indicates in this following passage:

> The lake is close to the fort, and the palace overlooks the water. In the palace there was a little garden, with a small building in it which my revered father used constantly to sit. At this period it appeared to me to be very much out of order and ruinous.... I ordered Mu'tamid Khan, who is a servant who knows my temperament, to make every effort to put the little garden in order and repair the building. In a short time, through his great assiduity, it acquired new beauty. In the garden he put up a lofty terrace thirty-two yards square, in three divisions (*qit'a*), and having repaired the building he adorned it with pictures by master hands, and so made it the envy of the picture gallery of China. I called this garden Nur-afzā (light increasing).[13]

Jahāngīr here attributes to Akbar a way of thinking of the garden as a space for meditation and contemplation, a refuge perhaps from the pomp and ceremony of the court. He, on the contrary, seems to have wanted to emblazon it with the seal of imperial glory. Although it is possible that he is exaggerating in order to turn the spotlight on his exploits, one can read between the lines that Jahāngīr here contrasts a power whose supremacy consists in eliminating nature (thereby confining it to the private sphere) to his practice, which incorporates the force of natural energies in the very definition of imperial dominion over the cosmos.

Shalimar and Nishat
Jahāngīr founded the garden of Shalimar at Srinagar for his wife, Nūr Jahān. Altered under Shāh Jahān then subjected to periods of abandonment, the place is now no more than a pale reflection of its onetime splendor. Laid out over a rectangle measuring almost 1,969 by 820 feet (600 by 250 meters), the garden is now connected to Lake Dal by way of a perfectly straight canal little more than two-thirds of a mile long. The center is highlighted by a rectilinear channel that extends over four terraces, each being subdivided in four parterres to either side of this median axis; cascades and pools attenuate the strict rigidity of the fundamental structure. The exuberance of the plants and water features is only sporadically tempered or interrupted by permanent constructions—except on the higher terrace, where an elegant *baradari* balances on black marble columns, covered, in a period after the reign of the monarch, with a roof divided into four double pitches. On one nocturnal visit, Vicomte Robert d'Humières described the garden thus:

> A kiosk with black marble columns [stands] in the middle of a square bason. From three sides of the square fell cascades, whose sheet of mobile crystal was illumined by lamps set behind them in recesses. The fourth side

The Nishat Bāgh, Srinagar, Kashmir, India, founded by Āsaf Khān, Jahāngīr's brother-in-law, first quarter of the seventeenth century.

opened out the perspective of a long canal bordered with lights, with a line of playing waters as an axis, the last of which ran out towards the lake in moonlit distances. Four other rows of spouting fountains in the bason itself raised as it were a forest of silver lances around the kiosk with its glittering marbles. We were surrounded by the splashing, by the efficient coolness of the heavenly water, the glory of consoling water, the feast and apotheosis of water.[14]

On the banks of Lake Dal stretches the Nishat Bāgh, a work by Āsaf Khān, Nūr Jahān's brother. Today, it boasts no remarkable buildings, but the sheer size of the space, with its ten terraces traversed by a central channel embellished with pools and fountains, remains awe-inspiring. Access to the garden was made by way of a jetty connecting to the lake.

The reign of Jahāngīr saw a huge increase in the number of such gardens (for example, Vernāg and Achabal), but the majority are now in a dreadful state of conservation and the verdant gems of Srinagar described above remain the most eloquent witnesses to the unrestrained and sensuous bonds our monarch managed to weave between natural forces and architectural constructions.

Restoration of the Rām Bāgh, Āgra
It was also at Jahāngīr's instigation that the layout of the garden called the Rām Bāgh (or Bāgh-e Eram) located in Āgra and mentioned in connection with Bābur's contribution was substantially modified, with the addition of pavilions on the terrace overlooking the Yamuna. The rectangular enclosure, measuring roughly 1,099 by 820 feet (335 by 250 meters), is subdivided into 42 squares, 6 wide and 7 deep. It is crossed by a central avenue intersecting a channel running east-west and punctuated by carefully positioned daises (*chabutara*) and pools that impart a measure of structure to its calculated chaos. The interior space of the garden is split into zones of variable accessibility, but, due to its present dilapidation, it remains difficult to reach any worthwhile conclusions as to its layout and planting.

Tomb architecture during the reign of Jahāngīr

The reign of Jahāngīr was enriched not only by the impulsion given architectural activity by the emperor himself, since several of the most prestigious monuments of the period were commissioned by the great and the good of his court.

The mausoleum of I'timād al-Dawla
Completed in 1628, the tomb of I'timād al-Dawla, for instance, was built in Āgra for her father on the initiative of Jahāngīr's wife, Nūr Jahān. The refined proportions of the monument blend intimate lavishness and exquisite grandeur, like a magnified version of an imaginary casket for the crown jewels. Encased in its original garden enclosure, this is the first Mughal building to be clad entirely in white marble inlayed with hardstone, and its unaltered perfection has earned the mausoleum the deserved moniker of the "little Tāj Mahal."

The red sandstone range of the gateway to the site with its white marble Motifs stands to the east of the garden to which it leads. While the access recalls the work of Sikandra, its dimensions are less grandiloquent. The white marble mausoleum on a red sandstone terrace is girded by a simple garden 525 feet (160 meters) along the side classically divided into four parterres (*chahār-bāgh*), the iconic form in spite of the small surface of the traditional Mughal garden. Avenues laid out in a Greek cross lead from the terrace to pavilions rising in the center of the north, south, and west walls of the enceinte, the last of these overlooking the Yamuna in the manner of a terrace. Norias concealed behind the walls supplied running water that flowed through a wall over a small cascade before babbling away along narrow channels and languishing in one of the pools.

With its square plan measuring about sixty-five feet along the side, the mausoleum nestles between minarets with two balconies topped by *chhatris* reinforcing it at each corner. In the center of the terrace the edifice is crowned by a square pavilion, prolonged by another humped-backed *chhatri* terminating in pinnacle finials. The external facings are decorated with motifs of plants and vases in a honey yellow hue executed in hardstone that cast intense, soft light over the snowy marble. The central funerary hall shelters the pair of yellow stone cenotaphs of the deceased and his wife. Eight secondary rooms surround the central hall, some containing tombs. Finally, the ceilings and the interior walls of the monument are adorned with paintings.

The mausoleums of the Khān-e Khānān and Chaunsath Khambā, Delhi
Built to shelter the remains of 'Abd al-Rahīm Khān, nicknamed Khān-e Khānān ("khan of khans"), one of the most significant figures of the courts of Akbar and then Jahāngīr, who died in 1626 or 1627, the eponymous mausoleum displays its compact monumentality not far from the complex of Humāyūn. The marble that once enriched its sturdy outline was removed and reused in the eighteenth century to decorate the mausoleum of Safdar Jang. The square-plan building invests the center of an ample terrace whose footings are hollowed out into cells around the perimeter. Each contains relief motifs that are different on each side of the curve of the arch through which it opens. A single staircase in the south allows access to the terrace. There, in the center of each of the four façades, tall *iwans* rise in majesty between a pair of double-tiered ranges adorned with geometric cartouches which originally framed the marble. These *iwans* are emblazoned with the motif of the six-pointed star (or "seal of Solomon"). An imposing central cupola crowns the building, bolstered at the corners of the roof by four plump *chhatris*.

In the vicinity, in the heart of the district of Nizamuddin, was erected a curious monument built entirely in white marble. Known as Chaunsath-Khambā ("Sixty-Four Columns"), it adopts a square plan of seventy-five feet (twenty-three meters) along the side and opens to each flank through five arcades. The one occupying the center is neatly pierced by a door, itself flanked by two arcades set with *jalis* that sculpt the light, whereas the panels at the quoins are closed off by partitions carved into motifs, but not in openwork. The interior opens into the volume of a columnated hall topped by twenty-five domes of identical size. Several tombs were placed in the monument, including that of Mirzā 'Azīz Kokaltāsh, son of Ataga

Detail of the *jali* and inlay decoration on marble, mausoleum of 'Itimād al-Dawla, Āgra, India, 1628.

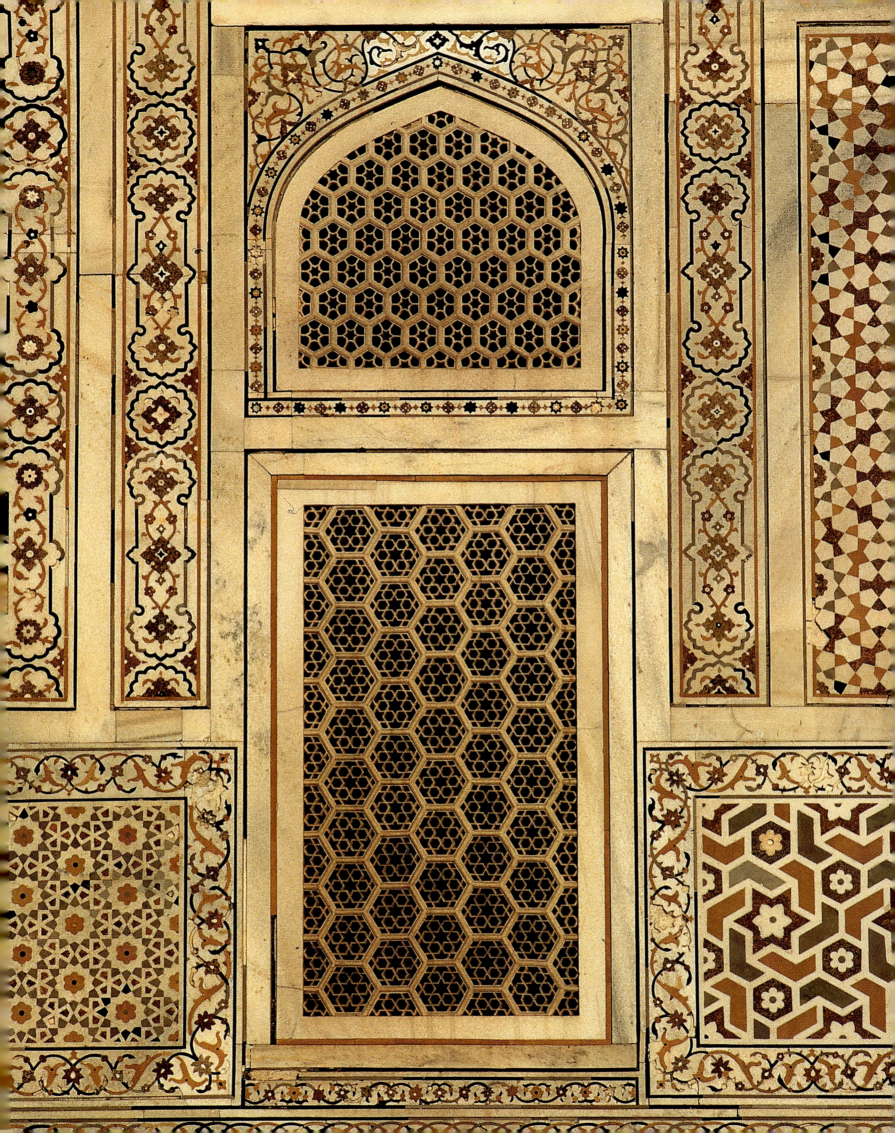

Khān, which bears the date AH 1033 (1623–24). Some are of the opinion that the original function of the building was not funerary, following in this Ebba Koch, who sees it as a possible model for Shāh Jahān's public audience halls.[15]

The imperial necropolis of Shahdārā

When, a victim of his excesses, Jahāngīr expired in 1628 aged fifty-eight, his powerful wife, Nūr Jahān, ordered the construction of a mausoleum now located in the suburbs of Lahore, in the locality of Shahdārā. In 1641 the tomb of the monarch's brother-in-law Āsaf Khān was built against the enclosure of the funerary garden, while not far off the vast complex is completed by a third funerary perimeter housing the remains of Nūr Jahān herself.

The mausoleum of Jahāngīr

The awesome proportions of the tomb of Jahāngīr are housed by a square garden of 1,558 feet (475 meters) down the side. Although descriptions of the monument often compare it to the mausoleum of I'timād al-Dawla, it does not have the balanced proportions of the latter and even gives the impression of being incomplete. The vast, square body of the building appears as if squashed into a single floor between the towering minarets at its corners with their four balconies topped with *chhatris* that accentuate the ramrod appearance of the immense barrels. At one point, the building would have been crowned by a white marble pavilion, but no trace of this remains. In the center of each façade, opening onto a corridor leading to the gateway of the funerary hall, an arcade curves in rhythmic vibration against five similar constructions to either side, forming a composition in which the freshness of marble alternates

with the blaze of sandstone. The funerary hall itself is ensconced beneath a vault with *muqarnas* underneath which reposes the marble cenotaph. A glorious red sandstone porch inlaid with marble in the western wall of the garden leads to Jahāngīr's seraglio, a rectangular planting of 771 by 574 feet (235 by 175 meters) whose enclosure also communicates with the exterior through monumental doors to the north and the south; to the west, meanwhile, it constitutes the *qibla* wall of a mosque whose prayer hall, introduced by a terrace with a pool for ablutions, is capped by three domes.

The mausoleum of Āsaf Khān

Leaning against the west wall of the seraglio, the tomb of Āsaf Khān (Mirzā Abu al-Hasan Āsaf Jāh, or Āsaf Khān, who died in 1634) is in the center of a square garden of 771 feet (235 meters) down the side. The edifice was built under Shāh Jahān, either by the monarch himself, since by marrying Arjūmand Bānū (later known as Mumtāz Mahal for whom the Tāj Mahal was built), he had become the deceased's son-in-law, or else, conceivably, at the instigation of his sister, Nūr Jahān. The monument is essentially built in brick and to a regular octagon plan; the fronts were formerly faced with glazed ceramics, but only scant vestiges cling to the walls today. The dignity of the interior was further enhanced by colorful ceramics and solemn marble dados, but the latter were plundered by Ranjit Singh and reused in the Golden Temple of Amritsar.

The mausoleum of Nūr Jahān

The funerary garden of Jahāngīr's widow was initially probably adjacent to that of her brother, but the ravages of time have not only amputated it of a substantial proportion of its original surface area—approximately 3,391 square feet (315 square meters)—but also scarred it with a railway track. It was the queen herself who supervised the project for the mausoleum in which she was buried after her death at the age of seventy-two in 1638. On a square terrace stands a building of the same ground plan, flanked by corner towers. Like the white marble and red sandstone facings, projecting doorways in the center of the façades slightly modulate their impassive rhythm. Only one floor of the building survives, including the towers in the corners. At the center to each side, framed by the firm curves of a triple arcade, an archway allows access to an interior formerly dressed with plaques of marble that Ranjit Singh purloined on the same occasion as for the preceding mausoleum.

Above and facing page.
The mausoleum of Jahāngīr, Shāhdara, Lahore, Pakistan, c. 1628.

Left. The mausoleum of Nūr Jahān, next to that of her husband Jahāngīr, Shāhdara, Lahore, c. 1638.

Shāh Jahān (1628–1657)

If Shāh Jahān betrayed some impatience to attain the throne, to the point of open conflict with his father, it was the death of Jahāngīr that sparked the real fight for the succession that opposed him and his brothers with their partisans. Dārā Bakhsh, the son of his deceased elder brother Prince Khusrau was the first designated successor, supported by the party of Queen Nūr Jahān, Jahāngīr's widow. The queen had no scruples about taking hostage two of the sons of Prince Khurram (the future Shāh Jahān, third son of Jahāngīr) to whom he had entrusted them on quitting Lahore to undertake a sortie into the Deccan. It was consequently only by turning to Āsaf Khān, the brother of the queen who was also her father-in-law, that Shāh Jahān succeeded in having his competitors assassinated and in seizing power.[16] Several months later he recovered his children, including the future Aurangzeb, brought back to Āgra under escort by Āsaf Khān. The first years of the new emperor's reign are remembered for the revolts in the Deccan that often forced the royal train to move wholesale to the south. There, near Burhānpur, Empress Arjūmand Bānū, known as Mumtāz Mahal, died giving birth to a fourteenth child. Without being devoured by ambition like her aunt, the empress was both a companion and a wise and faithful adviser, and her death hit her husband hard. He then sublimated his bereavement by building the incontrovertible masterpiece of world architecture that is the Tāj Mahal. This acme of technical and artistic perfection should not, however, obscure the exceptional degree of refinement already attained by palatial and religious buildings in capitals of the empire, such as Lahore, Āgra, and Delhi, then renamed Shāh Jahānābād. In plans often relying on faultless symmetry and generous perspectives, everywhere red sandstone and white marble vie with each other in luxury and subtlety. Overwhelming yet rigorous, his achievements turn stone into flesh, the better to convey unambiguous creative thoughts and precisely articulated designs.

Shāh Jahān appears as a monarch who succeeded in transcending both the untutored organizational skills of Akbar and the ethereal sensuality of Jahāngīr, restructuring them into the awe and grandeur that is so plainly visible in the constructions he commissioned or supervised.

Above. *Shāh Jahān Seated on the Peacock Throne*, gouache and gold on paper, Mughal India, c. 1655–58. Victoria and Albert Museum, London, no. IM.113–1921.

Facing page. The Tāj Mahal, Āgra, India, begun in 1632. Detail of the carved white marble paneling.

The Tāj Mahal

Incontestably the most famous monument on the subcontinent and recently declared a "wonder of the world," the Tāj Mahal, started in 1632, still remains for the most part a beauty enshrouded in mystery. Its prestige has nourished a wealth of legends that have become part and parcel of a history that now wallows in the romantic image of an inconsolable emperor giving vent to his grief and reflecting the love he felt for his empress in a monument of unsurpassable perfection.

There is, however, no evidence for the oft-rehearsed idea of a plan for a pendant, a black marble mausoleum to be built on the opposite bank of the Yamuna and linked to the Tāj Mahal over a bridge in which the remains of the bereaved sovereign were to have been interred. Shāh Jahān was in any case buried next to his wife, and, while the right bank of the Yamuna was indeed rehabilitated, it was in fact planted with a garden to provide a "belvedere." Actually, although there exists a plethora of documents relating to the construction of the masterpiece, much crucial information is still lacking—in particular the name of the chief architect.

To the rear of the bowery garden that encircles it, the mausoleum stands on a terrace dominating the river that runs past it in the distance, presenting a pure, snowy silhouette that changes hue over the hours and seasons, an entire palette caressed by a light that varies in a veiled or cloudless sky. On either side of the tomb, the composition is framed by a red sandstone mosque and an identical counterpart. The splendor of the ensemble owes as much to the irreproachable harmony of its proportions as to the nobility of the marble and the hardstone inlays verge on immateriality.[17]

The enceinte and the garden
The complex is accessible by a vast rectangular plaza of 984 by 459 feet (300 by 140 meters), divided into four seraglios and lined by shops. An enclosure cordons off this space from the rest of the city that one reaches through huge gates opening to the south, east, and west. The margins of the site, also embellished by a funerary mosque, have been enhanced over the years by some elegantly dignified mausoleums containing the remains of great ladies of the court. To the north, the imposing entrance points towards the main garden; all red sandstone and white marble and firmly anchored to the ground, the quadrangular tetrapylon sheathed with corner minarets bristling with *chhatris* rises to two stories. A broad *iwan* leads to an elliptical central hall emerging onto the garden front through a further *iwan* of equal dimensions. Their summits feature an enfilade of eleven small *chhatris* spiked by tapering pinnacles, reminiscent of the earlier Buland Darwāza of Fatehpur Sīkri.

The panoramic views in the garden in which the mausoleum is lodged are organized around a square 984 feet (300 meters) down the side and structured, as with the tombs of Humāyūn and Akbar, as a strictly composed *chahār-bāgh* (quadripartite garden). The four main surfaces are delimited by channels forming a Greek cross and are each divided into four parterres. The novelty here consists in the mausoleum's being situated on the riverfront and addressing the entrance range. In the center of the garden, the neat lines of an elevated white marble *chabutara* make room in the middle for the festooned contours of a pool of refreshing water. Less imposing, to the east and west gracious pavilions (one of which today houses a small museum) adjoining the outer wall echo one another. The enclosing wall is reinforced by four corner towers complemented by two further companions in front of the terrace overlooking the river, the whole suggesting that even the prospects discovered from the esplanade owe their grandeur solely to the harmony of the monument.

Below. Plan of the funerary complex, Tāj Mahal, Āgra, begun in 1632 (after C. Tadgell).

Facing page. The Tāj Mahal seen from the Yamuna.

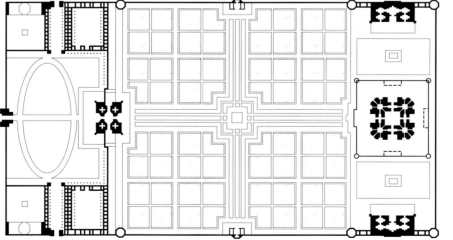

The terrace
With their hard, subdued, or variegated reflections that play over the stonework, the clear and perfect lines of the terrace dominating the river glitter like a stream of pure mineral. This is the culmination of the perspectives the garden has been building up since the entrance and is divided into three squares of 328 feet (100 meters) along the side. In the central zone, the mausoleum sits atop a white marble podium together with four corner minarets, while red sandstone predominates in the eastern and western squares. These are distributed in their turn into two zones that initially prolong at the center into a terrace before switching back against the enclosing wall, as if propelled by some tectonic force. To the west rises a mosque whose dark sandstone contrasts with the white marble of its three domes; to the east this is mirrored by a *jawāb* (literally, "answer"), a doppelganger of the first building that is, however, incompatible with the practice of prayer because of its orientation.

Beyond a monomaniacal taste for symmetry, this theatrical set piece was treated by Shāh Jahān as a frame and designed to be rigorously subservient to the glorification of the mausoleum itself.

The mausoleum
The point towards which all the various features of the complex converge, the great monument surges luminously from its podium in a burst of serene brightness. It is

arranged around an irregular octagon on a square base with 230-foot (70-meter) sides and rises to a dome whose strongly inflected form curves into an onion bulb, as if held up in offering from the tall drum supporting it. To the corners of a central dais with sides of some 340 feet (104 meters), the immaculate barrels of four "minarets" (they have no liturgical function) that are some 170 feet (52 meters) tall—that is, half of the aforementioned measurement—render the space encasing the edifice almost tangible and hint at a structure whose presence, though still invisible, can be sensed. The tomb emerges from the heart of the terrace, each front recessed by a large *iwan* whose firm and majestic curves occupy the entire elevation of the central zone, while two superposed arcades appear on the lateral registers; and likewise, and in identical proportions, on the shorter of the returns in the octagon. Amplifying the verticality, the arrises on the upper level surge into tapering pinnacles; while, with four large *chhatris* bolstering the dome, the ultimate impression on the topmost reaches is essentially that of a pyramid.

Inside as out, every visible surface is wrapped in white marble over which trails a melodious hardstone inlay of, on the one hand, a subtly kaleidoscopic repertory floral motifs, and, on the other, an impressive epigraphic program created by the famous calligrapher ʿAbd al-Haqq Shirāzi (called Amānat Khān) in black thuluth script that exalts the elegance of its aristocratic ascenders.[18] These decorative variations are set off by white marble skirting carved with low reliefs whose liveliness seems freely inspired by engravings in European herbals.

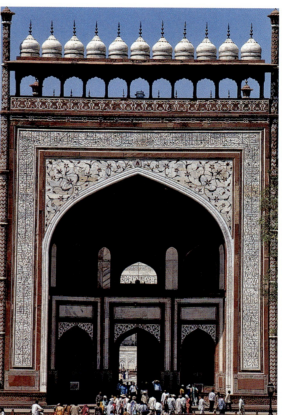

Facing page. The sole function of the counterpart, or *jawāb*, of the funerary mosque is to preserve the overall symmetry of the Tāj Mahal, Āgra.

Above left. *Iwan* of the white marble mausoleum, incrusted with hardstone. Right: entrance to the funerary complex topped by a cortege of miniature *chhatris*.

The funerary hall
Inside the mausoleum, while the tombs of Mumtāz Mahal and Shāh Jahān repose in the crypt, a hall seventy-nine feet (twenty-four meters) high and with a diameter of almost fifty-nine meters (eighteen meters) shelters their cenotaphs, which seem to be draped behind an openwork white marble screen as delicate as lace. The funerary backdrop is studded with hardstone incrustations shimmering with carnelian, lapis lazuli, malachite, jasper, and onyx in a composition repeated identically on the tombs in the crypt, deploying an unfussy floral brocade and exemplifying the taste for engraved botanical illustration that gripped the period. Notwithstanding, the surviving interior appears understated to the point of austerity compared to the decoration as it was originally embellished with silver-plated doors, gilded chandeliers, and silver and gold grilles set with precious stones, not to mention silk carpets and gilt bronze flambeaus. Following the depredations of Aurangzeb and generations of brigands, nothing remains of this treasure trove of ornament.

246

Facing page and above. The paneling of the *iwans* of the Tāj Mahal, Āgra, is finely carved with motifs reminiscent of European herbals; the borders are incrusted with hardstone.

The architect of the Tāj Mahal
Nothing in the mass of documents regarding the construction of the monument provides any reliable information as to the identity of the architect who designed it and oversaw the building work. Several indicators point to Augustin of Bordeaux or the Venetian Geronimo Veroneo, both Europeans whose names are often cited together with three other significant figures. The first of these is Ustād Ahmed, a mathematician and architect originally from Herāt and invested with the title Nādir al-'Asr ("wonder of his time"); the son of this scholar, named Lutfullāh and also a mathematician, claims the credit with his father for the construction of Tāj Mahal, but also of the Red Fort and the Jama' Masjid of Delhi. The second claimant is Mir 'Abd Al-Karīm, called Ma'mur Khān by Jahāngīr, who was commanded to build and restore certain palaces in Māndu; it seems that this was the man Shāh Jahān dispatched to Āgra in 1632 to serve on the site of the Tāj Mahal while he was engaged on additions the emperor had intended for the fort in Lahore. A further name mentioned in this connection is that of Mullā Murshid Shirāzi, also called Mukarrimat Khān, who reappears on later building sites at the palace of Delhi. In conclusion, it may reasonably be imagined that these three famous architects worked in concert on the site under the guidance of an omnipresent Shāh Jahān.

Viewpoints and perspectives
The impact of the Tāj Mahal is furthered by its integration into a skein of visual perspectives. Those generated by the rigorous geometrical construction of the site have been alluded to, but Shāh Jahān went beyond this in incorporating within his magnum opus viewpoints external to the tomb complex proper. Thus, the Bāgh-e Mahtāb ("garden in the moonlight") languishes on the northern bank of the Yamuna, along a low stretch of terrain bathed by the river and exactly opposite

the mausoleum. In the image of the Rām Bāgh, the locality was probably founded before the accession of the sovereign, but the relatively unbroken relief of the garden takes on special importance, the gently undulating greensward magnified in the shade of a building of great power. The link between the two sites is crystallized in the dedication of a large octagonal tank 164 feet (50 meters) across that the garden seems to present like a mirror to the mausoleum on the farther bank. Shortly after its installation, this was devastated by a flash flood, but, as restored today, it allows the Tāj Mahal to be viewed as if conjured up from some cosmic dream.

Above and facing page. Details of the paneling and corner colonnette with a chevron pattern inlay in hardstone on white marble, Tāj Mahal, Āgra.

Above and facing page. The mosque of Wazīr Khān, Lahore, Pakistan, 1635.

Religious architecture at the time of Shāh Jahān

During the reign of Shāh Jahān religious building flourished, reflecting the sovereign's self-appointed role as guardian of orthodoxy. Thus, a large number of great (or Friday) mosques sprung up in the more prosperous cities of the subcontinent, with often daring forms and audacious interiors. In this connection, the mosque of Wazīr Khān in Lahore and the Abdel Kafu Jami' of Thatta vie in conceptual originality and the richness of their glazed ceramic trim. Not to be outdone, the Jama' Masjid of Delhi and the mosque at Āgra, although they distance themselves less from the normal schema of the "imperial mosque," offer an insight into the newfound balance between ample proportions and delicate ornamentation, achieving a bipolarity oscillating between the understated yet dense notes of red sandstone and the brighter flurries of snow-white marble.

The mosque of Wazīr Khān in Lahore (1635)

Wazīr Khān (his real name was Hakīm 'Alī and he was from Chiniot), commenced his career as a physician, first becoming a minister before serving as governor of Punjab from 1633 to 1640. He served Prince Khurram for a long time before the latter seized power as Shāh Jahān. Since Lahore, the chief city of Punjab, was one of the capitals of the kingdom, Wazīr Khān decided to build a place of worship that incorporates some original features very different from the traditional lines of the Mughal great mosque, including a triple-domed prayer hall, minarets arranged in pairs, porticoes with a single aisle, and imposing axial portals.

The frame is brick, the characteristic material for major structures in the region, and is liberally bedecked with glazed ceramic panels for the most part made of cut-tile mosaic. The visible surfaces are chiefly strewn with plant themes that flirt with the vaguely naturalist influences of Western herbals, enhanced by crisply executed calligraphic panels in both Arabic and Persian.

The monument squats on a rectangular base of 278 by 157 feet (85 by 48 meters), opening onto a central court lined by a chain of porticoes, or *riwāqs*, occupied by cells implying that the building also functioned as a madrassa—a somewhat atypical remit in Indian religious architecture. To the east, a monumental gate opens into the courtyard as well as laterally to a covered bazaar with a host of storefronts on either side of the entryway; renting out such commercial concessions would have paid for the maintenance of the madrassa. Spiritual uplift is afforded by the graceful elevation of the minarets standing at the four corners, while the prayer hall occupies the western side of the courtyard. The large central *iwan* is framed by two arcades generating a total of five zones that blossom at roof level into the same number of cupolas.

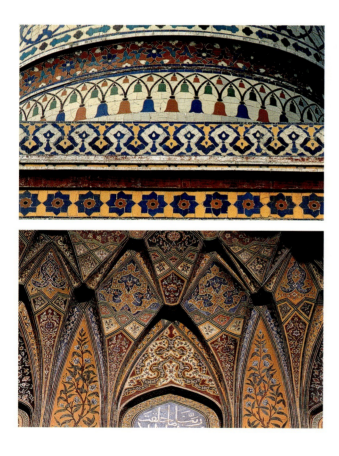

Facing page. Cut and inset ceramic decoration in the mosque of Wazīr Khān, Lahore.

Left. Portico (*riwāq*), Jama' Masjid, Thatta, Pakistan, 1647.

The Jama' Masjid of Thatta (1647) and the monuments of the Makli Hills
Thatta was the capital of Sindh, a province that—until 1627, the date of the arrival as head of state of Mirzā Issā Khān (who reigned until 1644), the founder of the Tarkhān line—remained relatively unhindered by the shackles of the centralized power. Unsurprisingly, the dynasty became intent on affirming its prestige by erecting various monuments, such as the Great Mosque, also known as Abdel Kafu Jami', in Thatta, completed during the reign of Shāh Jahān in 1647. The powerful form of the building stands firm on a plan inspired by the "Persian" mosque with four *iwans*. The brick is coursed in such a manner as to form a decoration in itself, but this ground is further illumined with a ceramic cladding that features geometrical or highly stylized motifs in a dense and luminous color scheme. This decoration was applied liberally, as much on the external façades as on the interior walls.

254

Above the dado running around the hall of the main mihrab—whose chiefly turquoise and blue enamel tile cladding plunges it into the unearthly glow of an undersea cave—a frieze of cartouches unfurls a thuluth epigraphic program in white on a cobalt ground. In the upper reaches, the curves of a dome on squinches are modulated though a delicate decoration which underscores the network of the force fields that give it structure.

The area of the Makli Hills to the west of the city boasts a veritable hive of mausoleums of members of the Tarkhān line, one of the more astonishing being the tomb of Mirzā Issā Khān, constructed in exposed stonework in a style not unlike that of Fatehpur Sīkri.

The Jama' Masjid of Āgra (1649)

This monument, built between 1644 and 1649 and supposedly financed by Jahānārā, the eldest daughter of Shāh Jahān, is contemporary with—if less imposing than—the great mosque of Delhi. Its rectangular plan of 328 by 269 feet (100 by 82 meters) sits on an earthwork so that the entrances are reached up staircases. The manner in which the porticoes are arranged into precincts to the north and south of the courtyard is compatible with its function as a Koranic school. Ringed by a band of black thuluth calligraphy over a white ground dating to 1648, the prayer hall is preceded by a broad *iwan*. To both sides of this porch stand "pseudo-minarets" or pinnacles, their bases decorated with a discreetly elegant repeated pattern of encrusted black and white stone palmettes contrasting with the flesh tints of the red sandstone. The decorously reserved mihrab is joined by a marble *minbar* whose back is incised with a scaled-down picture of the mosque itself. Except on the side with the main entryway, the parapets marking the summits of the façades are hemmed by a procession of energetic if small *chhatris*. The individual personality of the edifice derives primarily from the three onion-like domes, without drums, whose sinuous lines emerge from above the prayer hall and whose surfaces are plastered with a chevron pattern alternating white marble and red sandstone.

The Jama' Masjid at Delhi (1650–56)

When Shāh Jahān ordered the construction of this new place of worship, his intention was to outdo in size and magnificence all earlier achievements of the same type. The fact is that this Friday mosque is indeed the largest in India and only exceeded in scale on the subcontinent by the one Aurangzeb erected in Lahore, today in Pakistan. It took six years to complete and the combined energies of some five thousand workmen.

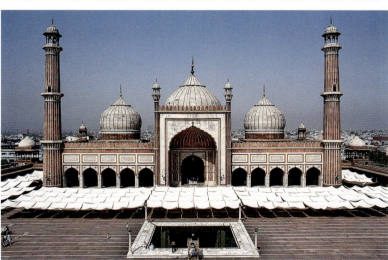

Facing page. Mausoleum of Mirzā 'Issā Khān, Makli Hills, Thatta, dated 1644.

Top, left and right. The Jama' Masjid, Āgra, India, 1649; the back of the *minbar* presents a view of the façade to the prayer hall.

Left. The Jama' Masjid, Delhi, India, 1650–56.

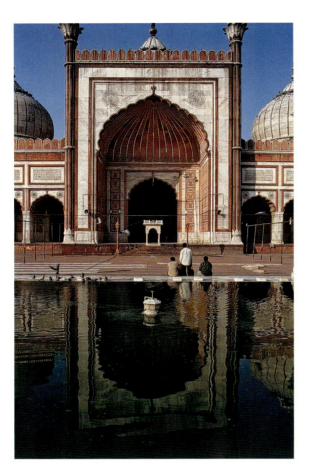

This enormous edifice stands on an approximate quadrilateral some 377 feet (115 meters) wide by 362 feet (110 meters) deep. It is approached and seen from below, the three gates accessible from broad flights of steps with the largest opening to the east. The immense paved courtyard is festooned on three sides by porticoes that give onto the outside, in particular to the east, opposite the *qibla* wall; this last façade is, moreover, reinforced by sturdy square towers topped by pretty corner pavilions.

The geometric mastery of the prayer hall unfolds to the rear of the main courtyard. In the center rises a large *iwan*, whose formal sobriety underlines the opulent yet unfussy verticality of its facings, where alternate braids of red sandstone and white marble mutually enhance their chromatic density. A similar color contrast surfaces on the five arcades to either side of the *iwan* that terminate in tall minarets studded with three balconies and capped with *chhatris*. Above the prayer hall, three white marble cupolas striated with slender bands of black stonework look like buds gorged with sap and ready to burst into flower; the most impressive of the three in the center towers over the space stretching before the main mihrab.

The imprint of Shāh Jahān in Lahore

The nomadic life of the Mughal court could not fail to lead Shāh Jahān to Lahore, where he resided from 1628. The city was one of the supreme glories of the kingdom and the emperor quickly sought to leave his mark there, too—if need be to the detriment of whatever was left by his predecessors. He was imitated in this by members of his entourage.

The fort of Lahore

The citadel was actually founded by Akbar, but Shāh Jahān stamped his mark on the defenses from 1628, soon modifying the appearance of an enceinte that is both more regular and on a smaller scale than its counterparts in Āgra or Delhi, extending to a rectangle some 1,198 by 1,001 feet (365 by 305 meters).

It is to this period that dates the cut-tile and inlay mosaic on the external brick façades on the northern wall and near the Hathi Pol ("Elephant Gate") to the west that give the monument its characteristic flavor. The ceramics assemble into a kind of picture gallery showing lively and impromptu scenes of fighting elephants or camels, military parades, and equestrian sports delightfully set off in clearly delimited compartments. The narrative dimension of this decoration is considerably enhanced both by the use of a restricted palette so that the actions stand out against a rather uniform ground and thanks to a graphic style that captures movement in tilework that is cut so meticulously that it suggests the compositional delicacy of manuscript painting.

The personality of Shāh Jahān also appears within the fort, as in the vast court leading to the Divān-e 'Āmm ("divan of public audience"), where an imposing colonnade shelters the imperial loggia. The private apartments extend the court to the north; the Bari Khwābgāh ("greater dormitory") was probably built by Jahāngīr before being reconfigured by Shāh Jahān, who was certainly responsible for the construction of the Choti Khwābgāh ("lesser dormitory"). Lastly, to the northeast of the public audience hall nestles the Motī Masjid ("Pearl Mosque"), built on Jahāngīr's initiative. This name was appropriated by his son for the great mosque of the fort of Āgra and by Aurangzeb for his small oratory in Delhi.

To the northwest corner of the citadel, the Musaman Burj ("octagonal tower") conceals some sumptuous apartments coiled up against an array of pavilions arranged into a half-octagon within a courtyard refreshed by the waters of a basin with *chabutara* in the center. Among them, the polylobe archways of the colonnade of the Shish Mahal to the north give onto a room "with walls clad in mirrors," while in the west the sensual curves of a *bangaldār* (humpbacked or "Bengali") roof burgeon into a white marble pavilion known as the Nawlakha.[19]

Facing page. Main *iwan* of the Jama' Masjid, Delhi, with its reflection in the pool.

Below. Plan of the fort at Lahore, Pakistan (after Kamil Khan Mumtaz): **(1)** Hazuri Bāgh **(2)** Musaman Burj **(3)** Jahāngir quadrangle **(4)** Divān-e ' Amm.

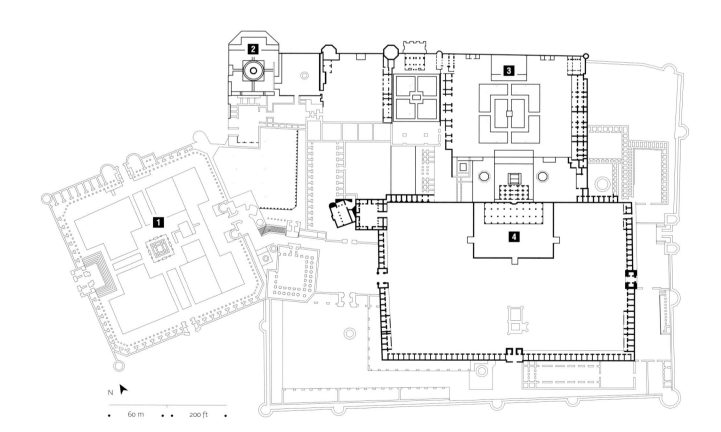

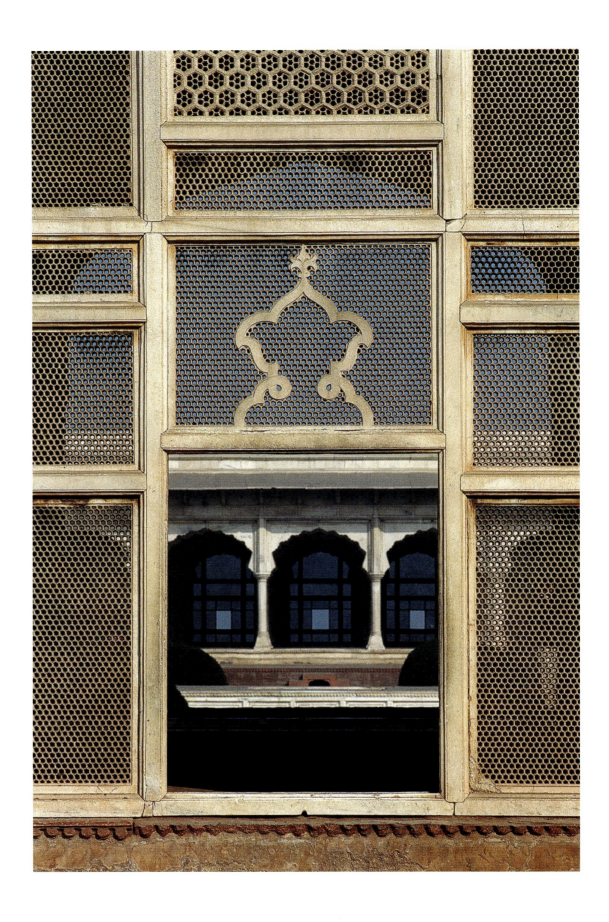

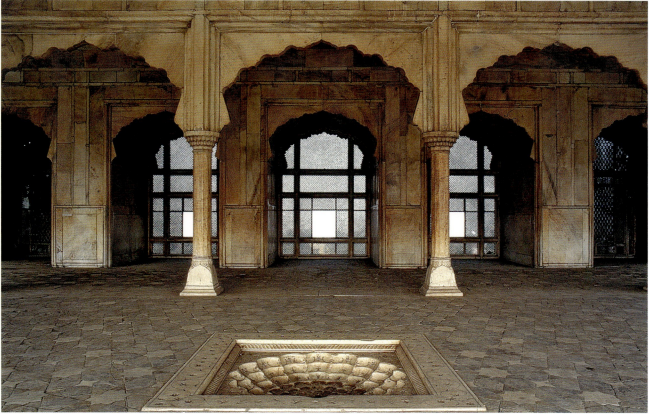

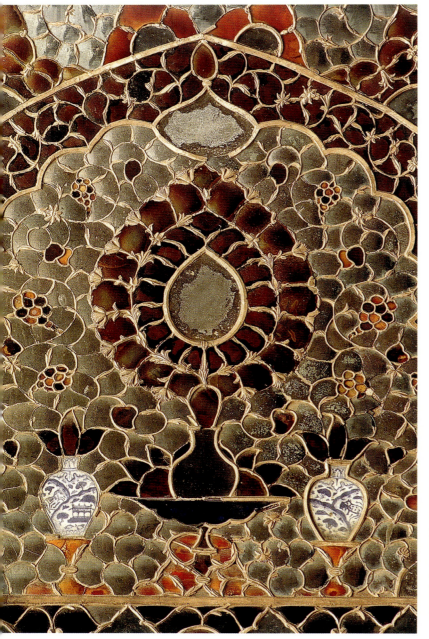

Pages 258–259. The fort at Lahore. The Shish Mahal and the Divān-e Khās; the latter was built under Shāh Jahān in 1645.

Above. Incrusted mirror-glass decoration, Shish Mahal, Lahore.

Facing page. View through the *jali* of the Divān-e Khās, Lahore, to the gardens below.

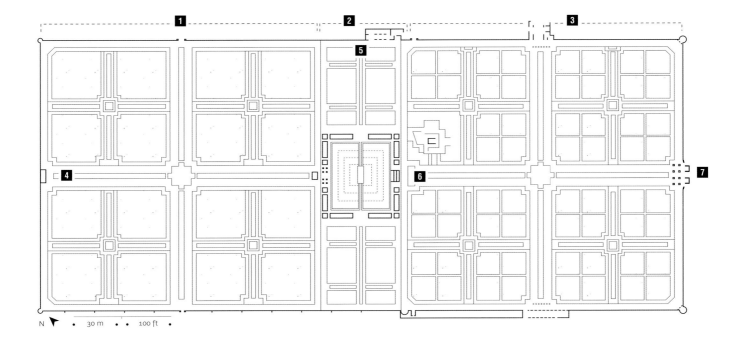

Above. Plan of the Shalimar gardens, Lahore, Pakistan (after Kamil Khan Mumtaz): **(1)** first terrace **(2)** second terrace **(3)** third terrace **(4)** entrance pavilion **(5)** hammam **(6)** pavilion **(7)** current entrance.

Facing page. The Red Fort, Āgra, India, viewed from the Musaman Burj ("Octagonal Tower").

The gardens of Lahore
The gardens of Shalimar in Lahore, planted between 1636 and 1642, are some of the most accomplished and best preserved. The crystalline fountains and sagaciously limpid waters of the pools are supplied by a channel completed in only 1648 under the aegis of the governor 'Alī Mardān Khān, while, in places, cut-out ceramic tilework adorned with floral patterns can be seen on the structural walls, responding in a half-realistic, half-stylized idiom to their natural cousins outside. This first planting paved the way in 1646 to that of the Chauburji Bāgh, executed at the instigation of Shāh Jahān's daughter, Jahānārā, and to others still, such as the Gulābi Bāgh in 1671. In the end, the city was encircled by a veritable "green belt," each garden competing in dazzling prospects and glittering waters with its neighbors.

The apogee of Āgra
If the Tāj Mahal remains the jewel in Shāh Jahān's Āgra crown, its prestige should not obscure the rest of a capital which in this time was ablaze with glory. In this respect, the Chini-ka-Rauza ("porcelain mausoleum") is indicative of the effervescent atmosphere that led high-ranking personages to select such places to trumpet their ambitions. Notwithstanding, the most eloquent testimonies of the political might of the city are the splendid works undertaken at the Red Fort at the instigation of the emperor himself. While the monument had already been substantially altered by Akbar, it is Shāh Jahān

who gave it its impressive contemporary appearance. The later destruction—following the Sepoy Mutiny of 1857—by the British of three-quarters of its surface area is a source of tremendous regret. This explains (among other depredations) the complete disappearance of the ancient *naqqāra-khāna* ("bandstand"), which would have greeted visitors where it opens onto the Delhi gate on the west side of the enceinte. The current entrance opens to the south, initially through a door on a dogleg and then through the Amar Singh gate, named after the brother of the maharaja of Jodhpur whom Shāh Jahān had executed on this very spot in 1644.

Divān-e 'Āmm and the Motī Masjid

Once through the gate of Amar Singh flanked by two imposing engaged towers whose bases are decorated with cartouches framing colored ceramic panels, one climbs the slope up which elephants used to enter the fort. The space then widens into a vast court bordered by porticoes in which thrones the Divān-e 'Āmm ("public audience hall"), the nerve center of the whole complex, since it is there that royal audiences were held, while the offices of the chancellery and the upper echelons of the political administration were housed under the surrounding porticoes. To the eastern side of the court, the red sandstone frame covered in white stucco of the Divān-e 'Āmm adjoins a building leading to the private apartments; from there one reaches the loggia, a lofty white marble construction adorned with floral motifs in hardstone inlay. The three other sides open grandly onto a hypostyle structure three bays deep by nine wide; its columns ascend with hieratic stiffness before opening out into gloriously clipped polylobe arches in what is a metaphor of royal might and munificence. The Āgra Divān is the largest such hall, taller even than those of the forts of Delhi and Lahore.

To the north of the court, one discovers the Motī Masjid ("Pearl Mosque"), erected between 1646 and 1653 by Shāh Jahān, as a Persian inscription makes clear. The name stems from the dazzlingly white marble that seems to lay a delicate sheen over the construction vibrating within its ruddy sandstone enceinte. Almost dazed by the glare of the immaculate domes towering over its three aisles, the pavement of the prayer hall is laid with black and yellow marble, one prevailing motif being that of the prayer mat.

Khās Mahal and private apartments

The monarch's private apartments extend east of the fort, screened off from the public audience hall by a closely guarded wall. The space is organized around a large court called the Machchi Bhawan ("Fish Pavilion"), which owes its current name to the pools teeming with life with which it was once adorned. Today framed with galleries of red sandstone, to the east it is dominated by the Divān-e Khās built in 1637, an elegant white marble pavilion borne on dodecagonal columns grouped in pairs. These columns widen at the summit into polyfoil arches as light as

264

Facing page, top. Ornamented column, Musaman Burj, Red Fort, Āgra.

Facing page, bottom. Paneling with carved floral decoration, Dīvān-e Khās, Red Fort, Āgra.

Left. Bases of the twin columns in the Khās Mahal decorated with incrusted hardstone, Red Fort, Āgra.

butterflies, while the lines in the lower sections, their barrels, and their capitals are set with motifs in colored stone. The Dīvān-e Khās introduces the visitors to an ample terrace on which stands a black marble throne installed by Jahāngīr opposite the river at the time of his accession in 1605. Shāh Jahān naturally responded with a white marble pendant on the courtyard side.

To the south, Dīvān-e Khās communicates with the Musaman Burj ("octagonal tower"), so-called because it stands on one of the towers of the fort enclosure. It looks like an octagonal pavilion, sumptuously clad in marble decorated with a rich inlay of hardstone motifs. After his son Aurangzeb usurped the throne in 1658, Shāh Jahān spent his last years here under house arrest until his death in 1666. At this time, he would have had at his disposal the small oratory lying between the tower and the Dīvān-e Khas.

Of the hammam that was attached to the private apartments and unfortunately in a severe state of disrepair, there remains the Shish Mahal (literally, "glass palace"), a building also rather badly preserved, but whose decoration consists of a blinding profusion of inlaid mirror glass; it is regrettable that such a work is so seldom accessible to the public.

Even so, the most ravishing jewel squirreled away among this impressive enfilade of white-marble lined apartments is probably the Khās Mahal ("private palace"). It rises above a terrace that, to the courtyard side, looks over the Anguri Bāgh ("grape garden") dug into a pool with leaping water jets. Rectangular pillars bearing five polylobe arches bring light to a marble front surmounted at roof level by a *chajja* and two diminutive *chhatris*. To either side of the terrace twin *bangaldār* pavilions—not identical twins, though, as one is marble and the other sandstone coated white—play hide and seek behind the marble screens partitioning off the courtyard. Their humpback roofs are covered like tortoises by a luxurious shell of gilt metal plates, originally topped by a crest of finials in the shape of golden apples.

The Chini-ka-Rauza
Outside the enclosure of the Red Fort on the right bank of the Yamuna rises a tomb known as, thanks to its glazed ceramic mural cladding, the "porcelain mausoleum." It shelters the remains of Shokr-allāh Shirāzi, known as Afzal Khān, a poet and officer who died in 1639. Though he enjoyed an enviable position at court, his brother, a

Facing page, top
Amar Singh gate, Red Fort, Āgra, 1644.

Facing page, bottom. The Chini-ka-Rauza, mausoleum of Afzal Khān, Āgra, after 1639.

Above. Cut-out and inlaid enameled ceramic decoration, Chini-ka-Rauza, Āgra.

calligrapher, is now better known.[20] This stocky and sturdy edifice stands on a square plan with a single imposing central dome reinforced by guardian pinnacles at the four corners of the main range. All the exterior surface was probably once dressed in a mosaic-type decoration in ceramics, while the majestic *iwans* were framed by epigraphic friezes, in all probability penned by the deceased's brother in a cobalt blue thuluth script on a white ground of which only the odd scrap can be deciphered today. The walls of the building are organized in rectangular or square compartments, with an abundance of ceramic decorations in colors ranging from white to the black, via cobalt blue and turquoise, chrome green, yellow (antimony?), and purple manganese to weave a lively floral pattern representative of an era especially fond of irises, fritillaries, and poppies.

Shāhjahānābād, or the consecration of Delhi

Although, during the sultanate era, the city of Delhi had long profited from political preeminence, its role as capital had been under threat from the ascendency of cities such as Āgra and Lahore, rising from its ashes after being sacked by Timur and other invaders. It was Shāh Jahān, probably in around 1638, who started the process leading to the consecration of Delhi as the unquestioned figurehead of the empire, both re-dedicating the city itself and rehabilitating its power centers. The sovereign led the work on reinstating the city on a new site, called Shāhjahānābād, corresponding to what we today call Old Delhi, the historic core of the current capital. For the first time in India on such a magnificent scale, it was city planning that guided the layout of an urban fabric, and this beyond the "classier" quarters. The transport network, provisioning, and drainage were thoroughly conceptualized, permitting the emergence of an embryonic planning policy governing the construction sites and a certain rationalization of population settlement arranged into districts. In this manner, the prince gave fresh impetus to the activities of the city that fueled an impressive economic boom. In parallel, he had monuments erected that symbolized the city's newly recovered luster, initially in the spiritual realm—with the Jama' Masjid already mentioned—then more especially in the temporal realm, with the changes made to the Red Fort that give it the grandiose appearance it enjoys today.[21]

The enceinte
The curved wall surrounding the complex measures 2,952 feet (900 meters) at its maximum width (north-south) by 1,558 feet (475 meters) deep (east-west). The imposingly lofty wall punctuated by towers that insulate it from the seething life of the nearby city is accompanied by a moat that reinforces its proud resolve. Two main gates, that of Delhi in the south and Lahore to the west, allow access to the nerve center within. At the time of Aurangzeb, the second gate was supplemented by a kind of barbican positioned in front of the vast entryway, itself crowned by seven small *chhatris* escorted by pinnacles, and prolonged outside the enceinte by a covered bazaar, Chatta Chowk. There, to both sides of a shaded walkway at the height of the domes, visitors could look down on various colorful stores selling quality groceries and curios, now sadly replaced by souvenir shops.

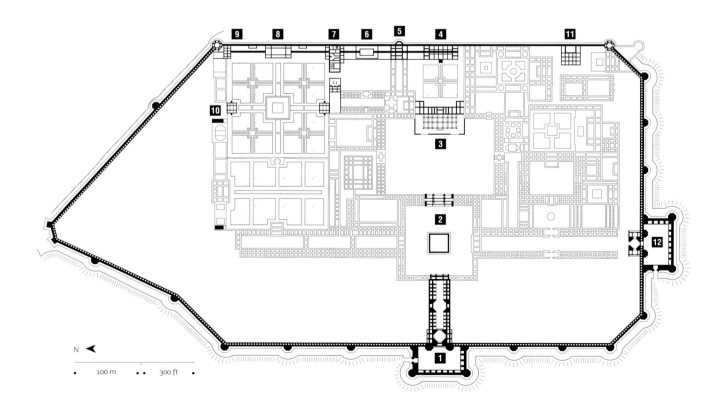

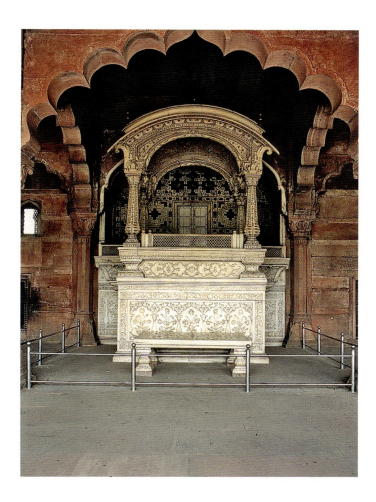

Facing page. Plan of the Red Fort, Delhi, India
(after C. Tadgell): **(1)** Lahore gate; **(2)** Naqqāra-Khāna;
(3) Divān-e 'Āmm; **(4)** Rang Mahal; **(5)** Musaman Burj;
(6) Divān-e Khās; **(7)** hammam; **(8)** Motī Masjid;
(9) Shāh Burj; **(10)** Bhadon pavilion; **(11)** Mumtāz Mahal;
(12) Delhi gate.

Facing. The Divān-e 'Āmm in the Red Fort at Delhi,
with the marble throne behind which one can glimpse
panels incrusted with hardstone.

Naqqāra-Khāna

Escaping the hustle and bustle of the bazaar, one enters a vast square containing buildings for the most part reserved for the chancellery and various administrations. To both sides of this space, along a north-south axis perpendicular to the commercial street, the supply and provision branches of the government were distributed in locales situated along the two thoroughfares; there were sheds and stables for every species of mount—horses, dromedaries, elephants—as well as "workshops" furnishing the great and the good with rugs, carpets, brocade, and gold- and silverwork. This elaborate system provisioning the train of the emperor and his court has long since vanished and only one building on the square survives: the Naqqāra-Khāna, or "bandstand," a prelude to interior spaces that were the unique preserve of a select handful. This building acted as much as a grand entryway as a pavilion for the court band that were lodged in an upper loggia and sounded the hours or played fanfares and flourishes for more distinguished visitors.

The register on the ground floor clearly stresses the curves of three archways; the one in the center opens into a passage providing pedestrian access to the court of public audience. On the elevation above, three further polylobe arches correspond to counterparts on the lower level. The external masonry walls are daubed with a coating, while the front facing the nobler sectors of the complex is faced with red sandstone

and divided into compartments embellished with niches and a flower show of carved motifs inspired by European herbals, with lilies, fritillaries, amaryllis, and irises as on a naturalist's engraving, their sensuous curves and dashes of green allowing a foretaste of the monarch's even more refined apartments.

Divān-e 'Āmm, the "public audience hall"
After the Naqqāra-Khāna one reaches the specifically royal realm of the fort, beginning with the ample esplanade that constitutes the court for public audiences, originally entirely girdled by a series of buildings, as in the example described in the preceding paragraph. None of these constructions has however resisted the depredations perpetrated by occupying troops who invested the site over the centuries, except for the Divān-e 'Āmm itself. The space reserved for the official audiences granted by the monarch, the monument was designed to highlight the privileged nature of such apparitions, as much as the might and incomparable eminence of his rule. In 1648, the sovereign thus replayed the formula already tried and tested in Lahore in 1628 and Āgra in 1637, with a colonnade occupying a broad and open parallelepiped projection. Imposingly hieratic and vertical, ten columns or column groups spout out from the façade, reappearing in several equally dynamic rows that generate four bays, the last abutting the wall separating this place from the private apartments—hence the name Chehel Sotūn ("forty columns") usually employed to refer to the building.[22] The hall itself is visible through the delicate yet bold outlines of nine polyfoil arches, while a *chajja* and a parapet ensure the transition to a roof with small *chhatris* at the quoins, like guardsmen in dress uniform. The sovereign's loggia rises majestically to face the central arcade. A white marble bench encrusted with hardstones stands at the foot of the baldachin, which for its part seems to hover a fair height above ordinary mortals, supported on baluster columns and surmounted by a curvilinear square roof redolent of the Bengali *chau-chala*. In the zone behind the baldachin against the wall there parades the splendor of the crown: ornaments in rich, almost virulent hardstone encased within an assemblage of black marble slabs, with intricate floral encrustations forming gleaming droplets of color picked out against the snowy marble. The birds composing the motifs on the black marble are probably of Florentine origin and the remarkable figure of Orpheus playing a violin, no less incongruous in this environment, must also surely hail from Italy.[23]

Facing page. The Rang Mahal with
its marble fountain, in the private area
of the Red Fort, Delhi.

Above. Enfilade of arcades
from the Divān-e Khās, Red Fort, Delhi.

The private apartments
Of still more strictly reserved access, the private domain of the sovereign extends eastwards from the court of public audience. Marking out a terrace built up against the eastern wall of the ramparts, an enfilade of pavilions and gardens was refreshed by a gently flowing channel graced with the evocative name of Nahr-e Behesht ("river of paradise").

Only a small proportion of these buildings has escaped destruction. The Mumtāz Mahal, the southernmost survivor of the unit as it is found today, originally served to house the women of the court, which explains the guarded protectiveness of its interior spaces, decorously enclosed on all four sides. Today it houses the collections of a small museum devoted to the Mughals. The female apartments are succeeded by the Rang Mahal ("palace of color"). Set up behind the Divān-e 'Āmm, it owes its name to its sumptuous ornamentation; it runs down the side of a quadripartite garden in the center of which is scooped into a basin, in turn answered by a second in the shape of a lotus within the pavilion that collects the waters of the noisy fountain in its center. The white marble paving can scarcely hint at the exuberant decoration that once invaded the walls and ceiling, the latter, for instance, being lined with silver sheeting made even more eye-catching by a wealth of floral motifs in gilt.

Above and facing page. Decoration in the private apartments of the Khās Mahal and carved marble *jali*, Red Fort, Delhi.

To the north of the Rang Mahal, the Khās Mahal ("private palace") is arranged into three sections. To the south, the *baithak*, or "living room," presents the architectural synthesis of a dialogue between the majesty of its master, expressed by the ample portico that opens to the south, and the intimacy of his private diversions, concealed from inquisitive eyes by the delicate *jalis* partially closing off the space to the west that let in a dappled light. In the wake of this initial space, the "dormitory" (*khwābgāh*) is organized as a succession of three rooms cordoned off from the external world (embodied here by the "room of the rosary," or Tasbih Khāna) by the gossamer lace of a claustra resembling a petrified veil; one of the motifs woven within its marble threads is an intriguing allegory of Justice with the scales balanced on a crescent moon. From the "dormitory," one finally reaches the Musaman Burj ("octagonal tower"), dedicated to the interface—which Mughal emperors since Akbar had long cherished—between the emperor in all his glory and his people, since it was here that was set up the *darshan jharokha*, a balcony devoted to the appearances of the monarch to his subjects.

Reserved for private audiences, the Divān-e Khās stands next to the Khās Mahal in a blaze of immaculate marble. To three sides rectangular pillars supporting cusped arches open broadly onto a grandiloquent portico that provides a sense of depth to the central space where the sovereign would be enthroned. The wall at the rear is worked entirely in *jalis* that carve the light from the outside, so surrounding the monarch with an immaterial yet bedazzling halo as he sat on the illustrious "the peacock throne"; the throne, a work of the finest goldsmiths of the period, including European artists, was purloined by Nādir Shāh in 1739 and has since disappeared. The corners of the roof terrace above surge into four elegant small *chhatris*.

The hammam that prolongs the preceding pavilion contains the most sumptuous baths that have come down to us from that era, but they can no longer be visited. Opposite, rises Aurangzeb's Motī Masjid, of which an account will provided below.

North of these two buildings lies the Hayāt Bakhsh garden ("that which gives life"), whose layout—and the pavilion emerging in the center of the pool—is the work of Bahādur Shāh Zafar. Farther out are two other structures, called Sawan and Bhadon, which date to the interventions of Shāh Jahān. Bhadon lies to the north and features, in the heart of a colonnade, a pool whose walls are lined with niches in which would have been stood nightlights; the fine film of water that tumbled like a curtain in front of these little recesses would have danced to a rhythm of shimmering amber, before descending the length of a cruciform channel and spouting out into fountains at garden level. On the northeast corner, the Shāh Burj ("royal tower") features one last aedicule, the initial receptacle for the water from the channel which scampers down an inclined plane (*chadar*) from there before skirting north-south along the entire terrace.

Aurangzeb (1658–1707) and his successors

By the time the aging Shāh Jahān designated his son Dārā Shikōh as his successor, he had already built the architectural treasures that added so much to the present fame of Mughal civilization and had brought the empire to the acme of its cultural eminence. The legitimacy of his heir, however, was soon being disputed by the sovereign's third son, who orchestrated the assassination of his rival, his other brothers, and their children, before seizing power in 1658 under the name of Aurangzeb and condemning his father to house arrest in the Red Fort of Āgra. Thus begun the last of the prestigious Mughal reigns, before a slow decrepitude set in, which, as emperor succeeded emperor, only came to an end with the dynasty being summarily ousted and replaced by the British colonial power.

Aurangzeb: absolute power and harbingers of decline

The new master of the empire's destiny was born in 1618 and usurped the royal function from his father when he was forty years old. Having had ample time to ponder his projects for government, Aurangzeb promptly put into practice an effective policy of territorial expansion in a blend of skillful negotiation and military arm-twisting. By seizing a substantial proportion of the Deccan, he enlarged Mughal territorial possessions to their greatest ever extent. However, the sheer size of the empire proved a weakness when it came to quelling the bids for liberty of local potentates, and many rebelled against a central authority that was becoming increasingly remote. Internal conflict and ceaseless external pressure was also a drain on the public purse, sapping the financial means of affirming the sovereign's power and majesty. Between the lines, harbingers of the inexorable collapse become perceptible, with architecture a telling omen: structural lines lost their energy, wilting into an accumulation of overloaded motifs, as testified by the curves of polyfoil arches scattered around pillars and drowned beneath teeming garlands of leaves evoking a pseudo-rocaille spirit that has led certain authors to lambast what they see as a Mughal "baroque." Aurangzeb did manage, however, to complete the construction of several great mosques, including that in Lahore, the largest ever built in the subcontinent. The extreme simplicity of his tomb near Aurangabad, where he had himself interred after a reign lasting fifty years, serves perhaps as an indication of a measure of detachment with regard to strictly material splendor and of a more introspective spirituality than that of his predecessors.

Above. *The Emperor Aurangzeb When Old*, gouache and gold on paper, Lucknow School, early eighteenth century. Fondation Custodia, Paris, no. 1974–T.32.

Facing page. The ʿĀlamgīr Masjid, or Mosque of Aurangzeb, overlooking the Panjaganga Ghat, Benares, India, late seventeenth century.

The mosques of Benares and Mathura

When Aurangzeb had a mosque built in Benares—a heartland of Hinduism if ever there was one—it was clearly an expression of his power over the city; a local chronicle reports that in the process, a temple erected in the seventeenth century in honor of Vishnu by a Marāthā chieftain, Beni Madhur Rao Scindia, was razed to the ground. Whatever credit one ascribes to this account, it is a fact that the building, complete with minarets rising 197 feet (sixty meters) above the Panjaganga Ghat, occupies an eminent site. The massive stonework on the sober and vigorous elevation extending to the crenellated roof recalls an austere fortified town that minarets with lanterns and tapering pinnacles seem to arm with spears. These protect the generous curves of three *iwans* hollowed out from an inner courtyard that prepare for the spiritual elevation of a prayer hall surmounted by the full, sturdy lines of three domes. Besieged yet imperturbable, the 'Ālamgīr Masjid appears as a metaphor for the sovereign, a proud giant of an all-conquering Islam whose very success made it prey to internecine strife.

The mosque of Mathura, a blend of Punjabi architectural techniques (brick and glazed ceramic) and specific features in the Mughal tradition (courtyard flanked by minarets), is a very different affair. The base of the earthwork on which the building stands contains shop-houses; a gallery runs around the upper level where, to the east, a monumental gateway clad in ceramic panels overflows with color. The courtyard widens out into a quadrilateral whose corners burst into minarets with twelve faces and five levels topped by a bloom of *chhatris*. The façade of the prayer hall for its part exhibits a wondrous display of ceramic paneling.

The Motī Masjid, Delhi (1662)

Built within the Red Fort of Delhi in 1662, the Motī Masjid ("Pearl Mosque"), with its white-coated walls, looks like a modest oratory from the outside. This apparent discretion, however, conceals a jewel of immaculate marble. Two cusped arches frame a taller and broader central archway above a courtyard paved entirely in marble slabs. On the upper register, this graceful zest is answered by three ribbed domes capped with sensuous inverted corollas and pinnacles tipped with gilded metal apples. The roof is enriched by a profusion of "pseudo-minarets" and a plethora of *guldastas* that verge on the baroque. Other complicated ornaments unroll their interlace among motifs carved in light relief that serve to underscore the structural lines of the architecture and grow in density to the point of luxuriance on the entrance doorway to the courtyard; there, the saw-like teeth of acanthus crisscross languorous banana leaves and clash with stalks laden with ears of wheat, while the cusped archways bend under the weight of baskets of fruit.

The Bādshāhī Masjid, Lahore (1673)
Capable of accommodating fifty-five thousand worshippers, this, the vastest of all Mughal mosques, was built under Muzaffar Hussain, Aurangzeb's brother-in-law and governor of Lahore, who was nicknamed Fidā'i Khān Kokā. Completed in 1673, it was initially used as a reliquary to house in particular a hair from the head of the Prophet. Its square plan of 558 feet (170 meters) down the side defines a kind of matrix that reinterprets the main lines of the Jama' Masjid in Delhi. Thus, the slim spindles of four minarets at the corners of the external precinct are echoed by four others, less lofty, that enclose a prayer hall of crisp design beneath the immaculate curves of three marble cupolas. The unfussy simplicity of its overall shape, perfectly adapted to the dimensions of the building, however, loses itself in ornamental modulations whose details drown out the martial sobriety of the whole.

Five arcades frame the principal *iwan* on the façade, introducing the prayer hall; the profile of the archways, as well as the moldings that fringe them, are braided into an original fusion between red sandstone and white adornments, in particular on the level

Below left and facing page. The Bādshāhī Mosque, Lahore, Pakistan, 1673. General view and detail of a white marble ornament incrusted in sandstone.

Below right. The Bibi-ki-Maqbara at Aurangabad, erected in 1678 for Aurangzeb's wife, Rabi'a Daurani.

of the polylobe arch of the *iwan*, but it lacks the free-flowing energy of monuments built under Shāh Jahān. The prayer hall itself is subjected to the supple cadence of an enfilade of polyfoil arches, leading rhythmically into the light and calming tones of a decoration awash with stucco motifs. To the west stands the great entryway, its corners guarded by minaret "sentries" of square section, helmeted with *chhatris*, and stuck into bulbous bases whose coiled motifs evoke the luxuriance of banana leaves.

The Bibi-ki-Maqbara, Aurangabad (1678)

Aurangzeb built this edifice, known as "mausoleum of the lady," in honor of one of his wives, Rabi'a Daurani. Such circumstances made references to the Tāj Mahal unavoidable, and the general allure of the monument remains imbued with this influence, although important divergences mean that this is no servile imitation. However, the genuine architectural qualities of the Bibi-ki-Maqbara obviously suffer by comparison with the still more illustrious masterpiece that inspired it.

The site benefits from an enclosed garden measuring 1,345 by 804 feet (410 by 245 meters), open to the south through a half-octagon gate with a dado lined with painted ceramic tiles (known as "encaustic tiles"), displaying a dazzling nosegay of flowering stems of elegant and sure execution on a white ground. The planted zone extends onto an almost double square traversed by two perpendicular avenues, with, at the crossroads, an elevated terrace on which stands the mausoleum, accompanied by four minarets at the corners of the embankment.[24] In the center of the paths, stretches a mirror-like channel, ruffled occasionally by fountains that chop its waters into slowly moving friezes; withdrawn to either side runs a double sidewalk, separated from the waters by a flowerbed punctuated by cypress trees. The avenues are skirted by a screen wall beyond which frolic parterres divided into four irregular sections.

The mausoleum emerges on a square plan; its bond is a mix in which white roughcast often seems to get the better of marble. The middle of each façade is interrupted by a great *iwan* that deploys its polyfoil arches between two narrow vertical registers over two banks of arches; these, however, seem somewhat frail beneath the *chhatris* with their outsized whipped-cream cupolas, overflowing almost with the tapering pinnacles that extend the building at its corners, and vainly competing for room with the rotundity of the central cupola. Finally an inclined slope starts from the terrace, serving the funerary room in the basement which, under a cupola overloaded with *muqarnas*, houses both cenotaph and tomb in its grotto-like atmosphere.

The heirs to the Great Mughals (1707–57)

The death of Aurangzeb elevated the power and the glory of the Mughal sovereigns to legendary status. However, from 1707—the year the emperor passed away—to the demise of the dynasty shattered by the Sepoy Mutiny of 1857, a succession of seventeen emperors of the line followed one another onto the throne, sometimes for very brief intervals, accompanying without great prestige the inexorable disintegration of a central authority constantly undermined by internecine squabbles and disputes over succession. Certain individuals were not above taking advantage of the situation and tore great chunks out of the tempting prey represented by a state staggering under its own wealth but enfeebled and gutless. The reign of Emperor Muhammad (1719–48) is in this respect emblematic of the depredations endured by the last Mughals. Thus, in 1739, Nādir Shāh, basking in his triumphs and having wrested power from the Safavids of Iran, swooped down on Delhi and plundered, thus earning a dubious mention in the annals of systematic large-scale vandalism, whose end result was to bestow fabulous treasure on the shahs of Persia.[25] Yet things only got worse for Muhammad: not only did he undergo the humiliating treatment by Nādir Shāh—of mercenary brutality—he was also confronted by raids orchestrated by groups of Jāts, Marāthās, and Sikhs, his reign coming to a sticky end after repeated battering from the Afghans of Ahmed Shāh Durrānī.[26]

As is frequently the case, the political collapse of one side presents others with the opportunities they are waiting for to emerge from obscurity or gain a new lease of life. So the waning star of the dynasty proved a boon for the great Rājput lineages and various Muslim potentates impatient to affront the central powers. This was all the more the case since, as the eighteenth century dawned, the British East India Company, intent on feathering its colonial nest, had no qualms about playing one off against the other using a mixture of alliances, tricks, coups, and negotiation. Heading out from Bengal and going through Oudh, by the end the company had nibbled away at the near totality of the Mughal territory, to the point that, by the time of Shāh 'Ālam II (1760–1806), a popular saying scoffed that such late sovereigns now ruled over a kingdom "stretching" from Delhi to Palam—where the airport is located in the present agglomeration of Delhi.

The very last Mughal sovereign, Bahādur Shāh Zafar (r. 1837–57), exerted little more than nominal power by the time that the colonizers, accusing him of sympathizing with the insurrectionists during the Sepoy Mutiny, exiled him to Rangoon, Burma, where he perished in the most extreme destitution, just as the East India Company itself made way for the British Empire proper.

Notwithstanding, the powers that so profited to the detriment of the Mughal state were soon susceptible to the strength, charm, and creativity of its monuments, and it was from these monuments that the buildings with which they now filled the land were to take their inspiration. Thus they paved the way for the fascination and influence that the art of the dazzling dynasty of Bābur exerts on the world even today.

The Rājput revival

Early on Mughal emperors had been careful to weave dynastic bonds with the great Rājput families, often taking a wife from among the princesses of their prestigious courts. Although kept in an unambiguous state of vassalage, certain clans, like that of Mān Singh of Amber (1589–1614), also provided their suzerains with powerful resources in the event of conflict. Since no man is an island, as these strategic or passionate alliances continued to intertwine, stylistic, linguistic, and historical complicities and convergences that can be discerned in the architecture developed. Mughal taste, developed in a Muslim context, thus imposed itself on the palatial building of the Rājputs, although they were Hindu, and in Amber, at the summit of the glory of the descendants of Bābur. When the dynasty began to stumble, Rājput palaces even mirrored the changes affecting the magnificent counterparts of their masters. Mehrangarh Fort in Jodhpur and—reflecting the late Mughal manner—the palace of Deeg are prime illustrations of the masterpieces that sprung up in a number of princely states in northern India during the period.

Amber

Humāyūn's authority had already extended to the territories of the raja of Amber, Bhar Mal, when, in 1527, the latter was put in command by the emperor of a body of troops, before going on to negotiate the marriage of his son to a Muslim princess. Mān Singh, too, became not only a general, but more importantly an adviser in Akbar's inner cabinet. In 1558, when he received the emperor in Amber, whose fort was the principal residence of the dynasty that founded the princely state of Jaipur, the courtier's acumen

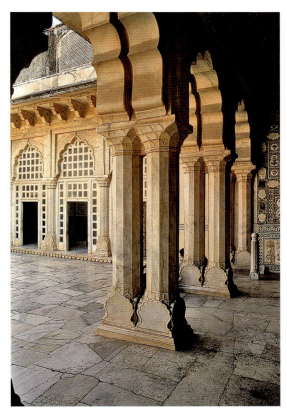

Above and left. The Shish Mahal at the fort of Amber, Rājasthān, decorated in the style of the Mughal court during the reign of Shāh Jahān, seventeenth century.

conspired with the assimilation of the dominant culture, and he decided to plant for the occasion a garden known as Delārām ("which unburdens the heart"). There, in the purest Mughal style, on a small island in a reservoir that reflects the fortress, terraces adorned with pavilions splinter into geometrical parterres with, at every corner, runnels that tumble into little cascades. In the same way, the taste of Shāh Jahān, who appointed Jai Singh I (r. 1621–67) governor of the Deccan, clearly influences the construction of his Divān-e 'Āmm, the gate of Ganesha and the Divān-e Khās, together with its Shish Mahal, where mirrors and lapping waters diffract the contrast between the greenery and the white marble of the inner courtyard into a sparkling riot of color.

Mehrangarh

In the fifteenth century, the heir to the Rathor clan, Rāo Jodha, founded the town of Jodhpur, which nestles in the shade of the impressing fortress of Mehrangarh. Akbar sealed his connections with the family by marrying Princess Jodh Bhai, thus initiating an alliance that endured for several generations. In the eighteenth century, however, the Rājput line regained its autonomy, a state of affairs it trumpeted by restoring various buildings in the fort. These drew the main lines of a hybrid style that blends the accomplishments of the indigenous tradition to contributions from imperial workshops. Thus, the aristocratic sensuality of the Mughals—embodied in Bengali roofs, ribbed domes puffing out into *chhatris* at the summit, cusped arches, etc.—plays host to a decoration of carved parrots perched on *chajjas* or monsters clinging to S-shaped consoles that were already nesting in the religious architecture of the region. As in the majority of the princely courts of the era, the Shish Mahal dazzles the visitor with a blaze of mirrors that magnify a host of paintings by the eighteenth-century school of Jodhpur.

Deeg

In the seventeenth and eighteenth centuries, the Jāts established a sizable citadel in the city of Bharatpur. Their alliances with the Rājput nobility and their prowess in war—particularly against the Mughals—guaranteed them a relative autonomy. After raiding Āgra in 1765, they returned with staggering spoils, including vast pieces of marble encrusted with

Mehrangarh Fort, further embellished in the eighteenth century, dominates the lower town of Jodhpur, India, with its blue-painted houses.

hardstones from the very palace of the Red Fort. Sūraj Mal, who, since the middle of the century, had been supervising the construction of Deeg, the second capital of the state, scattered these elements among the splendid pavilions and gardens for which the city is renowned.

Subtly balanced between the pool called the Gopāl Sāgar and the gardens that prolong its proportions so harmoniously, the remarkably preserved Gopāl Bhawan was occupied until the beginning of the 1970s by the maharajah of Bharatpur. Not far off, the columnated porticoes of the Nund Bhawan suggest that the building might have been used for audiences, but its roof conceals a colossal tank dug into a basin in the center of the terrace that it took several days to fill from a well. Its walls were bored with holes through which shot water jets. These apertures could additionally be fitted with filters impregnated with dye to produce multicolored and otherworldly aquatic effects that must have been a wonder to behold. The designers of the garden concealed a number of other extravagances among the more traditional plantations, such as a marble portico that could be fitted with a swing; the site from this viewpoint offers a vertiginous panorama.[27]

Composite variations in the Deccan

Over the centuries, the Deccan, where the Mughal yoke arrived late and was less burdensome, had been molded politically and spiritually by powerful Hindu kingdoms, to the point that, at the time of the sultanates, the region was steeped in an original culture. By the late seventeenth century, in the former territories of the Qutb Shāhīs and the 'Ādil Shāhīs, Aurangzeb had to confront the Marāthās, winning and seizing the lion's share of the peninsula. In 1692 he appointed Zulfikar 'Alī, an officer who had played a significant role in the victory, nabob of the Carnatic region, thus establishing a fallback position from which he might invest a vast sector south of the River Krishna and advance the banner of Islam still farther. The provinces of Mysore and Madras offer prime illustrations of the composite results of these events. Over the decades (like an amplified version of the heritage of Vijayanagar), the canons bequeathed by the genius of the Mughals, the creative brilliance of the preceding sultanates, and, last but not least, loans from various colonial styles, met and clashed. The eclectic architecture emerging from this maelstrom of fractured influences is not short of imagination, often to the detriment of structural purity, as in the case of the palace at Mysore (1897–1912), a pearl of what the British dub the "Indo-Saracen" style.[28]

The nabobs of Arcot

Taking advantage of the decline of the Hindu kingdom of Vijayanagar, Zulfikar 'Alī imprinted on his "fiefdom" an authority legitimated by his supposed descent from Caliph 'Umar. His successor Sa'ādatullah (r. 1710–32) then transferred the regional capital from Gingee to Arcot, near Madras; subsequently, Dust 'Alī Khān (r. 1732–40) annexed Madura in 1736.

Surviving monuments from the time are rare, but the palace of Tirumala Nayak in Madura testifies to an astonishing amalgam between "exotic" Islamic architectural characteristics and the fundamentals of indigenous construction techniques. Built in 1645 during the Hindu Nayak dynasty, from 1736 to the late eighteenth century, the palace served as the residence of the representatives of the Arcot nabob, whose line broke free from Mughal allegiance under Muhammad 'Alī Wallajah (r. 1749–95) only to be shorn of a great part of its territory by the East India Company in exchange for British assistance against Haydar 'Alī and the French.

The kingdom of Mysore
A possession of the Hindu Wadiyar dynasty from the fourteenth century to Independence in 1947, Mysore fell into the clutches of Haydar 'Alī from 1722 to 1782, then those of his son, Tippu Sultan, from 1782 to 1799.[29] The tumultuous lives of these two men and their feats of arms on the side of France against the British East India Company until their defeat in 1799 at Seringapatam, in what is commonly called the Mysore Wars, read like an adventure story and are celebrated in the writings of Le Maître de La Tour, who himself served under Haydar 'Alī.[30]

In Seringapatam, the capital of their states some six miles (10 kilometers) from Mysore, there survives the mausoleum of Tippu Sultan, an eponymous mosque, and a summer palace, the Daryā Daulat Bāgh, completed in 1784. This last edifice stands in a Mughal-style garden; it is built primarily out of teak, a traditional local material put in the service of techniques that integrate Islamic influences. The foundation of the Lāl Bāgh at Bangalore, now a botanical garden, also dates to the era of Haydar 'Āli, although it was his son who put on the finishing touches.

The nabobs of Oudh

Oudh is a province of the Doab, a territory extending between the Ganges and the Yamuna. The Mughal breadbasket, its economic importance meant that it often served as a political springboard from whence its governors could assert their prestige locally and/or advance their interests in Delhi. Hence, the region's first nabob, Sa'ādat Khān Burhān al-Mulk, added this function to that of vizier to his Mughal overlords, as did his successor, Abu al-Mansur Khān, known as Safdar Jang (r. 1737–53).[31] These allegiances, sometimes stormy and not exempt from double-dealing, led Burhān al-Mulk to create a brilliant court in his capital Faizābād that soon came to the fore as the political and cultural heartland of northern India until the local dynasty came to an end. His successor, meanwhile, having in all probability abused his prerogatives, was removed from his post by the emperor in 1753, dying the same year. Shujā' al-Dawla (r. 1753–97), the third nabob-vizier, after coming off second best in a battle with the powerful British East India Company, was forced to sign a disadvantageous treaty in 1765, but the power raised its head once more under Āsaf al-Dawla (r. 1775–97), who transferred the regional capital to Lucknow. The city was then in the throes of a creative effervescence and a building boom, a prelude to the sovereignty of Oudh that was proclaimed in 1819 against the emperor, only to be completely gobbled up a little later by the East India Company in 1856. The political bipolarity of the lineage, however, surfaces in the architectural heritage it bequeathed in both Delhi and Lucknow.

The mausoleum of Safdar Jang, Delhi
In addition to its intrinsic aesthetic qualities, the funerary complex of Safdar Jang, constructed in 1753–54 by his son Shujā al-Dawla, is also the grand finale of the architectural tradition of the descendants of Bābur. Standing at the western tip of

The City Palace of Mysore, India, built for the city's maharaja by Henry Irwin in the late nineteenth century in the hybrid "Indo-Saracenic" style.

Lodi Road, as if to echo the mausoleum of Humāyūn that occupies its eastern edge, the mausoleum closed the file on the glorious cortege of Mughal monuments that Humāyūn started. Notwithstanding, the building is a bundle of paradoxes: built according to the stylistic principles of the reigning lineage for a recipient who was not a member of it, it trumpets—in terms of materials and design—an opulence that arises partly from the marble plundered from the mausoleum of Khān-e Khānān.[32]

The building rises in the center of a square *chahār-bāgh* almost 984 feet (300 meters) along the side, reached through an imposing and elaborate entryway deployed over three levels, sheltering a generous atrium serving a series of rooms dedicated to services and maintenance. The building communicates to the north with a mosque topped by three sensuously swaying onion domes striated with bands alternating the flesh-tones of red sandstone with a less brazen white marble. In the center of the garden a broad terrace excavated into cells around the circumference shores up the base of the mausoleum. Of square plan, this construction is clad in a ceremonial coat of armor in marble and sandstone, framed on all four corners by minarets with two balconies sporting *chhatris* like rugged hafts. A triple vertical register adorns the façades, in the center of which, and over the whole height, there opens an *iwan* flanked by sections of the same width, divided into two levels. The arch-rings of the *iwans*, following the example of the bays, buckle into cusped flourishes, to which are added decorative details such as a profusion of saw-toothed moldings and *muqarnas*. In consequence, where the mausoleum of Humāyūn was all strength and innovative energy, here the structural lines are weighed down by a decorative overload that renders them flabby and "blurs" the elevation.

Āsaf al-Dawla in Lucknow, an architectural identity
When, in order to assert his power, Āsaf al-Dawla (r. 1775–97) resolved to make Lucknow his regional capital, he provided it with a significant economic and cultural boost. The city thus forged an original urban personality, embodied in iconic buildings

that lack neither robustness nor creativity. In about 1780, following a famine, the prince ordered the building of the funerary-cum-commemorative complex of Bara Imāmbārā (or Āsafi Imāmbārā), initially dedicated to the celebration of Muharram, the Shiite month of mourning, but which also houses the remains of the nabob, his first wife, and its architect.

The stately entrance with three lofty gateways whose spandrels are adorned with fish, which symbolize Oudh, leads to a court offering a majestic view onto the "great hall" some 328 feet (100 meters) away, while to the west and at a 45-degree angle stands the mosque. The impressive dimensions of the "great hall" unfold over a terrace provided with a staircase of regal breadth; 164 feet (50 meters) long, 52 feet (16 meters) wide, and 49 feet (15 meters) high, the main vaulted space was famous at the time as one of the largest in the world. The façade stretches 295 feet (90 meters) beneath an undulating cusped arcade whose order proclaims its singular elegance, while above runs a procession of little *chhatris*, as plump as putti, and then a second level formed by a gallery itself topped by a row of cheekily perched *chhatris*. The

Facing page. The mausoleum of Safdar Jang, Delhi, 1753–54.

Below. The monumental gate, Bara Imāmbārā, Lucknow, India, c. 1780.

Above left. The Rumi Darwāza of Lucknow and its exuberant decoration.
Above right. View from the esplanade in front of the mosque of the Bara Imāmbārā, Lucknow.

Facing page. Mausoleum of Sa'ādat 'Alī Khān, Lucknow, c. 1814.

gallery is reached by an external staircase that also opens onto the Bhulbhuliyan, a tortuous maze. This combination of monumental proportions and decorative "preciousness"—the vortex of diminutive *chhatris*, chains of cusps doubling the arch-rings, and stucco motifs—arouses the puzzling and contrasted impression of powerful currents of dynamic energy unhappily wedded to contrived convolutions. Placed before the complex of Imāmbārā, Rumi Darwāza derives its name from Constantinople (Rum), evoking the splendor of the Sublime Porte. All unbridled imagination, an overweight arcade crushes the beanpole "pseudo-minarets" flanking it, while outside it is bordered by a frieze fanning out into "trumpet" motifs, like a bizarre and petrified brass band.

Finally, the untoward originality of the architectural style of Lucknow is crowned by the decorative exuberance of the outsized Qaysar Bāgh, which was begun under Āsaf al-Dawla and completed by Wajid 'Alī Shāh (1847–56). It was severely damaged after the Mutiny of 1857, and only a few vestiges survive, such as the door known as the Chaulakha Darwāza and the spandrels ornamented with naive freshness in a fish motif in plaster.

Oriental eclecticism and European taste

From the late eighteenth century to the fall of the nabobs, Lucknow was gripped by intense building activity amid considerable stylistic turmoil. It was as if its princes, all the while marching towards independence and imposing ephemeral regimes, possessed a vague inkling of the transience of their triumphs—especially as compared to the architectural masterpieces that emblazoned the subcontinent throughout the centuries, seeking to make up for this historical transitoriness with an ill-digested hotchpotch of cultural influences.

Its silhouette rising among the tombs of the sovereigns and their wives adjacent to the Qaysar-Bāgh, the mausoleum of Sa'ādat 'Alī Khān (r. 1798–1814) is studded with domes and pyramidal *chhatris* more reminiscent of a "folly" than a burial place. Not far off, in an enceinte ringing a garden, towers the formidable Shāh Najaf Imāmbārā, where, beneath a dome with a diameter of seventy-two feet (twenty-two meters), repose Ghāzī al-Dīn Haydar, who died in 1827, together with his three wives, including Mubārak Begum, a European.

Around 1800, Sa'ādat 'Alī Khān also built the Residency, designed to house the local resident of the British East India Company. Built in an Italianate style, its ruins commemorate the massacres that followed the Sepoy Mutiny.

Close by the Bara Imāmbārā, the Hussainabad, or Chota Imāmbārā, complex was built by Muhammad 'Alī Shāh (1837–42). He now rests next to his mother in a mausoleum of less ambitious dimensions than its neighbor, but which combines an exterior inspired by the Royal Pavilion in Brighton and calligraphic decoration whose tranquil flourishes manage to instill an atmosphere of intimacy and peaceful meditation. In the garden with a 236-foot (72-meter) long basin are interred the daughter of the nabob and her husband within two unconvincing "scale models" of the Tāj Mahal—59 feet (18 meters) down each side. From the same period, the Jama' Masjid of Lucknow also features a profusion of decorative motifs in a mishmash of decorative idioms that illustrate why the term "decadence" often applied to the Awadhi dynasty.

Europeans also invested the city in this period, as shown by La Martinière, a palace built by a French general, Claude Martin. Once again eclecticism is the watchword, Romanesque arcades vie with Gothic ornamentation, and turrets fight it out with Corinthian columns topped by gargoyles.[33]

Bahādur Shāh Zafar (r. 1837–58), the last Mughal

Limited to a retrenchment around Delhi, the last heir to the throne of Bābur and Akbar exercised only nominal power, further corroded over the years by the prerogatives assumed by the British East India Company. Before being condemned to exile following the repression of the 1857 mutiny, however, he did succeed in erecting a handful of buildings. Some even escaped the wholesale destruction that accompanied the end of his reign and speak volumes about the faded luster of his age.

The Hayāt Bakhsh garden
To the north of the Pearl Mosque located at the heart of the Red Fort, Shāh Jahān had planted a quadripartite garden extending around a square central pool, while within, to the north and south, the zone was demarcated by two white marble pavilions (Sawan and Bhadon). In 1842 Bahādur Shāh added two new aediculae built in the same marble to the complex: the Motī ("pearl"), since disappeared, to the west, and the Hira ("diamond"), still standing, to the east. Finally a red sandstone pavilion on piles named the Zafar Mahal offers an island of serenity on the shimmering surface of the waters. Dropped basket arches opening broadly to the outside are accompanied by multifoil arches. Over time, however, the roof has caved in. When so many buildings and gardens within the Red Fort were razed to the ground to build ugly barracks, the

Facing page. Dargāh of Qutb Sāhib, Mehrauli, Delhi; much venerated by Bahādur Shāh Zafar, this sanctuary remains a focus for ardent devotion.

Left. Entrance to a well-heeled house in Old Delhi, late nineteenth century.

fact that this fragile haven was spared the spiteful rage that enflamed the British once the Sepoy Mutiny had been subdued seems positively miraculous.

The Zafar Mahal

The maze of lanes in the Mehrauli district conceals a little square that offers a glimpse of daylight for the vestiges of a palace probably founded by Akbar II (r. 1806–37), but named the Zafar Mahal because Bahādur Shāh Zafar was responsible for its final appearance. The building lies next to the *dargāh* of Qutb Sāhib whom the last Mughal greatly admired.[34] The façade still boasts its imposing sandstone gateway, of a deep red that contrasts with the bands of white marble that highlight the architectural structure. In the center, a blindingly white loggia with three arcades tops a cusped arch whose elevation projects between three levels of bays to either side, allowing access to the apartments through a roofed passageway, a pale reflection of the Chatta Chowk in the Red Fort. The interior is now in a state of ruin, though the occasional decoration still hangs from the crumbling walls: bizarrely incongruous chimneys bound with pilasters in the European style betray the influence of the European invaders, while bereft terra-cotta guardrails that long ago ringed a roof terrace now stand about aimlessly.

Conclusion
FROM IDENTITY TO UNIVERSALITY

Oddly enough, the overthrow of the Mughal dynasty by the British, far from bringing a cataclysmic curtain down on several centuries of Muslim creativity and demoting it forever to the rank of cultural dinosaur, in fact heralded a new era.

Since 1857, of course, the Indian pearl had sat firmly in the British Crown, which now governed its colony directly through the intermediary of a viceroy representing Her Majesty. Indo-Muslim culture, however, rather than representing an archaic atavism, a moribund identity frozen in admiration of its long-vanished years of triumph, started to appear in all its timeless grandeur and gain a status as a wellspring of inspiration. In architectural terms, even the contempt of the colonizers for their conquered peoples gradually evolved into an empathy with autochthon influences, particularly Mughal ones.

Consequently, following the almost Palladian lines of the Lucknow Residency and the Central Post Office in Calcutta, a plethora of monuments mushroomed whose hybrid architecture coalesced into the style known as "Indo-Saracenic."[35] The Baroda and Central Indian Railway building throws into this bubbling cauldron Gothic elements and bulbous domes, pinnacles with florets, two-tone voussoirs and twinned arches; for its part, Lahore Railway Station (designed by William Brunton) is a cross between Saracen castle and fortified mosque; in the High Court of Madras, Henry Irwin celebrated the improbable union of the styles of the late Deccan and English Gothic.[36] Not to be outdone, for the Victoria Memorial in Calcutta, Sir William Emerson borrowed the white marble and a soupçon of the Tāj Mahal, transmuting them into an echo of St. Peter's Basilica shilly-shallying between mannerism and baroque. The Venetian-Indian Clock Tower of Lucknow, designed by Sir George Couper and built in 1880, rises some 220 feet (67 meters), making it the highest in the country. And last but not least, Edwin Luytens's complex in New Delhi can be seen as the sanitized grand finale to all this stylistic crossbreeding.

Once Europe had learned to appreciate its originality, mastery, and majesty, Indo-Muslim culture could start to venture into other lands, feeding into the ideas of Orientalist architects and decorators, and steeping their creations in references, some direct, some heavily reworked. In the final analysis, and in the teeth of a turbulent and often violent history, the Indian genius was greatly elevated by the Islamic contribution from a long line of famous or anonymous planners of the monuments we have examined. It was they who invented a panoply of forms that blended, in breathtaking or subtle combinations (depending on the eras and regions concerned), indigenous and imported styles to forge a cultural and political personality that survived constant buffeting by the vagaries of history. Over the centuries, then, Mother India, offered a matrix in which contributions from her Arab, Mongol, Turco-Persian, and European invaders could intermix, while she for her part took from their artistic and technical expertise, exalting it to the point of the sublime.

By the period of sultanates, this quest for identity—shaped by concessions and often by brute force—had spawned a civilization in the true sense of the term which, blossoming during Mughal "classicism," entered an inevitable decline during the colonial period. Yet even then it never wholly lost its power to assimilate or to go beyond juxtaposition to creation. And thus, it still offers those with eyes to see a living fragment of the universal.

The Victoria Memorial, Calcutta, by William Emerson, late nineteenth century.

APPENDIXES

Enamel ceramic trim on one of the minarets
of the Mahmūd Gāwān Madrassa, Bīdar, India, 1472.

TIMELINE

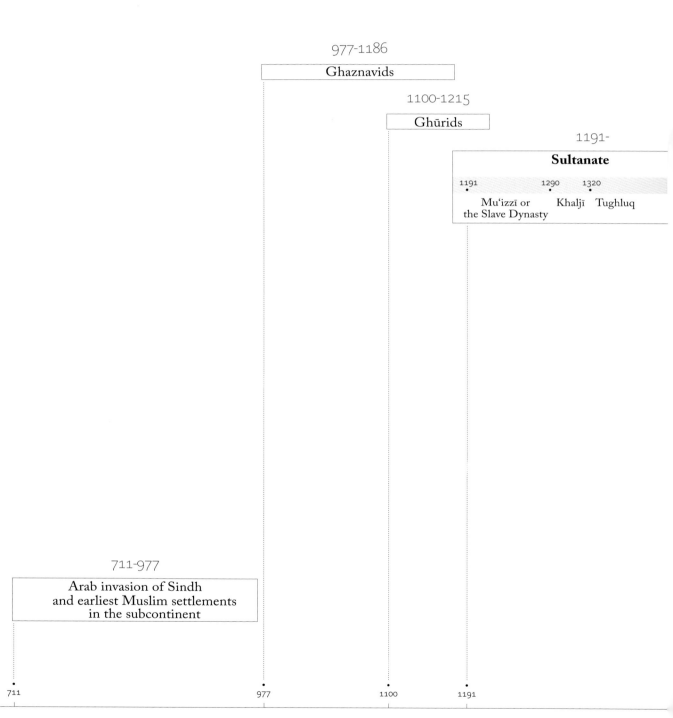

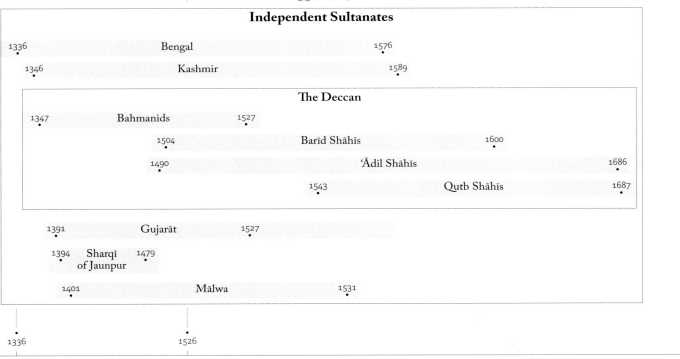

NOTES

From the Arab-Muslim Incursions
to the Foundation of the Mughal Empire

1. The history of this period is known especially through the *Shāh-nāme*, a work in Persian translated from an Arabic original by Mohammad 'Alī Kufi and completed in about 1216.

2. The identification of Bambhore with Daybul is not absolutely certain; see F. A. Khan, *Banbhore*, third revised ed. (Karachi: Department of Archaeology and Museums, Government of Pakistan, 1969), 24–30; see also K. Khan Mumtaz, *Architecture in Pakistan* (London: Butterworths Architecture, 1990), 35. See also, more recently, Monik Kervran, "Le port multiple des bouches de l'Indus: Barbariké, Dēb, Daybul, Lāhorī Bandar, Diul Sinde," *Res Orientales* 8 (1996): 45–92.

3. The old mosque of Kufa features a square plan with sides of 330 feet (100 meters)—a so-called "Bedouin" plan with, surrounding an open-air courtyard, porticoes on three sides and a prayer hall on the fourth side directed towards Mecca.

4. Henry Cousens, "Brahmanābād-Mansura in Sind," *Archaeological Survey of India, Annual Reports* (1903–04): 133–44; "Excavation at Brahmanābād," *Archaeological Survey of India, Annual Reports* (1908–09): 79–87; *The Antiquities of Sind*, ASI Imperial Series XLVI (1929): 50–51.

5. M. H. Pathan, *Arab Kingdom of Al-Mansura in Sind* (Hyderabad, 1974), 102.

6. Ahmad Nabi Khan, *Multān, History and Architecture* (Islamabad: Institute of Islamic History, Culture and Civilization, Islamic University, 1983), 34; see also M. Shokoohy, *Bhadreshvar: The Oldest Islamic Monuments in India* (Leiden: Brill, 1988), 5.

7. Louis Frédéric, *L'Inde de l'islam* (Paris: Arthaud, 1989), 23.

8. A. Maricq and G. Wiet, *Le Minaret de Djam. La découverte de la capitale des sultans Ghūrides (XIIe-XIIIe siècles)*, Mémoires de la Délégation archéologique française en Afghanistan XVI (1959).

9. D. Schlumberger, *Lashkari Bazar. L'architecture*, Mémoires de la Délégation archéologique française en Afghanistan XVIII, 1A (1978).

10. See M. Shokoohy, *Bhadreshvar: The Oldest Islamic Monuments in India*.

11. This fact is mentioned by Farrokhī, court poet to Mahmūd, who wrote a panegyric about crossing the desert in the Rann of Kachchh to Mansura, capital of Sindh; see ibid., 7.

12. Ibid., 10.

13. Ibid., 42–49.

14. M. Shokoohy, *Nāgaur: Sultanate and Early Mughal History and Architecture of the District of Nāgaur, India* (London: Royal Asiatic Society, 1993), 8.

15. The expression "Old" Delhi is an ambiguous one, since it today designates the city founded by Shāh Jahān in the seventeenth century located north of New Delhi; by "old" Delhi here, we mean the Chauhān citadel recovered by Qutb al-Dīn Aybak to the south of the British city.

16. Ibn Battuta, *Travels in Asia and Africa, 1325–1354*, vol. 3, trans. H. A. R. Gibb (New York: Augustus M. Kelley, 1969), 622.

17. Ibid., 624.

18. See especially, Ziyā' al-Dīn Barani, *Tārikh-e Firuz Shāhi* (Calcutta, 1862), 130.

19. Ibn Battuta, *Travels in Asia and Africa, 1325–1354*, vol. 3, 625–26.

20. Ibid., 195–96.

21. "Nizām al-Dīn" is the transcription of the name of the person; whereas we use "Nizamuddin" to indicate the district in which his sanctuary lies.

22. Esāmi, *Fotuh al-salātin* (Madras: University of Madras, 1948), 412 (our translation).

23. A pointed ("Gothic") arch is formed by the intersection of two arcs of a circle (two-centered arch); the Persian (horseshoe) arch is made up of four arcs of a circle (two larger and two smaller), and offers a broader opening; it can be compared with the English Tudor arch.

24. For additional details, see A. Nabi Khan, *Multān* (Islamabad: Institute of Islamic History, Culture and Civilization, Islamic University, 1983), 215–36.

25. Ibn Battuta, *Travels in Asia and Africa, 1325–1354*, vol. 3, 619–21.

26. See P. Brown, *Indian Architecture (Islamic Period)* (Bombay: D. B. Taraporevala Sons & Co., 1956), pl. XIV.

27. Shams-e Serāj 'Afif, *Tārikh-e Firuz Shāhi* (Calcutta, 1891), 295 (our translation).

28. This is a pun as, Hisār-e Fīrūza means both the "fort of turquoise" and "fort of Fīrūz"; on this site, see M. and N. H. Shokoohy, *Hisār-i Firuza: Sultanate and Early Mughal Architecture in the District of Hisār, India* (London: Monographs on Art, Archaeology and Architecture), 1988.

29. A few years later (in 1401), Dilāwar Khān Ghauri was actually to gain his independence and so found the sultanate of Mālwa.

30. *Malfuzat-i Timuri*, or *Tuzak-i Timuri*, by Amir Tīmūr-i-lang, in *The History of India as Told by Its Own Historians: The Posthumous Papers of the Late Sir H. M. Elliot*, vol. 2 (Calcutta: Susil Gupta, 1956), 8–98 [1867]; and quoted in French in L. Frédéric, *L'Inde de l'islam* (Paris: Arthaud, 1989), 99.

31. Concerning the site of Dholpur, Bābur notes that a dam built by the Lodī sultan can be seen; above the dam are dwellings and below, a garden. Bābur

was to have what became one of his favorite gardens planted on this same site (see below).

32. John Marshall, *Cambridge History of India*, vol. 3 (Cambridge: Cambridge University Press, 1928), 571–73.

33. *Bābur-Nāma*, trans. A. S. Beveridge (New Delhi: Oriental Books Reprint Society, 1979 [1922]), 531–32.

34. Ibid., 610.

35. Ibid., 531–32.

36. E. Moynihan, *Paradise as a Garden in Persia and Mughal India* (London: Scolar Press, 1980), 103–08.

37. *Bābur-Nāma*, 606–07.

38. See, for example, Fereshta, quoted in Gul-Badan Begum, *Le Livre de Humayun* (Paris: Gallimard, 1996), 60.

39. Ibid., 176.

40. P. Brown, *Indian Architecture (Islamic Period)*, 90.

41. For an account of the death of Humāyūn, see Gul-Badan Begum, *Le Livre de Humayun*, 166.

The Independent Sultanates

1. Up to the Mughal invasion of Bengal in the late sixteenth century, a steady output of princely manuscripts developed whose importance was only rediscovered in the late twentieth century, in particular thanks to the *Book of Alexander* by Nusrat Shāh (r. 1519–32); see Norah Titley, *Persian Miniature Painting* (London: The Library, 1983), pl. 32.

2. On this little-known monument, as well as on those mentioned subsequently, see the remarkable volume by S. M. Hassan, *Mosque Architecture of Pre-Mughal Bengal* (Dhaka: University Press, 1979), 127–31.

3. See S. M. Hassan, 144–46.

4. Ibid., p. 64.

5. See S. M. Hassan, 194–96.

6. See S. M. Hassan, pl. XXIIa (Indian Museum, Calcutta) and pl. XXIIb (Victoria and Albert Museum, London); for other examples in the Victoria and Albert Museum, see J. Guy and D. Swallow, *Arts of India: 1550–1900* (London: Victoria and Albert Museum, 1990), 45–46; for examples conserved in the British Museum, see V. Porter, *Islamic Tiles* (London: British Museum Press, 1995), 87–88.

7. P. Brown, *Indian Architecture (Islamic Period)* (Bombay: D. B. Taraporevala Sons & Co., 1956), 42.

8. S. M. Hassan, *Mosque Architecture of Pre-Mughal Bengal*, 152.

9. J. Burton-Page, "Daulatabad," in G. Michell, ed., *Islamic Heritage of the Deccan* (Bombay: Marg, 1986), 25.

10. See J. D. Hoag, *Architecture islamique* (Paris: Hachette, 1991), 145. Hoag adds to the list of elements influenced by Ottoman architecture, squinches presenting a cubic version of *muqarnas*.

11. Severely damaged, these ceramic panels are reconstituted in G. Yazdani, *Bidar, its History and Monuments*, Oxford University Press, 1947; see also Y. Crowe, "Coloured Tilework," in G. Michell, ed., *Islamic Heritage of the Deccan*, fig. 4.

12. The palatial zone has been excavated under the direction of the archeology department of the University of Baroda (1973–74); see *Indian Archaeology, 1974–1975: A Review*, Archaeological Survey of India, Delhi, 1979, 4–15.

13. See Y. Porter, "Jardins pré-moghols," *Res Orientales III, Jardins d'Orient* (1991): 51.

14. A. Führer in *The Sharqī Architecture of Jaunpur*, published in Calcutta in 1889, was the first to describe in detail this extraordinary architecture, together with its inscriptions.

15. See E. Brac de La Perrière, "Bihārī et naskhī-dīwānī: remarques sur deux calligraphies de l'Inde des sultanats," *Studia islamica* 96 (2004): 81–93.

16. "On the 9th of Rabi' II, 1070H. (14 December, A.D. 1659), the humble votary Lutfu'llāh, son of Master Ahmad, Architect of Shāhjahān, Khwājah Jadū Rā'i, Master Sheo Rām and Master Hāmid, came to show our reverence and wrote these few words by way of record." Quoted by G. Yazdani, *Mandū, the City of Joy* (Oxford: Oxford University Press, 1929), 48.

17. 'Alī bin Mahmud Kermāni, *Ma'āser-e Mahmud-shāhi*, translated by Y. Porter in "Khalji architecture of Mālwa in the light of the Ma'āser-e Mahmudshāhi," in F. N. Delvoye, ed., *Confluence of Cultures: French Contributions to Indo-Persian Studies* (Paris, 1994), 29.

18. Jahāngīr, *Tuzuk-i Jahāngiri or Memoirs of Jahāngir*, vol. 1 (Delhi, 1989), 381–82.

19. Y. Porter, "Jardins pré-moghols," 41.

20. Jahāngīr, *Tuzuk-i Jahāngiri or Memoirs of Jahāngir*, vol. 1, 385.

21. On these decorations, see Y. Porter, "Décors émaillés dans l'architecture de pierre de l'Inde centrale: les monuments islamiques de Mandu (XVe-XVIe siècles)." *Archéologie islamique* 7 (1997): 121–46.

22. See Y. Porter, "Khalji architecture of Mālwa in the light of the Ma'āser-e Mahmudshāhi," 34–35.

23. See Y. Porter, "Jardins pré-moghols," 50.

The Great Mughals and their Heirs

1. See Glenn D. Lowry, "Humayun's Tomb: Form, Function and Meaning in Early Mughal Architecture," *Muqarnas* 4 (1987): 133–48.

2. See W. G. Klingelhofer, "The Jahangiri-Mahal of Agra Fort: Expression and Experience in Early Mughal Architecture," *Muqarnas* 5 (1988): 153–69.

3. After P. Brown, *Indian Architecture (Islamic Period)* (Bombay: D. B. Taraporevala Sons & Co., 1956), 105.

4. The *dhrupad* is a sophisticated form of vocal music—still immensely prestigious—whose form was fixed by Tānsēn.

5. Literally "five palaces," *pānch* meaning "five."

6. See E. W. Smith, *The Moghul Architecture of Fatehpur Sikri* (Allahābād, 1894–97), pl. CIX.

7. A coin with his portrait, minted in 1611, shows him holding a cup. See B. Gascoigne, *The Great Moghuls* (London: Cape, 1971), 139.

8. In 1602, he traveled from Allahābād to Āgra at the head of an army of thirty thousand men; however, Akbar succeeded in avoiding open conflict; see B. Gascoigne, *The Great Moghuls*, 125.

9. Jahāngīr, *Tuzuk-i Jahāngiri or Memoirs of Jahāngir*, vol. 1 (Delhi, 1989), 152.

10. Quoted in E. W. Smith, *Akbar's Tomb, Sikandra* (Calcutta, 1909), 34; a remarkable monograph.

11. After pillaging the mausoleum in 1761, the Jāts of Bharatpur threw Akbar's ashes to the four winds.

12. Jahāngīr, *Tuzuk-i Jahāngiri or Memoirs of Jahāngīr*, 363–64.

13. Ibid., 150–51.

14. Robert d'Humières was a friend of Marcel Proust's and the French translator of Kipling; the text here is cited after E. Moynihan, *Paradise as a Garden in Persia and Mughal India* (London: Scolar Press, 1980), 125–26.

15. E. Koch, "Diwan-i 'Amm and Chihil Sutun: The Audience Halls of Shah Jahan," in *Mughal Art and Imperial Ideology* (New Delhi / Oxford: Oxford University Press, 2001), 249.

16. He was reminded of this bloodthirsty expedient when his son Aurangzeb seized power in his turn and eliminated his competitors.

17. The harmony of the proportions appears readily in diagrams published in W. E. Begley and Z. A. Desai, *Taj Mahal: The Illumined Tomb* (Cambridge, MA: Aga Khan Program for Islamic Architecture, Harvard University, 1989), 68–72.

18. These inscriptions, Koranic for the most part, are quoted in their entirety in Begley and Desai, *Taj Mahal: The Illumined Tomb*.

19. Lahore as a whole was further modified thereafter, in particular under the rule of the Sikhs.

20. Amānat Khān distinguished himself by producing the friezes at the entrance (*chār-minār*) of Sikandra, in 1613. In 1632 Shāh Jahān bestowed upon him the honorary title of Amānat Khān, and then, in about 1636–37, he designed the decorations for the Tāj Mahal, his greatest masterpiece. In about 1640 he retired to Punjab, near Amritsar, where he had built a small complex around a caravanserai that bears its name, decorated with glazed ceramics and calligraphic friezes; he died in about 1645. On this calligrapher and his work, see Begley and Desai, *Taj Mahal: The Illumined Tomb*, 247–57.

21. See L. Nicholson, *The Red Fort, Delhi* (London: Tauris Parke Books, 1989).

22. In fact, the columns are grouped in twos on the façade and in fours on the corners; on this subject, see E. Koch, "Diwan-i 'Amm and Chihil Sutun: The Audience Halls of Shah Jahan," in *Mughal Art and Imperial Ideology*, 229–54.

23. On this decoration, see E. Koch, *Shah Jahan and Orpheus* (Graz: Akademische Druck- u. Verlagsanstalt, 1988).

24. Unlike the Tāj Mahal, placed at the back of a perspective, the Bibi-ki-Maqbara is located in the center of the garden.

25. "Scraps" from this pillage still languish in the vaults of the central bank of Tehran. A notable exception concerns the famous Kūh-e Nūr (Koh-i-noor)—"mountain of light"—diamond, which, following a checkered history, is now in London.

26. Ahmed Shāh Durrānī (r. 1747–73) was the first sovereign king of Afghanistan.

27. For a detailed plan and a description of this garden, see C. M. Villiers Stuart, *Gardens of the Great Mughals* (London: Adam & Charles Black, 1913), 258–63.

28. In the same spirit, in the late nineteenth century the architect Robert Chisholm converted the Chepauk Palace (the residence of the Arcot nabobs in Madras) into the city department of public works, before going on to design the University Senate House, the highpoint of a style dubbed "Byzantino-Qutb-Shāhī"; see C. Tadgell, *The History of Architecture in India* (London: Architecture Design and Technology Press, 1990), 289.

29. Tippu Sultan became known as the "Tiger of Mysore."

30. M. Le Maître de La Tour, *Histoire d'Hayder-Ali Khan* (Paris, 1783).

31. The vizier is the equivalent of a prime minister; one can also note that, although the Mughal emperors were Sunnis, the nabobs of Oudh were Shiites.

32. It should be recalled that this mausoleum is located very close to that of Humāyūn.

33. Initially named Constantia, the buildings, now a boarding school, have sheltered the general's remains since 1800.

34. The place shelters the tombs of several sovereigns, including Bahādur Shāh I (r. 1707–12) and Akbar II. The tomb of their last heir was also to be placed here, but, as he died in Rangoon, it is unoccupied.

35. The Calcutta General Post Office was designed by Walter Granville.

36. The Baroda and Central India Railway building in Bombay is a work by the architect Frederick Stevens, who also designed the Victoria Terminus (1878–87) station in the same city.

BIBLIOGRAPHY

Afif, Shams-e Serāj. *Tārikh-e Firuz Shāhi*. Edited by M. V. Husain. Calcutta, 1891.

Bābur-nāma. Translated by A. S. Beveridge. New Delhi: Oriental Books Reprint Society, 1979 (1922).

Barani, Ziyā' al-Din. *Tārikh-e Firuz Shāhi*. Edited by S. Ahmad Khan. Calcutta, 1862.

Begley, W. E., and Z. A. Desai. *Taj Mahal: The Illumined Tomb*. Cambridge, MA: Aga Khan Program for Islamic Architecture, Harvard University, 1989.

Brac de La Perrière, Eloïse. "Bihārī et naskhī-dīwānī: remarques sur deux calligraphies de l'Inde des sultanats." *Studia islamica* 96 (2004): 81–93.

Brown, Percy. *Indian Architecture (Islamic Period)*. Bombay: D. B. Taraporevala Sons & Co., 1956.

Burton-Page, John. "Daulatabad." In G. Michell, ed. *Islamic Heritage of the Deccan*. Bombay: Marg, 1986.

Cousens, Henry. *The Antiquities of Sind*, ASI Imperial Series XLVI (1929): 50–51.

———. "Brahmanābād-Mansura in Sind." *Archaeological Survey of India, Annual Reports* (1903–4): 133–44.

———. "Excavation at Brahmanābād." *Archaeological Survey of India, Annual Reports* (1908–9): 79–87.

Crowe, Yolande. "Coloured Tilework." In G. Michell, ed. *Islamic Heritage of the Deccan*. Bombay: Marg, 1986.

Delvoye, F. Nalini, ed. *Confluence of Cultures: French Contributions to Indo-Persian Studies*. New Delhi / Tehran: Manohar: Centre for Human Sciences / Institut français de recherche en Iran, 1994.

'Esāmi. *Fotuh al-salātin*. Edited by A.S. Usha. Madras: University of Madras, 1948.

Frédéric, Louis. *L'Inde de l'Islam*. Paris: Arthaud, 1989.

Frykenberg, R. E., ed. *Delhi through the Ages*. Delhi / Oxford: Oxford University Press, 1986.

Führer, A. *The Sharqī Architecture of Jaunpur*. Calcutta, 1889.

Gascoigne, Bamber. *The Great Moghuls*. London: Cape, 1971.

Gul-Badan Baygam. *Le Livre de Humāyun*. Translated by P. Piffaretti. Paris: Gallimard, 1996.

Guy, John, and Deborah Swallow. *Arts of India: 1550–1900*. London: Victoria and Albert Museum, 1990.

Hassan, Syed Mahmudul. *Mosque Architecture of Pre-Mughal Bengal*. Dhaka: University Press, 1979.

Hoag, John D. *Architecture islamique*. Paris: Hachette, 1991.

Ibn Battuta. *Travels in Asia and Africa, 1325–1354*. Translated by H. A. R. Gibb. New York: Augustus M. Kelley, 1969.

Jahāngīr. *Tuzuk-i Jahāngiri or Memoirs of Jahāngir*. Translated by A. Rogers and H. Beveridge. Delhi, 1989 (reprint).

Kermāni, 'Ali bin Mahmud. *Ma'āser-e Mahmud-shāhi*. Edited by N. H. Ansari. Delhi, 1968.

Kervran, Monik. "Le port multiple des bouches de l'Indus: Barbariké, Dēb, Daybul, Lāhorī Bandar, Diul Sinde." *Res Orientales* 8 (1996): 45–92.

Khan, Ahmad Nabi. *Multan, History and Architecture*. Islamabad: Institute of Islamic History, Culture and Civilization, Islamic University, 1983.

Khan, F. A. *Banbhore*. Revised third ed. Karachi: Department of Archaeology and Museums, Government of Pakistan, 1969.

Klingelhofer, W. G. "The Jahangiri-Mahal of the Agra Fort: Expression and Experience in Early Mughal Architecture." *Muqarnas* 5 (1988): 153–69.

Koch, Ebba. "Diwan-i 'Amm and Chihil Sutun: The Audience Halls of Shah Jahan." *Mughal Art and Imperial Ideology*. New Delhi / Oxford: Oxford University Press, 2001.

———. *Mughal Art and Imperial Ideology: Collected Essays*. New Delhi / Oxford: Oxford University Press, 2001.

———. *Shah Jahan and Orpheus*. Graz: Akademische Druck- u. Verlagsanstalt, 1988.

Le Maître de La Tour, M. *Histoire de Hayder-Ali Khan*. Paris, 1783.

Lowry, Glenn D. "Humayun's Tomb: Form, Function and Meaning in Early Mughal Architecture." *Muqarnas* 4 (1987): 133–48.

Maricq, André and Gaston Wiet. "Le Minaret de Djam. La découverte de la capitale des sultans ghorides (XIIe-XIIIe siècles." *Mémoires de la Délégation archéologique française en Afghanistan* XVI (1959).

Marshall, John. "Monuments of Muslim India." *Cambridge History of India*. Vol. 3. Cambridge: Cambridge University Press, 1928.

Michell, George, ed. *Islamic Heritage of the Deccan*. Bombay: Marg, 1986.

Moynihan, Elizabeth B. *Paradise as a Garden in Persia and Mughal India*. London: Scolar Press, 1980.

Mumtaz, K. Khan. *Architecture in Pakistan*. London: Butterworths Architecture, 1990.

Nicholson, Louise. *The Red Fort, Delhi*. London: Tauris Parke Books, 1989.

Pathan, M. H. *Arab Kingdom of Al-Mansura in Sind*. Hyderabad, 1974.

Porter, Venetia. *Islamic Tiles*. London: British Museum Press, 1995.

Porter, Yves. "Décors émaillés dans l'architecture de pierre de l'Inde centrale: les monuments islamiques de Mandu (XVe-XVIe siècles)." *Archéologie islamique* 7 (1997): 121–46.

———. "Jardins pré-moghols." *Res Orientales III, Jardins d'Orient* (1991): 37–53.

———. "Khalji architecture of Mālwa in the light of the Ma'āser-e Mahmudshāhi." In *Confluence of Cultures: French Contributions to Indo-Persian Studies*. Edited by F. N. Delvoye. Paris, 1994.

Schlumberger, Daniel. *Lashkari Bazar. L'architecture*, *Mémoires de la Délégation archéologique française en Afghanistan* XVIII, 1A (1978).

Shokoohy, M. *Bhadreshvar: The Oldest Islamic Monuments in India*. Leiden: Brill, 1988.

———. *Nagaur: Sultanate and Early Mughal History and Architecture of the District of Nagaur, India*. London: Royal Asiatic Society, 1993.

Shokoohy, M. and N. H. Shokoohy. *Hisār-i Firuza: Sultanate and Early Mughal Architecture in the District of Hisar, India*. London: Monographs on Art, Archaeology and Architecture, 1988.

Smith, Edmund W. *Akbar's Tomb, Sikandra*. Calcutta, 1909.

———. *The Moghul Architecture of Fatehpur Sikri*. Allahābād, 1894–97.

Tadgell, Christopher. *The History of Architecture in India*. London: Architecture Design and Technology Press, 1990.

Titley, Norah. *Persian Miniature Painting*. London: The Library, 1983.

Villiers-Stuart, C. M. *Gardens of the Great Mughals*. London: Adam & Charles Black, 1913.

Yazdani, G. *Bidar, its History and Monuments*. Oxford University Press, 1947.

———. *Mandū, the City of Joy*. Oxford: Oxford University Press, 1929.

INDEX OF THE MONUMENTS

All place-names are in India, except where stated otherwise. Numbers in italics indicate illustrations.

Agra
Bāgh-e Mahtab 248
Chini-ka-Rauza 82, 262, 266, 267
Gardens 79
Jama' Masjid 254, 255, 268, 276, 287
Mausoleum of 'Itimād al-Dawla 235, 238
Musaman Burj 257, 265, 273,
Rām Bāgh (or Bāgh-e Eram, garden) 79, 80, 235, 248
Red Fort 70, 79, 210, 262, 263, 265, 266, 267, 274, 280, 281
   Divan-e 'Amm 132, 263, 269, 270, 280
   Divān-e Khās 196, 221, 260, 263, 265, 271, 273, 280
   Jahāngiri Mahal *210*
   Khās Mahal 263, 265, 266, 272, 273
   Machchi Bhawan 263
   Moti Masjid 257, 263, 273
Taj Mahal 9, 10, 187, 208, 231, 238, 240, 241, 242, 243, *245*, 247, 248, 262, 277, 287, 290

Ahmedabad
Bhadra Fort 153
Jama' Masjid 153, *154*, *155*
Kankaria (lake) 159
Mausoleum of Ahmed I and Rani-ka-Hujra 155
Mosque of Dada Hari *162*, *164*
Mosque of Dastur Khān 169
Mosque of Rani Rupmati *168*, *169*
Rani Sipri (funeral complex) 164, *165*, *166*, *167*
Sidi Sayyid Mosque 96, 102, 103, 170, *171*
Tin Darwaza 153
Wav of Dada Hari 162, 164

Ajmer
Arhai-din-ka-Jhonpra (mosque) 39, *40*
Dargāh of Mu'in-ud-Din Chishti 211
Palace of Akbar 210, 211

Allahabad
Chehel Sotun 212, 270
Fort 212
Garden of Khosrow 212

Amber
Delaram (garden, fort) 279, 280
Divān-e Amm 280
Gate of Ganesh 280
Shish Mahal 279

Awrangabad
Bibi-ki-Maqbara *276*, 277

Ayodhya
Babri Masjid 11, 77

Bagerhat (Bangladesh)
Saith Gumbaz Masjid 120

Bambhore (Pakistan)
Mosque 23

Benares
'Alamgir Masjid 275

Bhadreshvar
Chhatri 31
Chhoti Masjid 29, *30*
Dûdhâ Wâv 31
Mausoleum of Ibrahim or Dargāh La'l Shahbaz Mosque 29, 31
Solahkhambi 29, *30*
Solakhambi Masjid 29

Bharuch
Friday Mosque 153

Bidar
Diwan-i 'Āmm 132
Lal bāgh 131
Mahmud Gawan Madrassa 127, 130, *132*, 133
Rangin Mahal 132
Royal Bahmanid and Barid Shahi necropolises *133*
Solahkhambi Masjid *130*, 131
Takht Mahal 131

Bijapur
Friday Mosque of Yusuf 135
Gagan Mahal 136, 139
Gol Gumbaz 135, *139*, 142, 143
Jama' Masjid *100*, *101*, *136*, *137*
Karimuddin Masjid 135
Mausoleum of Ibrahim Rawza *138*
Mausoleum of Shāh Nawāz Khān 139
Mihtar Mahal 136, *137*
Mosque of Khwāja Jahān 135
Mosque of Malika Jahān 136, 137
Mosque of Mustafa Khan 139
Yaqut Dabuli Mosque and mausoleum 139

Bost (or Lashkari Bāzār, Afghanistan)
Palatial complex 29

Calcutta
Victoria Memorial Hall *291*

Cambay
Friday Mosque 153

Champaner
Jama' Masjid 158, 159, *160*, *161*

Mausoleum of la Nagina Masjid 170
Palace and gardens 158, 191
Saharwali Masjid 156, 157

Chanderi
Badal Mahal 193
Jama' Masjid 193
Kushk Mahal 193
Madrasa 193
Shahzadi ka Rawza 193

Chota Pandua
Friday Mosque and minaret 106

Daulatabad
Chand Minār 55, 126, 127
Chini Mahal (fort) 126, 127
Jama' Masjid (Friday Mosque) 11, 125, 127

Delhi
'Alā'i Darwāza 36, 38, 39, *46*, 48
Arab-Sarai 208
Begumpuri Masjid 56, 127, 153
Bijai-Mandal (palace) 57
Chaunsath-Khambā 236
Chehel Sotun 270
Chirāgh-i Dihli (*dargah*) 68
Citadelle of Dinpanāh 81, 86
Darwāza, Sher-Mandal 76, 81, 86, 87, 88,89, 90
Funerary complex of 'Alā' al-Din Khalji 48
Funerary complex of 'Issa Khān 90, *91*, 205
Funerary complex of Homayun, Chahār-bāgh,
    Arab-sarai 93, 205, 206,207, 208, 209, 224,
    242, 284
Ghandak-ki-baoli 44
Hawz-e Shamsi (pool) 43
Hawz-Khas (Hawz-i 'Ala'i) 45, 56, 57, *60*
Hayat Bakhsh (garden) 273, 288, 289
Jahānpanāh 49, 56, 153
Jama' Masjid 248, 250, 255, 257, 267, 276
Kalān Masjid 48, 62 63, 153, 205, 209
Kāle Khān-ka-Gunbad 72
Khirki Masjid 56, 62, 63
Kiloghari 44
Kotla Mubarakpur (mausoleum of Mubarak II)
    66, 67
Lodi Garden 14, 68, 72, 74, 82, 87
Mausoleum of Sabz-Burj 82
Mausoleum of Ataga Khān 82, 209
Mausoleum of Bahlul Khān Lodi 68
Mausoleum of Balban 44
Mausoleum of Chaunsath-Khamba 236
Mausoleum of Iltutmish 36, 42
Mausoleum of Khan-e Jahan Tilangani 66
Mausoleum of Khan-e Khanan 236, 284
Mausoleum of Nizam al-Din Chisti 49
Mausoleum of the "Barber" 205, 208
Mausoleum of Safdar Jang 236, 282, 283, *284*
Mausoleum of Sikandar Lodi 72
Mausoleum of Nila-Gunbad 82
Mosque and mausoleum of Bara-Gumbaz 20, 21,
    72, 74, 87
Mosque and mausoleum of l'Afsarwala 205, 208,
    209
Mosque and mausoleum of Jamāli-Kamāli 72, 76,
    81, 87
Mosque of Khayr al-Manāzil 90
Moth-ki-Masjid 76, 81, 87, 88

Muhammad of Shah Seyyed 66, 67, 68
Muhammad, son of Iltutmish 42
Nizamuddin *dargāh*, Jamā'at-Khāna and *baoli*, 49
Pavilions (Kushk Mahal, Mālcha Mahal)
Private apartments (Rang Mahal, Mumtaz Mahal 257,
    263, 270, 271, 272
Purana Qila (mosque) *87*, *88*, *89*
Qila Rai Pithora (Lāl Kot) 34
Qutb Minār 9, 12, *14*, *18*, 19, 21, 27, 29, 34, 36, 37,
    38, 39, 42, 46, 50, 76, 106
Qutb-Sāhib (*dargāh*) 77
Quwwat al-islām (mosque) 33, 34, 35, 36, 39, 42,
    46, *48*, 127, 154
Razuya Sultān 42
Red Fort 248, 268, 269, 271, 272, 275, 288, 289
    Bhadon 273
    Divān-e 'Āmm 257, 263, 270
    Divān-e Khās 271
    Moti Masjid 273, 275
    Naqqara-Khana 263, 269, 270
    Sawan 273
    Shah Burj 273
Satpula (dam and bridge) 56
Shāhjahānābād (Old Delhi) et Chatta Chowk
Sher Shāh (Lāl Darwāza) 87, 90
Shish-Gumbad (mausoleum) 72, *73*, 74, 82
Sultān Ghāri (mausoleum of Nasr al-Din)
Tomb of Rāziya Sultān 42
Wazirabad (dam and bridge) 59

Dholpur
Garden (Lotus Garden) 79, 193

Dig
Gopal Sagar et Gopal Bhawan (basins) 281
Palace and gardens 281

Djam (Afghanistan)
Minaret 28, 37, 39

Fatehpur Sikri
Ankh Michauli (kiosk of the Astrologer) 212, 220,
    221, 222
Anup Talao, pavilion of the Turkish Sultana, 212,
    220, 221, 222
Women's apartments 219, 223
Badshāhi Darwāza 218
Buland Darwāza 214, 218, 242
Court of Pachhisi 219, 220, 222, 223
Divān-e 'Āmm 212, 219
Divān-e khās 212, 218, 220
Palace compound 222, *225*
Great Mosque, The 196, 197, 213, 214, 217
Hawā Mahal 224
Hiran Minār 216, 218
House of Birbal and "stables" 212, 224, 225
House of Maryam 212, 223
Mausoleum of Salim Chishti 197, *202*, *203*, 217, 218
Mausoleum of Islam Khān 218
Nagina Masjid 224
Palace of Jodh Bhai 212, 223, 224
Panch Mahal 70, 222

Firuzabad
Khunin Darwāza 90
Kotla de Firuz Shāh (Lāt-Minār) 56, 57, 58,70, 90,
    222

Gaur (or Lakhnāwati)
Bara Sona Masjid *117*
Chika Masjid *116*
Chota Sona Masjid 117, *118*
Dākhil Darwāza *113*, 120
Gumti Gate *116*, *119*
Firuz Minār 114
Lotan Masjid 114
Mosque of Tantipara *114*
Qadam Rasul (mausoleum of Fateh Khān) *115*, 117, *119*

Ghazni (Afghanistan)
Minarets *26*, *27*, *29*

Golconda
Bala Hissar (citadelle) 145
Bala Hissar Darwāza 145, *146*
Fath Darwāza 145
Fort 143, *144*, *145*
Friday Mosque 146
Mausoleum of Yar Quli Jmashid 148
Mosque of Ibrahim Qutb Shāh *144*
Naya Qila 145
Qutb-shāhis necropolis *146*, *147*, *148*, 149

Gulbarga
Dargāh of Muhammad Gesu Deraz 128
Mosque 127, *129*

Gwalior
Garden of Rahim-dād 79
Man Mandir (palace of the fort) 14, 16, 17, *70*, 72, 211
Mausoleum of Muhammad Ghaus 92, *93*, *95*

Hisar (or Hisar-i Firuza)
Mosque 59

Hyderabad
Chār Minār *150*, 151, 231
Jama' Masjid *149*, 151, 153
Mecca Masjid 151
Purana Pul (bridge) 150
Toli Masjid 151

Jaunpur
Atala Masjid *173*, *174*, *175*, 176
Jama' Masjid 176, *177*, *178*
Jhanjhiri Masjid 177, *179*, *180*
Lal Darwāza Masjid *176*

Jodhpur
Mehrangarh Fort 279, *280*
Shish Mahal 280

Junagadh
Mosque 31

Kabul (Afghanistan)
Garden and mausoleum of Babur 77, *78*, 80
Mosque 28

Kufa (Irak)
Mosque 23

Lahore (Pakistan)
Bādshāhi Masjid *276*, 277
Fort 72, 210, 248, 256
  Bari Khwābgāh 257
  Chauburji Bāgh 262
  Choti Khwābgāh 257
  Divān-e 'Āmm 257
  Hathi Pol 232, 256
  Musaman Burj 257
  Nawlakha 257
  Shish Mahal 257
Great Mosque 274
Gulābi Bāgh 262
Mosque of Wazir Khān *250*, *252*, *253*
Moti Masjid 257
Shahdārā nêcropolis (mausoleum of Jahāngir, Asaf Khān and Nur Jahān) 228, *238*, *239*
Shalimar gardens 262

Lucknow
Bara Imambara 285, *286*, 287
Bhulbhuliyan 286
Chaulakhla Darwāza 286
Chota Imambara 287
Jama' Masjid 287
Mausoleum of Sa'ādat 'Ali Khān *287*
Qaysar-Bāgh 286, 287
Residency 287, 290
Rumi Darwāza *286*
Shah Najaf Imabara 287

Madras
Victoria Hall (National Art Gallery) 11

Madura
Tirumala Nayak 281

Mandu
Bāz Bahādur (palace) 194, *195*
Champa Baoli 192
Friday Mosque 98-99, 181, *184*, 185, *186*
Hindola Mahal 192, *193*
Jahāngir gardens 233
Jahangiri Mahal and house of Gada Shah190, 233
Jahāngiri-Mahal, Hathi Pol, Nahār Jharokā 232, 233
Jahāz Mahal (palace complex) 188, *190*, *191*, 232
Jal Mahal 193
Mausolem and mosque of Hushang 186, *187*
Mausoleum of Khalji (or Ashrafi Mahal) *98*, *99*, *188*, *189*
Mosque of Dilāwar Khān 182, 183, 190
Mosque of Malik Moghith 182, *183*
Munj-Talao (bassin) 190, 192, 193
Pavilion of Nilkhant 11, *191*, 194, *195*, 210

Mansura (ou *Brahmanābād*, Pakistan)
Friday Mosque 25

Mathura
Jama' Masjid 275

Mehrauli
Jahāz Mahal 44, 76
Mausoleum of Adham Khān 68, 92, 93
Mausoleum of Balban 44
Pavilion of Mahipalpur 59
Rājon-ki-baoli 76, 77
Zafar Mahal 288, 289

Multan (Pakistan)
Mausoleum of Bahā' al-Din Zakariyā 52, 53

Mausoleum of Rukn-i 'Alam 49, 52, 53, *54*, 55
Mausoleum of Shādnā Shahid 52
Mausoleum of Shāh Shams al-Dīn Tabrizi 52
Mausoleum of Yusuf Gardizi *52*

Mysore
Town Hall 11
Palace 281, 282, *283*

Orchha
Palace 72

Pandua
Adina Masjid 106, *107*, *108*, *109*, *110*, *111*, 120
Mausolem of Eklakhi 106, *112*
Qutb-shāhi Masjid *120*, *121*

Patan
Mausoleum of Shaykh Farid 153
Mosque of Adina (Friday Mosque) 153
Wāv of the Rani (wells) 153

Samarkand (Uzbekistan)
Mosque (Bibi Khanum) 57

Sarkhej
Complex of Sheikh Ahmed Khattri
Ganj Bakhsh *156*
Summer Palace 156

Sasaram
Khān and Salim Suri 83, 86, 94
Mausoleum of Arawal Khān *84*
Mausoleum of Hasan Khān 83, *84*, *94*
Mausoleum of Sher Shāh Suri *83*, 84

Seringapatam
Daryā Dawlat Bāgh 282
Mausoleum of Tipu Sultan 282

Sikandra
Baradari of Sikandar Lodi 69, 230
Char Minār 231
Mausoleum of Akbar 69, *200*, *201*, *228*, 231, 232, 242

Siri
Basin 45
Fort 45, 46, 50
Hezār Sotun (palace) 45

Srinagar
Hari Parbat 233
Jama' Masjid 123
Garden of Jama' Masjid 228, 233
Garden of Shalimar 234
Mausoleum of Zayn al-'Ābidin *124*
Nishat Bāgh 228, 234
Shāh Hamadān Masjid 122, *123*

Thatta
Abdel Kafu Jami'a 250, 253
Jama' Masjid 253, 255
Mausoleum of Makli Hills 253

Tribeni
Friday Mosque 106

Tughluqābād
Fortress 50, 51, 56
Mausoleum of Ghiyāth al-Din Tughluqābād *50*
Palace-citadel 56